Introduction to
Family Counseling

*This book is dedicated to our clinical mentors, Hildy Getz and
Larry Allman, and to all the clients and students who contributed to our knowledge
and to the creation of the Manning-Kelly and Jones families.*

Introduction to Family Counseling

A Case Study Approach

Judy Esposito
Elon University, North Carolina

Abbi Hattem
Private Practice, Chapel Hill, North Carolina

Los Angeles | London | New Delhi
Singapore | Washington DC

Los Angeles | London | New Delhi
Singapore | Washington DC

FOR INFORMATION:

SAGE Publications, Inc.
2455 Teller Road
Thousand Oaks, California 91320
E-mail: order@sagepub.com

SAGE Publications Ltd.
1 Oliver's Yard
55 City Road
London, EC1Y 1SP
United Kingdom

SAGE Publications India Pvt. Ltd.
B 1/I 1 Mohan Cooperative Industrial Area
Mathura Road, New Delhi 110 044
India

SAGE Publications Asia-Pacific Pte. Ltd.
3 Church Street
#10–04 Samsung Hub
Singapore 049483

Acquisitions Editor: Kassie Graves
Editorial Assistant: Carrie Montoya
Production Editor: Bennie Clark Allen
Copy Editor: Michelle Ponce
Typesetter: Hurix Systems Pvt. Ltd.
Proofreader: Susan Schon
Indexer: Maria Sosnowski
Cover Designer: Michael Dubowe
Marketing Manager: Shari Countryman

Printed in the United States of America

Library of Congress Cataloging-in-Publication Data

Esposito, Judy.

Introduction to family counseling : a case study approach / Judy Esposito, Elon University, USA, Abbi Hattem, Private Practice, Chapel Hill, North Carolina, USA.

pages cm

Includes bibliographical references and index.

ISBN 978-1-4833-5176-6 (pbk. : alk. paper)
1. Family psychotherapy. 2. Family counseling
I. Hattem, Abbi. II. Title.

RC488.5.E868 2016

616.89'156—dc23   2015029676

This book is printed on acid-free paper.

15 16 17 18 19 10 9 8 7 6 5 4 3 2 1

Brief Contents

Detailed Contents

Acknowledgments

As coauthors of this book, we are listed in alphabetical order, although we contributed equally to this collaborative writing. We each recognize and value the strengths and talents the other brought to this collaboration.

We also wish to thank the following people, without whom this book would not have been possible. You all helped us in some way, either through support, encouragement, inspiration, or a combination thereof. We are forever grateful.

Peter Felten, Deandra Little, Jessie Moore and the Elon University Center for the Advancement of Teaching and Learning

Tim Peeples, Associate Provost for Faculty Affairs

Elon University Faculty Research and Development Committee

Gabie Smith, Dean of Elon College, the College of Arts and Sciences

Paul Anderson, Director of Writing Across the University

Larry Basirico, Department of Sociology

Student researchers:
  Georgia Lee
  Madalyn Pinto
  Scott Powell

Students from Elon University HSS 212 classes 2013-2015

Our wonderful editor, Kassie Graves, and production editor, Bennie Clark Allen

Joshua and Benjamin Hattem and Bruce Hyman

Chad, Ben, and Patrick Esposito and the Folmar family

The many friends and colleagues who supported and encouraged us

SAGE Publications gratefully acknowledges the following reviewers:

Judith E. Beechler
Midwestern State University

Garry M. Breland
William Carey University

Kananur V. Chandras
Fort Valley State University

Jacalyn Claes
North Carolina A&T State University and University of North Carolina
Greensboro

Kevin A. Curtin
Alfred University

Drew A. Curtis
Angelo State University

Gloria Dansby-Giles
Jackson State University

Lakitta D. Johnson
Jackson State University

Janel Lucas
Lesley University

Judith G. Miranti
Xavier University of Louisiana

Michael R. Perkins
Columbia College

Diana-Christine Teodorescu
Saint Mary's University

Shannon Wolf
Dallas Baptist University

About the Authors

Judy Esposito, PhD, is an associate professor of Human Service Studies at Elon University in North Carolina. A licensed professional counselor and former school counselor, Dr. Esposito specializes in play therapy with children and families. She lives in Elon, North Carolina, with her husband, Chad, two sons, Ben and Patrick, Ellie the dog, Sadie the cat, and Ozzie, the bearded dragon.

Abbi Hattem, PhD, is an individual, marriage, and family therapist in private practice in Chapel Hill, North Carolina. She specializes in the mental health sequelae of acute and chronic trauma and of chronic illnesses, including eating and dissociative disorders, for individuals and their families.

She has been an adjunct faculty member at California State University at Northridge, the University of Southern California, and most recently Elon University. She has been a member of the faculties at Texas Tech University and the University of North Carolina at Chapel Hill School of Medicine. She has two grown sons and lives in Chapel Hill, North Carolina, with her fiancé, Bruce, and their dog, Trotsky, and three cats, Rumpelteazer, Ashrei, and SugarRei.

Introduction

This book is intended to serve as an introduction to family counseling. The collaborative writing of this book arose from a recurrent conversation between two instructors who teach a course entitled *Counseling Individuals and Families*, an undergraduate level course in the Human Service Studies Program. The main goal of the course is for students to learn various theories and methods used by helping professionals in their work with individuals and families facing problems. Over the years of teaching this course, we have searched for a text appropriate for our students and, instead, finally decided to write our own. As such, this text is in response to decades of teaching introductory counseling skills to students who want to work with families. Our intent for this text is that it provides a broad view of working with families, and, simultaneously, an in-depth look at a particular family's journey through the counseling process. We created this text for anyone interested in working with families in multiple contexts, including family therapy, human services, social work, public health, medicine, and family law.

Though broad and generalist in nature, this book presents a clear focus on multicultural competence in working with families, paying close attention to our changing times and the changing needs of our society. Additionally, this text presents examples of how professionals can connect families with the appropriate services available to them, based on their unique needs and keeping in mind the family's wishes and cultural values. This is what makes this text unique. While a typical book about family therapy would not be appropriate for a public health or education course, this book may prove to be quite useful in its careful examination of the complexities of the family system and its focus on how the larger systems in which families live impact each person in some way. Additionally, what makes this text different from other family counseling texts is its emphasis on family counseling concepts as they relate to one family, described in detail at the beginning of the book and followed throughout in transcripts from hypothetical counseling sessions, as well as in general discussion.

Before we go further into family counseling, there are a couple of terms we want to clarify. In this book, we refer to the practice of family counseling. The words *counselor* and *counseling* get thrown around a lot. Technically, counseling can mean giving advice, so people in various fields may choose to describe what they do by using the word counseling, such as financial counseling or college admissions counseling. However, there are also licensed counselors who are trained to do psychological counseling and are endorsed by the state in which they live to do so. Furthermore, counseling from a licensed mental health professional rarely actually involves giving advice. Rather, the process of counseling is a collaborative relationship between a credentialed mental health professional and a client, or clients, in which problems are explored, goals established, and interventions are chosen and used. Thus, the authors of this book encourage readers to investigate the training and preparation of counselors for licensure in the states in which they reside.

Psychotherapy and *counseling* are terms that are often used interchangeably. However, there are some distinctions between the two. Counseling by a licensed professional usually involves a short-term collaborative relationship in which a counselor and client focus on behavioral issues, such as how one functions in relationships or anxiety about changing careers. The term *psychotherapy* usually refers to long-term work focusing on deeper, more complex issues and disorders, such as dealing with the trauma of physical or sexual abuse. In both cases, a licensed counselor may be qualified to facilitate the client's work, depending on the training and expertise of that counselor. While counseling can be with individuals, couples, groups, and families, the focus of this book is on families, their dynamics, and the complexities of family functioning.

We begin our text with a description and genogram of our family case study: The Manning-Kelly and Jones family. Part of a blended family, we start with Christina, the identified patient and the family members she lives with. Each family member is described in detail in order to give students an idea of what a family counselor's first impressions might be during the first session with them. Excerpts from a transcript of the first session are included. The next chapter describes the family life stages of development, providing examples from the family case as illustrations of each stage and typical issues that accompany the stages. The developmental stages provide background for an assessment of the family, which, along with several assessment methods, is discussed in more detail in Chapter 3.

In Part II, we chose to emphasize four main theoretical approaches to family therapy, with an additional chapter providing a summary of selected other approaches. Part III explores the complexities of the counseling relationship when working with families, including working with special populations or issues, the counselor's personal challenges that may arise when working with a family, and the legal and ethical issues related to family counseling. During this section, we encourage students to examine their personal view of change. Understanding how people change, and what they need to be able to make positive changes, will inform one's theoretical orientation. Students who have studied theories for counseling individuals should continue to develop their preferred theoretical approaches while reading about the ones in this text.

Finally, in Part IV we explore potential situations that may warrant referring family clients to other agencies, referral resources and services available to families, and end with a look at how the family case is functioning and what their plans may be after a pivotal shift takes place.

In the next chapter you will be introduced to the Manning-Kelly and Jones family. This family, like so many others, includes multiple generations, a wide array of personalities, lots of challenges, and many, many strengths. While the family is fictional, we have created the family members with the intent of preparing students for working with real families with real issues. Your responses to reading about this family, and imagining yourself working with them, may surprise you. You will like some of the Manning-Kelly and Jones family members more than others. Some you will want to defend, and others you may despise. Regardless of how you feel about them, it is our hope that you will connect with this family in a way that helps you understand more fully the concepts related to family counseling, and, perhaps, gain some insight into your own family dynamics and your place in them.

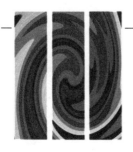

PART I

Introduction to the Family

CHAPTER 1

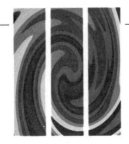

The Manning-Kelly Family

Working with families, whether as a human service or mental health professional, physician, or attorney, is challenging and exciting and will allow you to help others and will also leave you changed in the process. What you will learn immediately is that no two families are alike, although certain theories can help guide you as you approach each unique family situation. In this chapter, you will meet the Manning-Kelly family. You will learn about various members of the family, their presenting problem, their family history and dynamics, and how the family counselor put the information together to assess the family and conceptualize an intervention plan.

As you meet and read about the Manning-Kelly family and view its genogram in both this chapter and Chapter 3, you will notice that the family is large and complex, sometimes even confusing. Family counselors frequently discover more complexity than they anticipate when they ask about their clients' extended families. Fortunately, the tools and family concepts you will learn about help family counselors organize complicated information about the family in ways that are both relevant to the work of family counseling and easier to remember than lists of facts.

Finally, as you read this textbook, please remember that the Manning-Kelly family is not a real family. Rather, it has been created from the authors' combined experience working with families for the sole purpose of exemplifying the concepts, counseling theories and techniques, and practical considerations you'll learn about throughout this textbook.

CAST LIST

Christina:	Identified patient, 17-year-old high school junior
Liz:	Christina's mother, 44-year-old attorney
Martin:	Christina's father, 43-year-old research pharmacist
Mark:	Christina's step-father, 48-year-old attorney
Martin Jr (MJ):	Christina's brother, 14-year-old high school freshman
Emma:	Christina's half-sister, 4-year-old daughter of Liz and Mark, cerebral palsy
Daniella:	Christina's step-mother, 38-year-old stay-at-home mother
Jamal:	Christina's step-brother, 11-year-old son of Daniella
Dominique:	Christina's half-sister, 4-year-old daughter of Martin and Daniella
Matthew:	Christina's half-brother, 2-year-old son of Martin and Daniella
Shoshana:	Mark's first wife, 50-year-old librarian
Jason:	Christina's step-brother, Mark's 24-year-old son, MBA student
Ashley:	Christina's step-sister; Mark's 22-year-old daughter, boomerang
Barbara:	Christina's aunt, Liz's 48-year-old sister, housewife, breast cancer
Peter:	Barbara's husband, 48-year-old professor
Paul:	Christina's cousin, 26-year-old son of Barbara and Peter
Matt:	Paul's life partner, 30 years old, PTSD, discharged from military under Don't Ask Don't Tell
Patricia:	Christina's cousin, Paul's twin, 2-year-old daughter, pregnant
Gary:	Patricia's husband
David:	Christina's uncle, Liz's 46-year-old brother, poly-substance abuse, metabolic disease
Susan:	David's ex-wife, remarried, 2 children with her second husband
Carl:	Christina's cousin, David's 15-year-old estranged son
Sally:	Christina's grandmother, Liz's mother, 74 years old, elevated blood pressure

Jim:	Christina's stepgrandfather, Sally's second husband, Alzheimer's disease, TBI (traumatic brain injury)
Bill:	Christina's deceased grandfather, Liz's father, died in 2002 of cardiovascular disease, polysubstance abuse
Samuel:	Christina's grandfather, Martin's father, 68-year-old retired plumber
Roxanne:	Christina's grandmother, Martin's mother, 68 years old, cardiovascular disease
Bryan:	Christina's step-grandfather, Mark's 87-year-old father
Emily:	Christina's step-grandmother, Mark's 86-year-old mother
Lynette:	Christina's aunt, Martin's 47-year-old sister, nurse, elevated blood pressure, married with twins Jeannette and Jeanine
Daisy:	Christina's aunt, Martin's 40-year-old sister, 4 children
Selena:	Christina's aunt, Martin's 37-year-old sister, blood pressure and mobility issues, lives with her parents and her 15-year-old son

Figure 1.1   Genogram: Christina's Immediate Family

Note: CP = cerebral palsy; etoh = alcohol abuse; r/o = ruling out; TBI = traumatic brain injury.

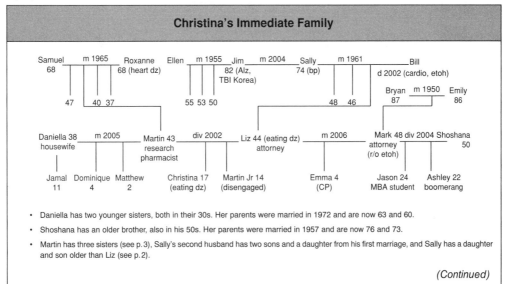

Christina's Immediate Family

Samuel 68 — m 1965 — Roxanne 68 (heart dz) — Ellen — m 1955 — Jim 82 (Alz, TBI Korea) — m 2004 — Sally 74 (bp) — m 1961 — Bill d 2002 (cardio, etoh)

Bryan 87 — m 1950 — Emily 86

47   40 37   55 53 50   48 46

Daniella 38 housewife — m 2005 — Martin 43 research pharmacist — div 2002 — Liz 44 (eating dz) attorney — m 2006 — Mark 48 div 2004 attorney (r/o etoh) — Shoshana 50

Jamal 11   Dominique 4   Matthew 2   Christina 17 (eating dz)   Martin Jr 14 (disengaged)   Emma 4 (CP)   Jason 24 MBA student   Ashley 22 boomerang

- Daniella has two younger sisters, both in their 30s. Her parents were married in 1972 and are now 63 and 60.
- Shoshana has an older brother, also in his 50s. Her parents were married in 1957 and are now 76 and 73.
- Martin has three sisters (see p. 3), Sally's second husband has two sons and a daughter from his first marriage, and Sally has a daughter and son older than Liz (see p. 2).

(Continued)

(Continued)

Christina's Mother's Family

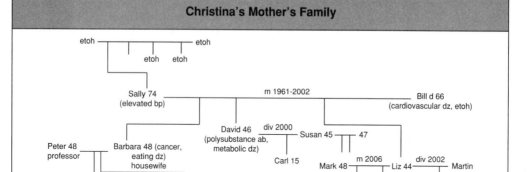

- David's ex-wife is remarried, but since he is cut off from his son he also doesn't have contact with her and so not much is known about her second husband and their two children.
- Bill's parents were both dead by the time Liz was born, and little is known about them. Liz thinks her grandfather, Bill's father, was killed when Bill was in high school, and his mother died of health issues related to substance abuse around the time of Bill's marriage to Sally. If he had siblings, Liz does not know about them.
- Sally has three younger brothers.

Christina's Father's Family

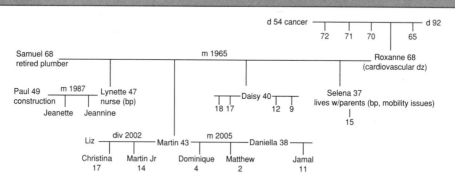

- Samuel joined the military at 18, served briefly in Vietnam, and met and married Roxanne upon his return to the United States.
  He seems to have lost touch with his mother and brother; Martin has no memory of his father talking about either one of them.
- Martin's mother, Roxanne, is the fourth of five children. She has two older brothers and both an older and younger sister.

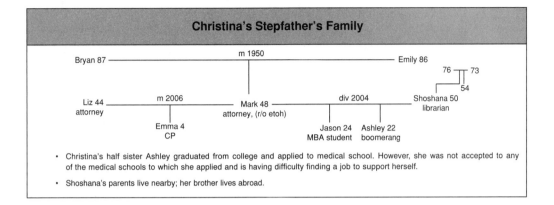

Christina's Stepfather's Family

- Christina's half sister Ashley graduated from college and applied to medical school. However, she was not accepted to any of the medical schools to which she applied and is having difficulty finding a job to support herself.
- Shoshana's parents live nearby; her brother lives abroad.

PRESENTING PROBLEM

Families present for counseling with a particular problem they have identified, which family counselors refer to as the *presenting problem*. The presenting problem usually involves an issue, event, or series of events that has resulted in changed behavior, thoughts, feelings, and external consequences, all of which have resulted in emotional pain.

Family counselors are especially interested in three aspects of the decision to seek counseling. The first involves the details of the presenting problem. Many family counselors ask all family members to describe the reasons they think the family came to counseling. The family counselor might begin with the parent who did not make the initial phone call and then move on to the parent who called. Once both parents have spoken, the counselor asks the children, sometimes beginning with the identified patient and other times beginning with her or his siblings. Sometimes, however, the family counselor asks the children before asking the parent who called to arrange the session.

Some clients are very specific when describing the presenting problem. For example, Liz Manning, the mother in the family we are about to describe, could have answered the family counselor's question about what brought the family to counseling by listing the challenges the family had experienced over the past few years. She might then have gone on to say that these challenges have led to increased tension throughout the family, and, as a result, she and her husband, Mark, have been distracted from parenting, and their children have suffered.

On the other hand, she could have been vague about the problem. She might have said her children don't listen and then have been unable to specify what she meant by not listening. Or, she might have relayed that her older daughter's physician thought they should come to counseling, even though no one else thought there was a problem.

STOP AND THINK:

Think about these examples of how the client could describe the presenting problem.

1. Which can you more easily picture?

2. Explain the differences that account for your answer.

 Finally, while it is important for family counselors to know the reasons a family has sought counseling, most family counselors would agree with the following statements:

1. A client family is far more than the symptoms and problems that bring the family to counseling, though these symptoms and problems are certainly important. Family members experience emotional, behavioral, and cognitive symptoms that they ascribe to their problems. And their symptoms are, at least in part, a product of these problems. However, just as someone who is depressed may also be a loving spouse and parent, a talented musician or computer programmer, and a valued member of her or his social network, so a family can produce very successful members while experiencing such misery in their interactions that they become depressed, abusive, or withdrawn. To ignore these other aspects, or strengths, of clients and their families dehumanizes them and limits the information available to the counselor and the scope of treatment.

2. When a family counselor conflates the symptom or problem with the people in the family, a self-fulfilling prophecy may be created. In other words, the expectation that one or more family member(s) is/are the problem may emerge, further entrapping them in problematic behaviors. Alternatively, when strengths and resources the family already

has are utilized to alter family functioning and reduce the symptoms, another, more positive self-fulfilling prophecy may result. Narrative family counselors (see Chapter 8) specifically focus on separating the family from its problem(s) so that the latter can be viewed more objectively and their meaning altered.

The Manning-Kelly family was referred for counseling by their primary care physician (PCP). During a routine physical examination of the 17-year-old daughter, Christina, the doctor noted significant weight loss, irregular menstruation, and some scars on her upper arms and thighs. These observations suggested to the physician that there existed mental health issues beyond what she had time and resources to treat in her practice.

Liz Manning, Christina's mother, called the family counselor to make an appointment for Christina. Liz told the family counselor she thought the physician was overreacting, but she wanted to make one appointment for her. She indicated that she thought her daughter would be better served by encouragement than by being diagnosed and put into treatment. She said she hoped the family counselor would agree. Liz also stated that she was uncertain Christina would benefit from counseling even if she needed it.

Many questions arose from this description. However, family counselors usually refrain from asking questions in an initial telephone conversation, especially when it is with one person seeking counseling either for someone else or for the family.

Most, though not all, family counselors ask to see the entire family, at least at the first session, because hearing about family dynamics from one member is very different than observing them. Because Christina is an older adolescent, some family counselors might agree to see her individually in recognition of her impending independence, or *launching*, as family scholars call the stage of the family life cycle during which young adult children leave home (see Chapter 2).

Clients who do not voluntarily seek counseling are often reluctant to fully engage in the process. Christina's mother initiated the call on the advice of the PCP, rather than at Christina's request. Thus, enlisting the parents in the process of counseling might increase, though not ensure, the likelihood that Christina would also commit to it.

Like many parents, Liz did not agree with the family counselor's recommendation to meet with the entire family. Liz warned the counselor that it would be difficult, if not impossible, to coordinate schedules. She indicated that her husband, Mark, did not have time to attend family counseling sessions; her son, Martin Jr., would not be interested; and her younger daughter, Emma, was too young to be there. She then asked whether she could bring Christina for a session without the rest of the family. The family counselor reiterated that she needed to see the entire family, knowing it was important for her to observe the family dynamics in which the mother-daughter dynamics occurred.

At the family counselor's insistence, Liz agreed to bring the entire family with whom Christina lived to family counseling, and she and the family counselor then arranged a time to meet. The family counselor urged Liz to do everything possible to get everyone there; although she knew, but did not tell Liz, she would see whoever came.

STOP AND THINK:

1. What would you find difficult about insisting an entire family come to counseling if the person on the phone resisted?

2. What skills could you learn that might help?

3. How might you learn and practice those skills?

When the family counselor met with the Manning-Kelly family, she learned from Christina's stepfather, Mark Kelly, that he thought Christina's concern about her weight was very similar to her mother's, that neither of them had a weight problem even despite Christina's thinness, and the real problem was Christina's arguments with Liz about college. Christina's mother, Liz, said she agreed that Christina's weight was not a problem, and Christina's refusal to explore college options was a concern not warranting family counseling.

Christina's brother, Martin Jr., said his mother and sister argue most days, and he thought Christina needed to eat more. He said he and Christina rarely talked, and both thought their parents were too controlling. Emma, when asked what she thought, snuggled closer to her mother and looked at her lap.

Identified Patient

Christina was a 17-year-old high school junior, 5'8" tall. She was visibly underweight, having lost more than 10% of her body weight according to her

PCP. She appeared wary of the counseling situation. She wore loose, heavy clothing, with long sleeves and long pants despite the warmth of the spring day on which the family was first seen. Christina and her 14-year-old brother, Martin Jr., are ethnically biracial (White and African American).

Christina Jones was in the role family counselors refer to as the *identified patient*. She brought the family to counseling when her symptoms were noticed by her PCP. While families often present with a number of issues and problematic dynamics, one member usually needs to act out (get in trouble) or act in (harm herself or himself) to alert the family that a need for help exists and motivate them to seek it. While some couples might arrive at couple counseling saying they are fighting too much or do not have communication skills, families are rarely able to identify their family dynamics. For example, Christina acting in may have distracted her parents from repeatedly engaging in arguments that they do not resolve. It would also be unrealistic to expect that Liz would have recognized how polysubstance abuse in her family history (father Bill and brother David) may have impacted her behavior and her current family's dynamics, even though she complained about her husband, Mark's, drinking. She would be unlikely to respond to the question of what brought the family to counseling by saying she grew up in an abusive family, was mistrustful of intimate relationships, felt the need to control her weight when other aspects of her life felt out of control, had become hyperfocused on her career in part to identify herself as distinct from the other women in her family, colluded with everyone in her family to deny these things, and worried that all of this was affecting her children. Similarly, Mark would be unlikely to say he felt the pattern in his first marriage was repeating itself now that he and Liz have a child together, regretted starting a second family with Liz, self-medicated with alcohol in ways that reminded Liz of her own father and brother, and contributed to the family's avoidance of these and other issues. Even if he acknowledged drinking more than might be desirable, he would be unlikely to recognize the complexity of multigenerational patterns in both his and Liz's extended families being played out in the Manning-Kelly family.

As you read about systems theory (see Chapter 4) and learn about family counseling theories, tools, and techniques (see Chapters 5-8), the variety of ways in which family dynamics undermine family functioning and contribute to symptoms in family members will become more apparent. Additionally, it will become clear that Christina's symptoms, however dangerous and distressing they may be for her, are also the family's way of asking for help for more global family issues. And that is why it is important for family counselors to view the presenting problem and the identified patient as symptoms of family dynamics and processes that may be not only too subtle for family members to identify themselves but also difficult to recognize without observing the entire family together. It is for this reason that family counselors often insist the entire family come to counseling sessions together, at least initially.

STOP AND THINK:

1. What have you learned about Christina?

2. What do you already know about the family that might help explain the presenting problem?

3. What else do you want to know about the family to fully understand the problem?

Why Now?

Once a family counselor has been told about the family's view of the identified patient and the presenting problem, other questions emerge. The first is, why did the family choose to seek counseling at this particular point in time? For the Manning-Kelly family, the obvious answer is that their PCP recommended counseling and knew the professionals she recommended would insist on seeing the entire family.

For other families, the question of why now may be less obvious. They may have experienced a difficult time and expected to return to their previous level of functioning, realizing the need for help only after a specific event clarified that they had not. Or, one or more of the children may be acting out or acting in for reasons the family cannot identify, and some event has rendered the child's behavior unacceptable.

Sometimes, the duration of the presenting problem prior to seeking counseling has created more problems. In that case, the question "why now?" yields the information that *not* addressing the presenting problem has resulted in additional problems for the family. For example, you will learn that not addressing the distance in Mark and Liz's marriage since Emma's birth may be associated with Liz's overinvolvement with Emma, Mark's drinking, which further separated them emotionally, and thus exacerbates Liz's overinvolvement and Mark's drinking. You will also learn that both Mark and Liz have unresolved issues with their first spouses that affect their relationships with each other and their own and each other's children. In other words, unresolved presenting problems can create an escalating cycle of symptoms, or positive feedback loop (see Chapter 4).

It is also important for the family counselor to know what the family has already done to address the presenting problem. The question, "What have you already tried?" yields information about how the problem has been handled or avoided prior to the event that led the family to seek counseling, as well as what has not been effective.

The Manning-Kelly family's answer to "why now" is clear: Christina's PCP urged them to seek mental health treatment for her. Not all families would have sought counseling even in their situation, and it is fine for the family counselor to commend the family for following the physician's advice. When asked what they had already done to address the presenting problem, Liz reminded the family counselor that they were unsure they agreed with the PCP that Christina's weight was a problem that required addressing. Later, it emerged that Liz thought convincing Christina to explore college would make her happier and thus symptom free, and Liz had been unsuccessfully arguing with Christina about college for months.

STOP AND THINK:

1. Think about what you knew about the Manning-Kelly family before and after you learned their answer to "why now." How does their answer to "why now" help explain them?

2. How did the answer that eventually emerged regarding what they had already done provide new information or help you organize the information you had differently?

Family's Goal(s)

A final aspect of the presenting problem that is of interest to the family counselor is the family's goal for the outcome of counseling. As with the presenting problem and what the family has already done to attempt to alleviate it, families vary in terms of how specific members are able to be when describing their goals. Some clients simply want to feel better; while they say they want the problem or symptom to stop, they cannot describe what they or their lives would be like without it. In these cases, family counselors need to help them become more specific. If an individual or family cannot envision where they are going, then they are not very likely to get there. Additionally, if the symptom is serving a function in the family (Chapter 4), then another way to fulfill the function must be found to replace the symptom.

Some families are able to be much more specific. When asked what they would like their lives to be like when they finish counseling, family members are able to describe details such as enjoying a meal without feeling guilty about what they have eaten or without anyone leaving the table in anger.

While clients rarely list a goal with which the counselor disagrees, goals are sometimes either unrealistic or limited. For example, it is unrealistic to imagine that family members will never again feel sad or angry, and the family dynamics will not change if the goal is simply to reduce the frequency of the same argument. The family counselor can help the family adapt their goals to the reality of the human condition.

Family counselors frequently notice more subtle aspects of how the family works than family members do, such as how the family interacts and its resultant dynamics; the meaning members attach to events; certain behaviors in sequence with certain other behaviors; how the family manages emotions; members' unrealistic expectations for one another; attributions; and the wording, tone, and timing of communications. Addressing these more subtle factors might be more effective in bringing about the desired change than tackling either the presenting problem or the family's goals.

Some family counselors believe that all goals must be specified and agreed upon by the family. Others prefer to facilitate changes that may be most helpful in achieving their clients' specified goals, sharing their own goals only when relevant or asked. If you become a family counselor, your views about discussing all your goals with clients will be influenced by the ethical codes and practices of your particular profession, the policies of your employer, and the theoretical approach you use with clients.

At the beginning of family counseling, the Manning-Kelly family's goal was to obtain confirmation that Christina did not require counseling. However, during the course of the first session, enough family members reached consensus that Liz and Christina's ongoing argument about college was a problem that it became the initial focus of family counseling. While family members wanted the arguing to stop, the family counselor hoped that family counseling would also allow them to change the family dynamics that supported the arguments and impeded their resolution, so that their work in counseling would not only reduce the frequency of the arguments between Christina and her mother but also allow them to be resolved. She also hoped that changes in the family's dynamics would generalize beyond discussions between Liz and Christina about college.

As family counseling continued, the members of the Manning-Kelly family also began to recognize the benefits of changing the ways in which they interacted. However, the family counselor believed that had she expressed these goals in the first session, the family would not have endorsed their importance.

> **STOP AND THINK:**
>
> 1. How might a family counselor's goals differ from the family's goals?
>
> 2. If you were the family counselor, would you share your impressions about what the Manning-Kelly family might need from counseling as soon as you identified them? Why? Why not?

HISTORY OF THE PRESENTING PROBLEM

History of the Identified Patient

To be effective, the family counselor must also understand the history of both the identified patient and the presenting problem. Most family counselors want to know how and when the presenting problem arose, how the identified patient and the family have already attempted to cope with it, and what else may have occurred in the identified patient's and family's history that could have affected the presenting problem's origin and development. Family counselors also want to know about the identified patient's functioning outside the family, both at the time the family initiated counseling and prior to the presenting problem.

Christina was 7 years old when her parents divorced. She reported missing her father and remembered worrying about her mother. She remembered her mother crying at night and looking sad when Christina and Martin Jr. left to visit their father, Martin. Liz was already seeing Mark when Martin and Daniella became engaged. However, Christina said her mother was anxious and distracted about Martin and Daniella's marriage. Christina believed her mother had not fully recovered from her divorce and still missed and loved Martin.

Christina told the family counselor she thought marriage was a bad thing for women, because it hurt them more than it hurts men. She said that although her stepfather, Mark, appeared upset and angry at how his first wife, Shoshana, undermined his relationship with their children, Jason and Ashley, she did not believe he was as upset about his divorce as either her mother or as Shoshana were about their divorces. She thought Susan, her Uncle David's ex-wife, was more unhappy about her divorce from him than he was.

Christina said she appreciated her father's involvement in her life and also thought he used involvement to control his children. Her father wanted her to go to college when she graduated from high school, and Christina consistently stated that she did not want to go to college until she had more life experience. At that time, she was arguing with her mother about whether she would apply to college in the fall. She said her father had given up talking to her about it, though she knew he was unhappy with her decision. She said his disapproval had affected her confidence in herself. She said her parents thought she would enjoy college less if she was older than her classmates. Christina disagreed with them.

Christina did not think Liz's career made her happy, and said she would rather be happy than do what other people thought she should do. She said she was a thinking person, rather than a mindless follower like her parents and stepfather. She said her father's wife, Daniella, and her mother's sister, Barbara, were different. She reports that Daniella was doing what she wanted by staying at home with her children, just as Barbara did. When asked whether she would like to get married and be a stay-at-home mother, she looked appalled and immediately said, "No way. I don't like little kids." Apropos of this statement, Christina has three half-siblings under the age of six.

Christina began restricting her caloric intake and depriving herself of foods she had previously enjoyed during her last year of middle school, about the time her half sister, Emma, was born. Although Christina said she thought it was coincidental, the timing interested the family counselor. Christina said she was unconcerned about her health, even though her periods had become irregular and she felt tired a lot. Instead of eating more as her physician suggested and her father urged, she had chosen to exercise more, saying that exercise gave her more energy and she had read that many female athletes do not have regular periods. She found she occasionally eats more than she wants and, disgusted with herself, began attempting to purge about a year ago. She discovered she needed to overeat in order to effectively purge and so occasionally planned binges. Angry at her lack of control and disliking the boredom she felt when her friends talked about college, she had also experimented with cutting herself. She reported that it did not hurt but also only briefly helped her feel better. As with purging, she felt pressure to do it, could not describe her experience while purging or cutting, and felt relief and disgust with herself afterward.

Although Liz expressed concern about her daughter's health as these facts emerged, Christina pointed out that her mother also restricted what she ate and exercised more than Christina's friends' mothers did. She acknowledged that her father and do not understand her preoccupation with her appearance, food intake, and exercise. "It's my White half," she explained with a slight sneer at Liz and then a smile at the counselor.

Christina had always been an excellent student and, despite these challenges at home, she maintained high grades. She had a number of friends who she saw regularly, and talked to through various social media and texts. She ran track until the fall of that year, her junior year, when studying began taking more of her time and she decided to focus on grades despite her desire not to go to college immediately upon graduation from high school. When she was not studying, she enjoyed being with her friends, although she said she sometimes felt more disconnected than her popularity suggested. She also played violin, although she stopped taking lessons and practicing regularly at the beginning of her junior year.

When Christina talked about college, she repeated two apparently unrelated reasons for not wanting to explore going then. First, she wanted more "life experiences," although she said she was uncertain what that would entail other than working and living on her own. She had not yet considered whether a high school diploma would get her a job that would support her living independently. Second, she did not believe she needed a college education to achieve her stated goal to be like her Aunt Barbara and her stepmother, Daniella, and stay home when raising the children she also said she did not want.

STOP AND THINK:

1. How does this history of the identified patient help clarify the presenting problem?

2. There are several contradictions in what Christina says. What are they?

History of the Patient's Nuclear Family

Most family counselors also want to know about the history of the family. A family history includes information about the people in the family and their individual histories, as well as changes that have occurred in the family through time and how the family has coped with these. Some families have strong coping skills that have been overwhelmed by recent events, and knowing about these strengths allows the family counselor to help the family adapt to their current situation.

Christina's mother, Liz Manning, is a 44-year-old staff attorney for a local corporation and mother of three. She is the youngest of her parents' three children. Her father died 8 years prior to the family beginning counseling, and her mother remarried 2 years after his death. Liz's stepfather, Jim, sustained a traumatic brain injury (TBI) while on active duty in Korea and had recently been diagnosed with Alzheimer's Disease.

Liz's older sister, Barbara, and her family, as well as her mother and stepfather, lived nearby. Her older brother, David, also lived in the area and remained somewhat dependent on Sally and Jim. Barbara's son's life partner was an Iraq war veteran with Post Traumatic Stress Disorder who was dishonorably discharged from the military during Don't Ask Don't Tell. Barbara's daughter was married and pregnant with her second child. David had a child from whom he was estranged.

Liz met and married her first husband, Martin Jones, while they were both in professional school. After Christina was born, Liz left her job with a prestigious law firm to take a job with less demanding hours and less possibility for career and income growth.

Liz expressed very definite thoughts about how family life should look. Divorce was not something she expected, and she said she resented Martin for not fighting harder for the marriage. She did not mention her own role in its demise.

Liz thought Barbara was of another generation, even though she was only 4 years older than Liz. She said she could not understand her decision to stop working when she had children. She also said she thought that was what Martin wanted her to do and noted it was exactly what his second wife was doing.

Martin Jones is Christina's father. He was 43 years old and worked as a research pharmacist for a large pharmaceutical company. When the family counselor met him at a subsequent session, he said he was glad to be there and glad Christina was in counseling. He showed none of the hesitancy or wariness his first wife and older children displayed.

Martin is the second of four children. His parents were both in their 60s and active, although his mother had cardiovascular disease. They lived nearby, as did his three sisters and their families.

Despite his divorce from Liz and his commitment to his current wife, Daniella, young children, Dominique (4) and Matthew (2), and stepson Jamal (11), Martin had remained involved in his older children's lives. He attended sports and school events, paid child support, and maintained a regular visitation schedule including holidays and vacations. He described his home and family as welcoming and said he wished his older children lived with him. He said that at the time of the divorce, he went along with Liz's assertion that living in one house and visiting the other would be less confusing for the children, thinking it made some sense and not wanting more conflict with Liz to upset the children. Since then, he wished he had insisted on the joint residential custody preferred by the courts of the state in which they lived.

Martin Jr., or MJ, is Christina's 14-year-old brother. Martin Jr. says he doesn't remember the time when his parents lived together. He referred to Mark as the father he lives with and Martin as the father he goes to visit.

He thought Christina fought with Liz because she was overly concerned about what the family thought of her. Like his sister, he maintained a high grade point average. He had played soccer since elementary school and talked to his friends more than he talked to adults or his sister. He said he especially liked Jamal, and the young half siblings were alright, although he did not think about them when not with them. Martin Jr. believed that, as a child and teenager, life happened to him. He looked forward to becoming an adult, living independently, and being in charge of his own life.

As previously mentioned, Liz and Martin divorced when Christina was 9 years old, and Martin Jr. was six. Liz said the divorce was amicable, although she and Martin disagreed about sharing the financial consequences of her limiting her career to be more available to their children. She remembered Christina and Martin Jr. being alright when they were told their father was moving. She did not remember subsequent behavior problems.

Liz began dating, at friends' insistence, a year after her divorce and met Mark almost a year after that. When they decided to marry, they also decided they wanted a child together. In retrospect, she hesitantly said she probably wanted another child more than he did. Once Emma was conceived, they set a wedding date and married.

Liz's pregnancy with Christina's half sister Emma was difficult, although there was no indication of age-related genetic problems. She was on bed rest the last 2 months. This limited their extracurricular and social activities during their middle school years, as neither could drive. Both Christina and Martin Jr. believed their mother was more committed to her new life with Mark and Emma than to them, and both expressed a nonchalant attitude about the situation. They were old enough to take care of themselves and did not need Liz's parenting.

Liz remembered that Mark's older children were angry about his remarriage and her pregnancy. She said Christina and Martin Jr. had not had any difficulty with either parent's remarriage. Although neither interacted with Emma in any way during family counseling sessions, Liz assured the family counselor they loved and cared about her.

Mark Kelly, Liz's second husband and Christina and Martin Jr.'s stepfather, was 48 years old and worked as an attorney. He had declined opportunities to take more responsibility in the firm. He appeared less ambitious than Liz.

Mark is an only child. His parents, Emily and Bryan Kelly, lived about 600 miles from Mark and Liz. They were both in their mid-80s and in poor health. Because he was an only child, Mark was responsible for their care. He said they can no longer manage their house and did not have the resources to hire the help they needed. However, he had not considered moving them closer to him.

Mark sat apart from his wife, daughter, and stepchildren in the office. When asked about his involvement with the family at home, Liz said he becomes increasingly disengaged from all of them as the evening wears on. Neither Liz nor Mark believed his behavior toward his wife and children was related to his drinking, which included a drink when he got home, a bottle of wine shared with Liz at dinner, and additional drinks throughout the evening. Mark said alcohol helped him relax after the stress of the day and when Liz and Christina argued in the evening.

STOP AND THINK:

The family counselor was surprised that Liz did not respond to Mark's statement regarding why he drank with a statement such as, "Don't blame me for your drinking." Were you? Why, or why not?

Mark and Liz agreed that Mark used his available time and financial resources for his older children since his divorce from their mother. This included giving them money when they asked, inviting them on family vacations, and taking them to visit his parents. Liz thought Mark encouraged age-inappropriate dependence on him, and both she and Mark acknowledged they argued about them. Liz was especially concerned that he would pay for his daughter's medical education and was already upset that he funded his son's MBA program. Mark considered Liz's complaints about the time and money he gave his older children to be hypocritical, given that her older children lived with them and he therefore helped support and care for them. He also said he would like her empathy for his strained relationships with his older children. He said his first wife, Shoshana, and her parents alienated the children from him, and he felt guilty for allowing them to do so.

Liz and Mark had been married for 4 years. Christina and Martin Jr. did not interact with Mark during sessions, unless prompted by the family counselor. Mark sometimes looked at them when they spoke and otherwise focused his gaze on Liz and Emma or stared out the window. Christina and Martin Jr. indicated their dislike of Mark with their facial expressions, rather than words. Christina interacted only with her mother, usually in a dismissive or argumentative way, and Martin Jr. rarely made eye contact with or talked to anyone in the family during sessions. Liz, for her part, approached Christina with suggestions that were delivered in such a way that it was easy for the family counselor to see how Christina interpreted them as criticism and control.

Four-year-old Emma was born when Martin Jr. was 10, and Christina was 13. She had been diagnosed with cerebral palsy, a central nervous system disorder that is not progressive. She walked on her toes and favored her left side. Her lack of clear articulation made her speech difficult to understand. She usually sat close to her mother and was either silent or whispered to Liz. The two older children ignored her. Mark looked at her, although he made no attempt to interact with her.

Christina's father, Martin, is married to Daniella. Daniella, 38, was African-American. She had an 11-year-old son, Jamal, from a previous relationship. She was working as a medical writer in the pharmaceutical industry when she and Martin met. After their children were born, Martin and Daniella agreed that she would stay home with the 3 children and be available to her 2 step-children. She was happy as a stay-at-home mom, although she imagined she would be ready to work at least part time when her preschool aged children started school.

Daniella is the oldest of 3 sisters. Her parents were in their early 60s, and they and her two younger sisters also lived locally. Like Martin, she valued time with extended family, and her family had welcomed Christina and Martin Jr. into their midst.

Martin and Daniella had two preschool-aged children, Dominique, who was 4 years old and Matthew, who was 2 years old, both of whom they described as active, happy children. Dominique began attending preschool 3 mornings a week when she was 3, because Daniella and Martin believed that social contact with peers and adults other than parents and extended family members was good for children. Matthew would start preschool the next year. Although Daniella loved being a mother, she and Martin had agreed to stop adding to their family.

Jamal was 4 years old when his mother married Martin. He had lived alone with her prior to that time and had mixed feelings about sharing her, first with Martin and the older stepsiblings and then with his younger half siblings. His biological father was never very involved in his life, in part because he and Daniella found they could not live together. He paid child support and was friendly to Martin and the other children when he came to pick up Jamal for monthly day visits.

Daniella attended one or two sessions with Martin. She said that while her parents were still married, they were separated for several years while she was growing up and she therefore appreciated the difficulty of being children of divorce. She said she had made every effort to be welcoming to her husband's older children and to include them in the life of their family whenever possible. She always asked to say hello to them when Martin called them, sent cards and gifts when they were with their mother on their birthdays or holidays, and arranged alternative celebrations when they next visited. She referred to Christina and Martin Jr. as "your big sister" and "your big brother" when talking to Jamal and the two younger children. She and Martin cared about each other, and she hoped this made the remarriage easier for his older children, who she introduced to friends and family as "my stepdaughter and stepson." Language is important, and the distinction between calling them Martin's children or her stepchildren was significant.

Christina and Martin Jr. both said they were close to their stepmother, young half siblings, stepbrother, and their grandparents, aunts, uncles, and cousins on Martin and Daniella's sides of the family. Jamal and Martin Jr. were close in age and had become friends. Martin Jr. once told Jamal he wished he could live with Jamal's family and said he planned to talk to his father about it when Christina moved away the following year.

STOP AND THINK:

1. How does the history of the identified patient's family help clarify the presenting problem?

2. How does the history of the identified patient's family help you more fully understand the identified patient?

3. As you read the history of the identified patient, her family, and the presenting problem, what were you curious to learn more about?

History of the Patient's Extended Family

You have already read quite a bit about Christina's extended family. As you will learn in Chapters 2, 3, and 5, family counselors ask for information about extended family members in order to assess what multigenerational issues might be influencing the identified patient and the family's dynamics.

Christina's extended family, as previously mentioned, is large and complex. We will examine aspects of this family when relevant to topics throughout this textbook. For the moment, there are four issues, two of them multigenerational, that may impact Christina's family's dynamic and thus the presenting problem. These are substance abuse, eating disorders, biomedical illnesses, and aging.

Substance Abuse. Substance abuse has a multigenerational history in Christina's mother's family. Christina's maternal grandfather, Bill Manning, died of cardiovascular disease at the age of 66, the same year Liz and Martin divorced. There is evidence that Bill's health may have been compromised by alcohol and prescription medication abuse. Liz acknowledged her father's alcohol abuse and reported that her mother, Sally, grew up in an alcoholic family. She speculated that Bill's drinking may have felt familiar to her, although she did not think Mark's drinking feels similarly familiar to her.

Christina's maternal uncle, David, is, like his father, a polysubstance abuser. He was in his mid-40s and suffered from metabolic disease, which is a combination of high blood pressure, elevated cholesterol, and type 2 diabetes. This biomedical disease may be related to his polysubstance abuse. His ex-wife, Susan, and their 16-year-old son, Carl, lived in another state with Susan's second husband and their two children. David had no contact with him, and Christina said she had not seen her cousin Carl since they were very young children. David worked intermittently and had financial problems related to his polysubstance abuse. He relied financially on his mother and stepfather.

Eating Disorders. There is also a multigenerational appearance of eating disorders in Christina's extended family. Liz said her mother, Sally, had always been concerned with appearance and viewed thinness as admirable. Liz reported that Sally was critical when she or her sister, Barbara, gained weight, something she had attempted to avoid with Christina. Both Liz and Barbara have struggled with distorted body image and resultant restricting and overexercising. Both Barbara and Liz were critical of their appearances. They said one or both usually disparaged herself for what she had eaten at family gatherings, and Sally pursed her lips and said, "Tsk" when she disagreed with their choices of what or how much to eat.

No one had previously sought counseling for either substance abuse or eating disorders. This was significant, given Liz's reluctance to bring her daughter to counseling for an eating disorder and her apparent lack of concern for Mark's drinking.

Biomedical Illnesses. In recent years, Christina and her family have also witnessed her Aunt Barbara's struggle with cancer. Liz's older sister, Barbara Mills, was 48 and in remission from stage II (early metastatic) breast cancer. She lived nearby with her husband, Pete Mills. They had 26-year-old twins, Paul and Patricia.

Christina had watched her beloved aunt in pain as she went through surgery, chemotherapy, and radiation treatments. She also observed her Uncle

Pete caring lovingly for Barbara and her two older cousins, Paul and Patricia, helping their parents. She says as sad and scared as everyone was, she thought it would be nice to live in such a loving family.

Other family members have been diagnosed with a variety of biomedical conditions, including Emma's cerebral palsy, Martin's mother's heart disease, Liz's brother's metabolic disease, and Liz's stepfather's Alzheimer's disease.

Aging. Christina's stepgrandfather, Jim, had been diagnosed with Alzheimer's disease. He was able to live independently with Sally, but he was becoming increasingly forgetful, irritable, disoriented, and disinterested in their life together. Sally was showing signs of stress, with elevated blood pressure and complaints that she could not sleep. Liz said she was concerned about the toll on her mother, but Sally said she was not yet old enough to need her children involved in her or her husband's health care. Christina was aware of the changes in her grandparents, as well as of her mother's worry.

Christina said she had vague memories of her maternal grandfather, Bill, and loved her grandmother and stepgrandfather. She remembered her grandparents were busy and happy when they were younger, perhaps because the grandparents were more energetic or perhaps because Jim's disease had changed him and exhausted Sally. She also said it was fun to visit her grandmother's animals. Sally had always seemed more involved with the animals than with people, according to Christina and Liz.

Mark's parents are also in declining health, and he was solely responsible for their care. Liz said he was sometimes irritable and distracted by his concern for them and sometimes visited and helped them over a weekend. When he was away, Christina said Liz became short-tempered. Even though Christina did not know these stepgrandparents well, her family was affected by their deteriorating health.

STOP AND THINK:

How does the history of the extended family help you more fully understand the identified patient and presenting problem?

SOCIAL SUPPORT

Research has consistently shown that social support is a buffer for a variety of stressors. Social support has been correlated with outcomes such as birth weight and the mental health impact of chronic illnesses.

Social Support

Social support involves both the number of people with whom individuals and families interact and the quality of those interactions. It is important for families like Christina's to have a network of health professionals, acquaintances, close friends, and family members. It is also helpful to feel part of a community that lends identity, whether it is a religious or spiritual community, a neighborhood, a school or professional organization, or a social, athletic, or service club.

Identified Patient's Peer Relationships

Because social support is associated with a variety of positive outcomes, it is important for family counselors to ask about the identified patient's support network. If the identified patient is well connected, then the family counselor can encourage the identified patient to use her or his network. If the identified patient is more isolated, the family counselor can facilitate her or his efforts to develop a network.

Christina had a history of connectedness. She had friends, had been part of an athletic team and the orchestra at school, and was close to her aunt and stepmother. More recently, however, she left both the athletic team and the orchestra. She also described feeling detached from friends as they planned for college. These changes suggested decreased social support, possibly related to increased cutting and purging. Christina said she could not talk to Daniella because she did not wish to worry her father, and, even though her disease was in remission, Christina had been hesitant to talk to her Aunt Barbara.

Family's Support Networks

Like individuals, families have support networks of friends; colleagues; neighbors; members of their religious, school, and service communities; and extended family members. The quality, as well as the existence, of these connections must be examined in order for the family counselor to fully understand whether the family's support network is or could become a buffer for the stress of the presenting problem.

The Manning-Kelly family had a large network of extended family members. However, there was distress throughout this network. Liz's siblings and her mother struggled with their own health issues, Mark's parents needed his help, and he was disconnected from his children. Christina and her brother, Martin Jr., were connected to their father and Daniella's extended family network, lending them extended family support the rest of the Manning-Kelly family lacked.

It emerged that Liz and Mark had a number of couple friends. However, Liz was reluctant to leave Emma and so they no longer socialized with their friends. They each had friends at work and went to annual holiday parties for each other's jobs. They did not belong to a religious or spiritual community and rarely volunteered in their community. Their neighbors socialized regularly, although most were families of school-aged children with whom the Manning-Kelly family did not fit. They appeared to view Emma's condition as a source of isolation for the entire family.

With a deteriorating social network, the Manning-Kelly family had less buffer for stress. One goal of family counseling could be to shift their view of Emma's cerebral palsy to allow the family greater social connection.

CLINICAL OBSERVATIONS AND IMPRESSIONS

To effectively practice family counseling, you will need to not only get to know the individual family members but also to observe the patterns of interactions among members, discover information about multiple generations of the extended family, determine how all this may impact the individuals and the problems they bring to counseling, and decide how to intervene to address those problems as well as the family dynamics. You will begin to learn these skills as you read this book.

In this section of this chapter, we share our clinical impressions about the Manning-Kelly family. We will repeat aspects of this description to refresh your memory and further develop the case when relevant as we address specific theories and interventions in future chapters. You can also refer back to this chapter.

Although the family counselor had told Liz that she wanted to see the entire family, the five people who entered her office on a warm, spring afternoon in 2010 were only those who lived with the identified patient, Christina. The family counselor invited Christina's father and stepmother to attend family sessions, and after one session with both families, allowed them to decide with Mark and Liz whether they wanted to meet together or separately after that. She occasionally saw one or two members of the extended family. Additionally, members of the nuclear and extended families were referred for other family and related services as appropriate. The Manning-Kelly family is a blended family. In other words, Christina and Martin Jr. do not live with their two biological parents but rather with their mother and stepfather. They also live with one of their three half siblings. Additionally, they regularly visit their biological father, his second wife, their two children, and their father's stepson. Finally, their other two stepsiblings, the children from their stepfather's first marriage, occasionally visit them at Mark and Liz's.

The Manning-Kelly family interacts frequently with extended family members. These include Liz Manning's mother and her husband and Liz's older sister, brother-in-law, and their two adult children and their families. Christina and Martin Jr. also interact frequently with their father's extended family members, including his parents, siblings, nieces, and nephews, and with his second wife's parents, siblings, nieces, and nephews. There is virtually no interaction with their stepfather Mark's parents.

When the Manning-Kelly family first entered family counseling, no one appeared interested in being there. Liz had expressed skepticism that counseling was necessary or potentially useful. Mark deferred to Liz and Christina. Christina did not endorse that her eating, exercise, or cutting were issues and initially said the scars her physician had seen were due to exercise. Martin Jr. did not make eye contact with anyone and was reluctant to speak when asked questions. His answers were initially shrugs, "I don't knows," or single-word answers. Emma sat close to her mother, looked at her lap when the counselor smiled at her or asked her what she thought, and spoke only to her mother and in soft whispers.

While few families want to go to counseling, many are relieved to be getting help. The family counselor's impression of the Manning-Kelly family was that not only did they not want to be in her office but also they did not want to be with each other. No one looked happy, no one but Emma turned to anyone else for connection or comfort, and no one stepped forward as the family spokesperson.

This presentation stood out to the family counselor as unusual, although consistent with the fact that no one in the family had been in treatment for either substance abuse or eating disorders despite the presence of both in multiple generations of the family. Liz reflected the family's reluctance to seek mental health treatment when Christina's physician recommended it, and the entire family exemplified hesitation in the family counselor's office.

The family counselor's initial clinical impressions of the Manning-Kelly family also identified issues of control and conflict avoidance. After a discussion of these issues, we will examine her initial working hypothesis, or assessment of the family's interactions. This assessment will be further developed as you learn about tools for assessing families (Chapter 3) and experiment with ways to facilitate change within the family (Part II). Most family counselors would identify a preferred and appropriate theoretical approach to intervention as a starting point for helping the family to change. However, because you will learn about several possible theoretical approaches to the Manning-Kelly family later in this book, a variety of possible theoretical approaches to intervention will be explored (Part II).

Control

Did you notice that both Christina and Martin Jr. said they experienced their parents as controlling? Yet, Liz, Mark, and Martin all acknowledged feeling out of control.

Liz. Liz feels she cannot control anyone in her family. She pressured Christina to apply to college, while Christina demonstrated she cannot be controlled by refusing to explore even the possibility of going to college. She argued with Mark about the time and resources he devoted to his older children, apparently attempting to convince him to change, and he didn't. And she cannot change Emma's cerebral palsy.

Liz said she would like to be closer to her son, although is disinclined to reach out and risk rejection from him. Liz believed Martin Jr. is more engaged with his father than he was with her and was resentful of their relationship.

None of this sounds like a woman who feels able to control her family. She could not convince Mark to change, Christina to go to college, or Martin Jr. to be closer to her.

The possible exception for Liz is Emma. Because Emma appeared emotionally dependent and avoided any physical distance from Liz, Liz likely felt in control of Emma despite lack of control of her cerebral palsy. However, Emma appeared to lack the confidence and age-appropriate maturity of many 4 year olds. Without information from allied health care professionals, it is impossible to know whether her speech is immature or affected by her central nervous system disorder. It is also difficult to know exactly how independent she could be. The family counselor asked the family for permission to contact Emma's pediatrician at the same time that she asked permission to exchange information with Christina's PCP in order to get a better idea of the extent of Emma's disability.

Martin. It appeared that Martin had given up attempting to control what Christina did after she graduated from high school. At no time did anyone suggest Martin attempted to control Daniella, her son Jamal, or their two younger children. However, according to Liz, she and Martin struggled for control of her career decisions during their marriage, and Daniella had avoided a similar conflict by not working outside the home.

Mark. Mark felt out of control of his first wife's behavior while they were married and now of his own relationships with his older children. As a result of his complex feelings about his older children, Mark appeared helpless to repair those relationships. He also felt out of control of Liz when she precipitated conflict with Christina, worried that if he shared his annoyance at her hypocrisy about food and weight or his belief that arguing with Christina served to further entrench her in her position, the fights would only worsen. He was also reluctant to let Liz know he would like them to spend more time together because he believed they would argue about whether she needed to spend so much time with Emma, which he believed she does not.

Christina. Christina was very much in control of her family, even though she did not experience herself as such. Although Liz often initiated conversations that led to open conflict, Christina decided when their arguments stopped by leaving the room.

By contrast, Christina believed she was in control of her college decision and may not be. Imagine that Liz convinces Christina or Christina wants to go to college with her friends. If she were to change her position, the dynamics within the family would also change. Liz might declare victory, and Christina might feel controlled by her mother in a way she thinks is inappropriate for her age.

Part of the argument for Christina is about her mother's career. Saying she doesn't want to go to college because she wants to stay at home with children like her Aunt Barbara and stepmother conflicts with both the reality of their lives and other things Christina has said. Both her aunt and her stepmother went to college and held professional jobs. Barbara returned to work when her children were grown, and Daniella not only worked after Jamal was born but also plans to work part time when her younger children are in school.

Additionally, Christina said she thinks marriage is a bad deal for women and does not like small children. These statements conflict with her desire to stay home with small children because, in addition to the small children she says she does not like, staying home requires considerable financial support from the children's other parent that rarely comes without marriage or cohabitation with the intent of permanence. And finally, Liz shifted the trajectory of her own career after Christina was born specifically to increase her time with her children. While Christina may feel the time remained insufficient, Liz hardly ignored her role of mother in favor of career building. The family counselor wondered whether Christina felt she would be agreeing with Liz's career choices and betraying her aunt and stepmother if she relented about college.

Christina also saw that her father did not attempt to control Daniella, whose role as a full-time mother was clear, while Liz says he fought to control her when she attempted to balance career and parenting. It is possible Christina decided that seeking a traditional role would avoid a battle for control with her father or partner.

The family counselor concluded Christina does not control her decision about college but rather is influenced by her *family's dynamics*. Similarly, Christina's various self-harming behaviors appeared to be out of her control, yet she experienced them as choices. For many people, restricting food intake and exercising excessively feel like behaviors over which they have control. There is the implicit assumption that the person who engages in them feels out of control in other areas of her or his life and thus seeks control in ways that incidentally involve self-harm. This is not about the self-discipline one needs to exercise regularly and avoid overeating most of the time. Rather, it involves one doing these things to excess and thus inflicting self-harm. Cutting and the binge-purge cycle are less likely to be experienced as control. Rather, people usually feel great internal pressure to cut or binge, and that pressure is relieved by cutting or by the binge-purge cycle. At some point, the family counselor will need to address Christina's lack of control and those factors in her family that exacerbate her symptoms as well as locking her into resisting going to college.

Martin Jr. Martin Jr. appears to be in control of his interactions with his family. However, as with Christina's refusal to go to college, appearances may be deceiving. While he describes leaving to visit friends and avoids interacting with family members, he is 14 years old and not yet able to live independently of his family. Thus, he seems to have learned to distance himself in the midst of his family. But, like Christina, this apparent control belies a lack of control over the family dynamics that leave him with disengagement from the family as his perceived best option.

Because control is an issue identified by most members of the Manning-Kelly family, it can be used as a tool to question their assumptions and a metaphor when they are stuck. It is therefore useful for the family counselor to develop her impressions about how each family member views her or his own control, as well as her assessment about their paradoxical lack of it.

Conflict Avoidance

There appears to be a multigenerational tendency throughout the Manning-Kelly family to avoid conflict. Sally, Christina's maternal grandmother, had been passive and accepting about her first husband and son's polysubstance abuse and related behaviors and health consequences. And while Liz had been more assertive with her husbands, children, and professional colleagues, she colludes with Christina to avoid continuing the conflict after a certain point. For example, she could tell Christina not to walk away until the argument is resolved. Or she could listen to Christina's viewpoint, express her own, and work with Christina to understand one another and find a solution. Liz does none of these but rather colludes with Christina to stop their fights before they can be resolved and before whatever she fears can emerge.

Additionally, the family was organized around allowing the conflict between Liz and Christina to remain unresolved. Mark sometimes deflected it onto himself, by interrupting Liz when she already was angry. And he did not stop Emma from interrupting, although he could have told her that her mother was busy and focused her attention on him instead.

Liz and Mark reported minimal conflict between the two of them. Yet, Liz as unhappy with Mark's withdrawal from the family over the course of an evening, and while she said she did not attribute it to his alcohol use, she also did not address her concerns with him. She occasionally displayed anger at him about how he managed his older children, although in much the same way she expressed frustration with Christina about college: She stated her opinion and then got angry when someone disagreed. There was no listening, no dialogue, and no resolution. As a result, while conflict was precipitated, it was not resolved. Additionally, negative feelings about the unresolved conflict are piled onto negative feelings about the content of the argument. This is an example of how a family's attempt to resolve the presenting problem can create more problems.

Mark, for his part, was not pleased with the way Liz was handling Christina or Emma. He thought she babied Emma and bullied Christina. He also resented her anger at him about his older children, particularly in light of the fact that he was helping to support her children. He told the family counselor he expected empathy from Liz about the challenges in his relationships with his children. Despite all this, he had never discussed these concerns with Liz. Additionally, when things became uncomfortably heated for him, he attempted to stop, rather than resolve, them. The family counselor wondered whether he also numbed his frustration and thus the possibility that it would lead to conflict with alcohol.

The identified patient had the job of preventing conflict from going so far underground that the family never resolves it and eventually dissolves. She did not function in this role when her parents were married. Although school-aged children sometimes act out to distract their parents from marital problems, Christina was acting in, and that behavior is frequently less developed in younger children.

Martin, Christina's father, may or may not avoid conflict. He said that Liz never wanted to talk about their problems, while Liz said he would have refused to do anything about them. Christina and Martin Jr. said they do not remember. However, Martin had stopped talking to Christina about college, not because he agreed with her decision but because he saw no point in arguing about it because her decision appeared final. The family counselor did not ask whether he and Christina had ever had a productive conversation about her lack of college plans. The answer might help to differentiate conflict resolution from avoidance between Christina and her father.

While there was no open conflict with Martin Jr., there also appeared to be only superficial contact between him and his mother and stepfather. Martin Jr. was present but not actively engaged in family life or in the family counseling sessions. Disengagement may have been his method for avoiding the family conflict.

Emma also appeared to successfully avoid the family's conflict. The family counselor had insufficient information to know whether she was uncomfortable when Liz was upset, whether her role in the family was to distract Liz, thus preventing conflict, or whether she needed Liz's attention focused on her. The family counselor decided to observe Emma more closely in future sessions.

Family Dynamics

As will be discussed in Chapter 4, family members interact in repetitive ways to create a dynamic that exists independently of its members. Many of the family counselor's impressions already discussed in this section focus on family dynamics, for example, the question of Emma, Mark, and Martin Jr.'s roles in the ongoing argument between Liz and Christina, as well as the power and control issues that underlied whether Christina would explore college options then, during the spring of her junior year of high school.

STOP AND THINK:

1. Discuss your thoughts about the family counselor's impressions.

2. What other impressions would you like to add? Explain why they are important.

PRELIMINARY ASSESSMENT

The family counselor's preliminary assessment has already been touched upon. She believes that Christina's symptoms—restricting what she ate, overexercising, and cutting—are symptomatic of deeper issues within the family. These include multigenerational appearances of eating disorders and substance abuse, intergenerational struggles about the role of women, failure to resolve conflict by avoiding and distracting from it, marital distress, unresolved divorce issues, and what family counselors call coalitions and triangles (see Chapter 6).

A more complete assessment would require you to already know what you will learn as you study this textbook. You will learn about assessment tools in Chapter 3 and how various theoretical approaches to family counseling view assessment in Section 2.

THEORETICAL CONCEPTUALIZATION

Once a preliminary assessment is made, family counselors then decide what theoretical approach best fits a particular family. The preliminary assessment can be viewed as a working hypothesis and changed as the family counselor discovers new information about the family through further assessment and observation of the family's responses to various interventions. In Section 2 of this book, you will learn about the interventions to the Manning-Kelly family's presenting and relevant problems suggested by several theoretical approaches.

CONCLUSION

This chapter introduced you to the Manning-Kelly family, who you will follow throughout this textbook. It is a large and complex family. Family counselors do not need to remember every detail. What they do need to remember are the family dynamics, so they can guide client families toward changing the ways in which members interact that have led to the problems the family and family counselor have identified and that have prevented the family from changing on its own.

> ## STOP AND THINK:
>
> 1. What do you know now about the Manning-Kelly family?
>
> 2. What are your assumptions about the Manning-Kelly family?
>
> 3. How might you distinguish what you know from what you assume?
>
> 4. What else might you need to know in order to understand this family?

As we continue to follow the Manning-Kelly family, we will describe how their dynamics illustrate family concepts and the various schools of family counseling and observe the family counselor interacting with them. We will describe her thoughts about what happened in counseling sessions, as well as her reaction to it. You will also learn about other social services the Manning-Kelly family require and about how to refer for these services. For now, you have an introduction to who the family members are and how they approached family counseling.

Chapters 2 and 3 will describe the concept of the family life cycle, which helps family counselors understand some of the challenges most families face, and tools for further assessing families. Being as large and complex as it is, the extended Manning-Kelly and Jones family illustrates every stage of the family life cycle. You will also see how the tools described in Chapter 3 provide new information about family.

FOR FURTHER STUDY

Basirico, L. A., Cashion, B. G., & Eshleman, J. R. (2014). *Introduction to sociology (6th ed.)*. Redding, CA: BVT.

Gehart, D. (2010). *Mastering competencies in family therapy* (1st ed.). Belmont, CA: Brooks/Cole.

Nichols, M. (1984). *Family therapy. Concepts and methods*. New York, NY: Gardner Press.

Yalom, I. (2003). *The gift of therapy. An open letter to a new generation of therapists and their patients*. New York, NY: Harper.

CHAPTER 2

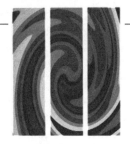

Families and
the Family Life Cycle

As you learn more about Christina and the rest of the Manning-Kelly and Jones families, it is important to keep in mind the developmental stages families experience, both as individuals and as a unit. As children, our families are usually part of our first memories, the yardstick against which we measure ourselves at each stage of development and our go-to place for protection, encouragement, and support. In this chapter, we present the concept of the family life cycle and its utility in understanding many of the challenges families face. Additionally, we explore how the ways families respond to these challenges may impact them both individually and as a unit. The Manning-Kelly family is a blended family, with biological parents remarried and with young half siblings. There are also aging parents and teenagers. Every stage of the family life cycle is illustrated by one of the nuclear families that, together, comprise this blended, multigenerational family.

Families serve many functions and fulfill numerous needs for individuals. The family "produces and socializes children, acts as a unit of economic cooperation, gives us significant roles as children, husbands, wives, and parents, and provides a source of intimacy" (Strong & DeVault, 1986, p.4). Specific psychological characteristics of families include the following:

(a.) A sense of mutual commitment—time, energy, money

(b.) A sense of history and continuity—stories, family folklore, private jokes, family trips, and important events (a sense of stability in the midst of change)

(c.) A potential for and expectation of long-lasting relationships—-not fleeting, in for the long haul, through thick and thin (d.) Extensive and intense relationships—multidimensional and intense emotions, intense joy and intense sorrow, intense passion and anger

(e.) Responsibility for the welfare of each other—parents are expected to care for their children, and their children are expected to watch out for each other as they grow and become adults, as well as caring for their parents when they get old (Berg-Cross, 2000).

Ideally, families provide each other support, ensure that basic needs are met, and have stronger members who protect the weaker ones from harm. Problems may arise when these functions are not taking place and when needs are not being met.

Families come in many shapes and sizes, from the traditional two-parent heterosexual household with 2+ children, to same sex couples with adopted children, single-parent families, blended families, multiple generation families living under one roof, and many more. Some families are limited to persons who are related through biology or marriage, while others include honorary family members who are neither blood relatives nor related by marriage but who have served the roles that family members typically serve. The 2011 American Community Survey, conducted by the United States Census Bureau and in conjunction with the 2012 Census, revealed some interesting trends in how families in the United States have changed in the past few decades. These trends include smaller families, an increase in single-parent households, an increase in older adults living alone, and an increase in adult children living at home with their parent or parents (U.S. Census Bureau, 2012). Although family structures and roles have changed considerably over the decades, the purposes and functions of the family are still applicable for many people.

STOP AND THINK:

1. Think of your own family. Whom does that include when you picture them in your mind?

2. How did you all come together?

3. Are all members biologically or legally related, or do you have any honorary family members?

4. If there are honorary family members, how did they become "family," and what distinguishes them from those outside the family?

5. What purposes and functions does your family serve and provide for you? For others in the family?

6. Now look at the Manning-Kelly family. How are they different from your family?

7. What strengths do you notice right away?

8. What areas concern you?

THE FAMILY LIFE CYCLE

Families, just like individuals, progress through stages of development in which roles and behaviors change, new decisions and choices are made, and new situations require adjustments, often for everyone in the family. The Manning-Kelly family was no exception, with several life stages being present at once. The family life cycle describes stages of development that take place within the family over time (Carter & McGoldrick, 1980). Because the Manning-Kelly family was a multiracial, middle class family, it is important to remember that many families will not fit this model. Counselors should be encouraged to look for other culturally relevant and universal models to aid in conceptualizing families.

As human service professionals it is crucial to consider the stages of family development, along with the individual stages of development. Each developmental stage brings with it a new set of challenges and potential problems; and each stage is a common, anticipated part of life providing unique experiences and insights.

Stage 1: The unattached young adult leaving home. Having been recently launched by their own families, most college students can identify with this stage of the family life cycle, as it is the time when they leave their families and venture out into the world on their own. This corresponds with Erikson's (1959) psychosocial *intimacy versus isolation* stage of individual development, in which young adults focus on intimate relationships as well as career interests. A major developmental task for young adults is to be able to create and maintain an identity separate from their family of origin. Murray Bowen (1971, 1972, 1976) refers to this process and the struggles therein as the *differentiation of self*. According to Bowen, the goal of the individual's development is to learn to use one's intellect fully, "unimpeded by the conflicting pressures of family sanctioning mechanisms" (As cited in Berg-Cross, 2000, p. 45).

According to Berg-Cross (2000), "young adults have to be able to think and act autonomously," and "[those] who cannot achieve psychological independence from their families will be ill-equipped for marriage" (p. 11). For young single adults whose ideas and plans for their future conflict with those of their parents, this can create a struggle. Single adults represent nearly 47% of the United States population as of 2012 (U.S. Census Bureau, 2012), and therefore the age-old questions of "When are you getting married?" and "When are you having children?" are simultaneously troubling and way off base to young adults who have completely different plans in mind. As you refer to the Manning-Kelly family, you will note that Christina was on the verge of entering this stage, although her mental and physical health at the time may have interfered with her successful entry and completion of this stage. As such, she needed to be prepared for the questions from other adults who expected her to leave home and settle down on her own or with a partner and start a family during this stage of her life. Support from her family and friends during this time was crucial for her success in treatment.

Stage 2: The joining of families through marriage or pair bonding. Choosing and "settling down" with a life partner is common during this next stage of development. For couples who decide to live together in a committed relationship, the major task of this stage is adjusting to the new demands inherent in the new living situation. The couple has to develop their relationship while differentiating and separating from their families of origin or previous families. Typically this stage involves its share of conflict, compromise, and negotiating of roles and rules until couples find a rhythm and routine that works for them. Each must learn how to deal with the everyday moods and problems of another person, and household tasks must be organized, divided, and agreed upon (Berg-Cross, 2000). Family rituals and traditions must also be negotiated, as this stage of life presents the merging of two (or more, if either of them comes from blended families) families, with each person bringing their own beliefs, values, and traditions. The holidays are often challenging during this time, as the couple have to decide how they will divide their holiday time between families. Christina's cousin, Matt, and his partner, Paul, were in this stage as they had committed to starting a family together. In Mark's and Liz's case, they had each already entered this stage with their first marriages. They were then in this stage again, however, being in their second marriage and already having children from previous marriages, the dynamics were much more complicated and most likely required more attention and negotiation.

Stage 3: Families with young children. This stage is often the most difficult for couples, particularly due to the impact on the couple's relationship, as they experience the acceptance of a new person into their dyad. Once again, rules, roles, and relationships are renegotiated as they were at the beginning of the couple's agreement to enter into their committed relationship. However, for many couples, the birth or adoption of a child legitimizes their unit as a socially sanctioned family. Several factors can influence the impact of this stage on the couple's relationship, for example, whether or not the birth or adoption of a child was a mutual decision, such as a planned pregnancy, if the child arrived before the couple had agreed to enter a committed relationship, the financial stability of the couple, and the extent to which the couple has discussed child-rearing beliefs and practices ahead of time. In addition, this developmental stage is much more complex than other stages because it encompasses multiple stages of development all at once: the family life cycle, the couple's life cycle, the individual life cycle of each adult, the child's life cycle, the cycle of each partner's family of origin, and the extended family life cycle (Rasheed, Rasheed, & Marley, 2011). Martin was in this stage with his second wife, as they had two small children, Dominique and Matthew. The fact that Martin was simultaneously in this stage as well as in a family with teenagers (from his first marriage) further complicated this already challenging stage of family development.

Stage 4: Families with school-aged children. This stage of family development corresponds with Erikson's (1959) *generativity versus stagnation* stage of individual psychosocial development. This is a period of time when the focus of most individuals is on raising children and building their careers. The idea behind this stage is that the individual is building a legacy to leave behind. It helps us deal with our own mortality, knowing that our existence has contributed to the world either through producing and raising children who become valuable citizens or through meaningful work.

When children enter their school years, their parents are faced with letting go of constant care and supervision and have to allow for more independence in their children. Parents during this stage often worry about how their children will be treated by teachers and other adults during their school day, as well as the child-rearing practices and beliefs of the institution they are in. Feelings of protectiveness and anxiety surface, and often parents have trouble sharing some of the authority they are accustomed to having over their children with teachers and other adults involved in their education (Rasheed et al., 2011). Additionally, parents' social lives and daily routines are often consumed by their children's school and extracurricular commitments.

Both sides of the Manning-Kelly and Jones families had school-aged children. Liz and Martin's divorce, as well as Shoshana and Mark's, and their respective remarriages, most likely had a significant impact on the children's schooling as they adjusted to alternating between households and therefore complicating routines. Additionally, Emma's special needs (related to her cerebral palsy diagnosis) required more time and energy to manage as her parents were faced with providing as normal an educational process as possible.

Stage 5: Families with teenagers. Adolescence is a stage fraught with many changes: biological, cognitive, social, and psychological. According to Erik Erikson, a major developmental task of the teenager is to establish an identity independent of his or her family (1959). The child's peers become more important and more influential than they were in previous years. Often a challenge for the parents is to figure out how to provide enough space for the teen to explore his or her independence, while maintaining appropriate closeness and boundaries to ensure the child's safety. Christina and Martin Jr. were right in the middle of this stage. As such, their parents were faced with the normal challenges that come with having a teenage daughter, while also dealing with the mental and physical health issues Christina had presented recently, in addition to issues related to their divorce. The parents had worked out a custody arrangement that provided the children with frequent time with both parents, something crucial for teenagers. Still, Martin Jr. had fallen into a pattern of avoiding his parents as much as possible. Avoidant behavior is not unusual among teens. In fact, it is quite normal for teenagers to withdraw a little from their parents as they explore their individual identities. The challenge for Mark, Liz, Martin, and Daniella was to persist in creating opportunities for time and communication with Martin Jr. while he continued to push them away. The same could be said for Christina. Although she had no problem saying that she could not wait to get away from her parents' control, this was the stage at which she needed them the most, especially with her current problems. The most effective parents of teens remain involved and interested in their children's lives even though they are being pushed away; continue to "bug" and "nag" their kids even though they face eye rolling, heavy sighs, and slamming doors; and remain available and consistent throughout the difficult times. For Liz and Martin and their respective new spouses, this was particularly challenging since they both had younger children in their new marriages, and their attention was pulled in multiple directions.

Stage 6: Launching and moving on. This stage, usually prompted by adult children going off to college or leaving home for a job, involves the continued process of a young adult establishing his or her identity separate from his or her family of origin. Corresponding with Erikson's (1959) stage of *intimacy versus isolation* in which young adults search for meaningful relationships with other people and focus on work and developing a career, this stage also signifies the official "launching" of one's children into adulthood. This stage can often be marked by what's known as "empty nest" syndrome, as parents struggle with letting go of their grown children and renegotiating their relationship with their spouse or partner. At the time, Christina's family would normally have been preparing for her launching, however, her issues were halting the developmental progression. It was possible that she would postpone college until her eating disorder and other issues were under control or that she would choose another path altogether. Because of her strong desire to separate from her parents, it was possible that she would try to launch before she was ready, which could have caused even more problems for herself.

Boomerang Children. The term *boomerang children* refers to grown children who have been launched and then return home again to live with their parents. There are many reasons why an adult child may return home including illness, relationship problems, and financial issues. This stage is one that became increasingly common with the economic downturn of 2009. When adult children leave the home and then return, all of the adults in the household may be faced with new challenges in their relationships as they try to cope with new roles and rules. One mistake parents can make is to try and hold onto the parent-child relationship they had before, rather than move into a new adult-adult relationship. It is important for all of the adults in this new living arrangement to agree on the new rules and on the levels of financial and household contributions each family member is expected to make. Boomerang children can have a negative impact on their parents' marriage, if the parents allow them to intrude on their need for time together. The launching stage is typically a time when couples reconnect and focus on each other, making up for lost time and preparing for their golden years. Having a child return to the nest can throw a wrench in the couples' plans for intimacy. Although Christina's stepsister, Ashley, was successfully launched to college, the fact that she was then living at home with Shoshana made her launching incomplete and therefore she was a boomerang child. Liz's brother, David, could also have been considered a boomerang child. Although he still lived in his own apartment, he was dependent on his parents for financial support and therefore affected their plans as a couple.

Stage 7: The family in later life. The final stage of the family life cycle occurs after the children have left home. Often, families are in more than one stage at a time during this point, as the grown children have moved beyond the launching stage either to the first or second family life cycle stage, perhaps starting their own families, while their parents are in later life, focusing on retirement; reflecting on their lives and past experiences and perhaps a "bucket list" of wishes to fulfill before they die; health issues; and end-of-life issues. This stage corresponds with Erikson's (1959) *integrity versus despair* stage of individual development, in which individuals reflect on their lives and search for meaning, while contemplating their own impending mortality. All of Christina's grandparents and stepgrandparents were in this stage of the family life cycle. Sally, Liz's mother, had already been widowed and was caring for her second husband as his cognitive functioning declined. Mark's parents were even older, and both were facing declining health, functioning, and death. By contrast, Martin's parents were in an earlier phase of retirement in which they were active and reasonably healthy. They were able to live independently, care for themselves as they always had, and actively participated in the lives of their adult children, grandchildren, friends, and their community. This stage for the Manning-Kelly family is discussed in more detail in the next section.

The Sandwich Generation. With the economic downturn of 2009, as well as an increasing number of senior citizens living well into their 90s and later, an increasing number of families are finding themselves in more than one stage at a time during what we call the *sandwich generation.* This is when parents are simultaneously the caregivers for their children and their aging parents. This can cause tremendous strain for the caregivers, as they frequently feel pulled in different directions and unable to fulfill everyone's needs as they would like. Both Liz and Mark were facing issues related to their parents' aging processes. Liz's stepfather, Jim, had recently been diagnosed with Alzheimer's disease. Mark's parents, Emily and Bryan, presented a different set of challenges. They both had age-related health problems, though neither suffered from either dementia or a life-threatening disease. They were less able to care for their home than they used to be and yet did not wish to move to an apartment or retirement community. Mark was concerned about their nutrition, as Emily, who had been a traditional housewife, no longer liked to cook or go to the grocery store. Mark was also busy with his career, wife, children, and stepchildren and did not live close enough to help his parents with routine chores such as changing heat and air filters, running errands, or taking them to appointments.

Martin's parents were both in their mid-60s and working. They were the center of Martin's extended family, which included his younger brother and two younger sisters and their children. Martin's father's health was excellent, but his mother had suffered cardiac problems for a number of years. She became very ill about the time her youngest child, Selena, left for college, which may have had repercussions for her daughter's adjustment to living away from home. Since then, her condition had been well managed, and she was active and independent.

Death and Dying. A natural part of living is of course dealing with the death of loved ones and acknowledging our own mortality. The pain of losing a loved one is difficult at any stage of development, but it is especially difficult when the death of a loved one goes against one's perception of the natural order of things. Death of a family member can also be the catalyst for all sorts of family drama, especially when there is a dispute over the estate of the deceased or unresolved issues between family members that are resurrected when the family members are brought together again to mourn their loss. Grieving the loss of a loved one is a complex and highly individualized process. Family counselors can help individual family members recognize their own grief processes, as well as those of their loved ones, and ways to cope effectively.

INDIVIDUAL COPING WITH GRIEF

How people grieve is as unique as our personalities. There is no correct or incorrect way to grieve. Still, some methods of coping with grief help return a person to a state of functioning similar to their preloss state, just as some methods may impair a person's functioning more than others. Some people throw themselves into work or other distractions in order to help them avoid dealing with their pain. Others may fall into a deep depression and withdraw from social activities. Both of these are understandable responses: Grief is painful. However, the problem is that trying to avoid pain doesn't make the pain go away. Although talking about one's loss can be difficult and may be scary for many people, it helps ease the pain and gets easier with more frequency. In her (1969) book, *On Death and Dying*, Elizabeth Kubler-Ross described the grief process as having 5 stages that many people experience:

1. Denial: This refers to how an individual is labeling his or her response to the death of a loved one. Of course the initial response to a death is usually one of shock or disbelief. However, many times people can convince themselves that they are "fine" and able to move on without difficulty. This may be a denial of their true feelings or an uncertainty of how to share their feelings with others. While people can and do cope with their grief and are able to resume prior functioning eventually, it generally takes some time and lots of adjustment to be able to return to a state of normalcy, or feeling "fine."

2. Anger: Not all people experience anger as a part of the grief process. Still, some may experience anger at the person they have lost, at the situation they are left to face, or at themselves. Finding effective ways to express this anger can help move a person toward resolution.

3. Bargaining: Generally with a higher power, bargaining takes place when an individual believes that an all-powerful being can change the

situation he or she is in. This is more common with people experiencing a terminal illness, divorce, or some other kind of loss, rather than after a death has occurred. A person trying to bargain with a higher power will promise to do something or change something significant in exchange for removal of the impending loss.

4. Depression: The word *depression* is used to describe the feeling of intense sorrow that occurs during the grief process. The symptoms of grief are also similar to those of clinical depression, therefore it is important for the counselor to distinguish the clients' symptoms as grief related or related to a major depressive episode. According to the DSM-V, the symptoms of grief typically include feelings of emptiness and loss when thinking about the lost loved one. While in a major depressive episode, the depression is persistent, and the individual is unable to experience or anticipate happiness or pleasure. A person who is grieving is usually able to experience some joy and pleasure in the midst of the pain and sorrow related to the loss, and one's self-esteem is intact, while a person in a major depressive episode will commonly experience feelings of worthlessness, self-loathing, or an inability to cope with the pain of depression (American Psychiatric Association, 2013).

5. Acceptance: In this period, the grieving person is coming to terms with the fact that while life after the loss will be forever changed, there is still hope that life ahead will include joy and new possibilities. The pangs of grief will most likely surface with reminders of the lost loved one, but the feelings of intense sorrow and pain are likely to decrease over time.

Not all people progress through all of the stages, nor is the grief process solely linear. In fact, some argue that the classification of the grieving process into stages is an unfortunate and inaccurate occurrence. Okun and Nowinski (2011) hold that the abovementioned stages of grief are applicable for what is now called "traditional grief." Advances in modern medicine have increased the lifespan for most, and a terminal illness is no longer an immediate death sentence. Because of this, Okun and Nowinski believe the Kubler-Ross (1969) stages of grief may no longer be appropriate for more contemporary types of loss. They developed five stages of the *new grief*, which include crisis, unity, upheaval, resolution, and renewal. More information on these and other information related to contemporary grief issues may be found in their book *Saying Goodbye: How Families Can Find Renewal Through Loss*.

Regardless of where a person is in the grieving process, there is support available. Some recommended ways people may cope with grief are listed below:

1. Reaching out to a support group for people dealing with a loss; many local churches, nonprofit agencies (such as hospice), and mental health centers offer such groups.

2. Finding and choosing ways to say goodbye to the loved one, such as holding a ceremony, creating a memory book, a burial ritual, or another way of celebrating the person's life and the grieving individual's relationship with that person, often helps with the grieving process.

3. Acknowledging that one's relationship with that person isn't over simply because he or she is no longer living; many people have unfinished business with their lost loved ones and need to find a way to communicate with them in order to be able to let them, or their issues, go. Writing a letter, journaling, or visiting the burial site may facilitate the communication that needs to take place in order to resolve this unfinished business.

4. Taking care of oneself both physically and mentally is key. Making sure that one is getting enough sleep, exercising, eating well, and connecting with others is essential for effective coping. Seeing a counselor may also be a good idea, especially if a person is having trouble coping on his or her own.

Children's Grief

When talking to children about a family member's death, honesty is important. It is not a good idea to try to mask the death by keeping it a secret or describing it in other terms, such as telling the child that "grandpa went to sleep." This causes great confusion and may even cause children to be afraid to go to sleep (and no parent wants that). Adults should give the children just enough information so they understand that death is permanent and that the lost loved one won't be coming back. Some adults worry about telling children how a person died, afraid that it will be too much for them to handle. This may be true depending on what the details are. Specific details about the death, such as the nature of a disease or events such as a car crash or suicide are not necessary for the child to understand that the person is gone and not returning. They simply need to know that the person died. Beyond that, adults may answer the children's questions about the death, being careful not to provide more information than they are requesting.

Children are similar to adults in that when a family member or close friend dies, they need to have something to do. Just like many adults often need to attend funerals or find other ways to say goodbye to the lost loved one, children need to have their own process of saying goodbye. Encouraging children to find their ways of saying goodbye, in addition to giving them the option of attending the other funeral or burial events, will help them work through their own grief.

Suggested children's activities for grieving include:

1. Making a memory photo book or special box that holds mementos related to the lost loved one

2. Planting a tree or flower in honor of the lost loved one

3. Writing a letter to the lost one, and placing it somewhere special, such as at a grave, buried in the ground, or burned as part of a goodbye ceremony

4. Working with a counselor (Talk therapy or play therapy may be effective ways to help children cope.)

5. Playing (Whether in therapy or on their own, children work through emotions and thoughts when they play. Allowing the time and space to play through their grief is crucial to their healing.)

Ambiguous Loss

Another type of loss that is becoming more commonly recognized is *ambiguous loss*. This is a loss where the circumstances of the loss, such as in the case of a miscarriage, loss of one's job, infertility, a disability, a missing person, an undetermined cause of death, or the loss of a relationship due to dementia, are making it difficult for a person to grieve. People experiencing ambiguous loss feel stuck and unable to move forward in their grief because of unanswered questions or lack of clear understanding related to the loss (Betz & Thorngren, 2006).

Ambiguous loss is especially common in cases of Alzheimer's disease and dementia. While dementia is not a disease, it refers to a set of symptoms including memory loss and other cognitive and social functioning deficits that are severe enough to interfere with daily living. Examples include getting lost while driving in a previously familiar area or becoming confused, agitated, or unable to recognize one's own family members. Imagine facing the reality of your own mother, with whom you have always had a close relationship, not recognizing you and you not being able to talk with her the way you used to and knowing that this relationship is changed forever. For some adult children this brings on the realization that they are now the memory keepers for the parents, and it is up to them to make sure that their parents' stories are told so that their stories don't die with them. This type of loss is especially complicated, because the person is still alive and visible, but the loss of the person as they knew him or her, and the relationship they had, is very real. *Complicated grief* applies to deaths due to suicide or murder, because of the other emotions such as anger and confusion that accompany the feelings of intense sadness. Grief is also complicated when the relationship with the lost person is not resolved, or there are things that were left unsaid. Just because a person is dead, doesn't mean your relationship with them ends. Your feelings of joy, sadness, frustration, anger, even rage, may continue. However, because the person is no longer there as a target for those feelings, one may feel conflicted and confused. "I should be sad because she's dead, but I'm still just so angry at her!" It is important for the family counselor to assure each family member that no matter what feelings they are having about losing their loved one, their feelings are their own and justified. Still, if a person cannot seem to move on through the grieving process for a considerable amount of time (i.e., 1 to 2 years later the person has not resumed their normal activities), and he or she is not able to function in daily tasks, he or she should be referred for treatment for clinical depression or some other diagnosis.

CONCLUSION

Because people are constantly growing and changing, families experience many milestones, changes, crises, painful losses, and joyous successes. New trends in family structures within the last few decades, as well as life-prolonging advances in medicine, have impacted both the family structure and the family life stages of development. For family counselors it is essential to understand the developmental processes that are typical and expected and to recognize when responses to family events warrant treatment.

STOP AND THINK:

1. Why is the family life cycle important?

2. Why is it important to study both individual and family development?

3. What stage of family development do you think is the most difficult for families? Why?

4. What stage of development was the most challenging for you? Why?

5. How have you or your family dealt with loss?

6. What was your first experience with death? How did the adults in your life handle the death?

7. What do you think people need in order to move on after losing a family member?

8. Discuss the potential issues that may arise when parents or children of empty nesters need to move in either for economic or health reasons, just when the empty nesters are ready to focus on themselves or their relationship. Use Martin and Liz's families as examples, and compare them to your own.

Extend Your Learning:

1. Notice families in public, at the grocery store, at athletic events, or at the park. What developmental stages are present? Are there any challenges evident during your observation?

2. Talk with a friend or family member. What stage of development was/is most difficult for him or her and why?

3. Look for evidence of developmental stages in your favorite television shows and movies about families. Note the difficulties discussed in this book, as well as any new ones presented.

4. Do a library search on developmental theories. Compare how the theories address individuals versus families.

REFERENCES

American Psychiatric Association. (2013). *Diagnostic and statistical manual of mental disorders*. Washington, DC: Author.

Berg-Cross, L. (2000). *Basic concepts in family therapy: An introductory text, second edition*. Binghamton, NY: Haworth Press.

Betz, G., & Thorngren, J. (2006). Ambiguous loss and the family grieving process. *The Family Journal: Counseling and Therapy for Couples and Families, 14*(4), 359–365.

Bowen, M. (1971). The use of family theory in clinical practice. In J. Haley (Ed.), *Changing families: A family therapy reader* (p. 159–192). New York, NY: Grune and Stratton.

Bowen, M. (1972). On the differentiation of self. In I. Framo (Ed.), *Family interactions: A dialogue between family researchers and family therapists.* New York, NY: Springer.

Bowen, M. (1976). Theory in the practice of psychotherapy. In P. Guerin (Ed.), *Family therapy and practice* (p. 42–90). New York, NY: Gardner Press.

Carter, E., & McGoldrick, M. (1980). *Genograms in family assessment.* New York, NY: W. W. Norton & Company.

Kubler-Ross, E. (1969). *On death and dying.* New York, NY: Macmillan.

Okun, B., & Nowinski, J. (2011). *Saying goodbye: How families can find renewal through loss.* New York, NY: Penguin Group.

Erikson, E. H. (1959). *Identity and the life cycle.* New York, NY: International Universities Press.

Rasheed, J. M., Rasheed, M. N., & Marley, J. A. (2011). *Family therapy: Models and techniques.* Thousand Oaks, CA: Sage.

Strong, B., & DeVault, C. (1986). *The marriage and family experience.* New York, NY: West.

U.S. Census Bureau. (2012). *Age & sex composition in the United States.* Retrieved from http://www.census.gov/population/age/data/2012comp.html

FOR FURTHER STUDY

Anderson, S. A., Russell, C. S., & Schumm, W. R. (1983). Perceived marital quality and family life-cycle categories: A further analysis. *Journal of Marriage and Family, 45*(1), 127–139. doi: 10.2307/351301

Becvar, D. S., & Becvar, R. J. (2009). *Family therapy: A systemic integration* (7th ed.). New York, NY: Pearson Education.

Chan, H. M. (2004). Sharing death and dying: Advance directives, autonomy and the family. *Bioethics, 18*(2), 87–103. doi: 10.1111/j.1467-8519.2004.00383.x

Glick, P. C. (1977). Updating the life cycle of the family. *Journal of Marriage and Family, 39*(1), 5–13. doi: 10.2307/351058

Grotevant, H. D., & Cooper, C. R. (1985). Patterns of interaction in family relationships and the development of identity exploration in adolescence. *Child Development, 56*(2), 415–428. doi: 10.2307/1129730

Grundy, E., & Henretta, J. C. (2006). Between elderly parents and adult children: A new look at the intergenerational care provided by the 'sandwich generation.' *Aging and Society, 26*(5), 707–722. doi: 10.2307/351301

Hill, R. (1986). Life cycle stages for types of single parent families: Of family development theory. *Family Relations, 35*(1), 19–29. doi: 10.2307/584278

Kilpatrick, A. C., & Holland, T. P. (2009). *Working with families: An integrative model by level of need* (5th ed.). New York, NY: Pearson Education.

Lynn, J., & Teno, J. M. (1997). Perceptions by family members of the dying experience of older and seriously ill patients. *Annals of Internal Medicine, 126*(2), 97–106. doi: 10.7326/0003-4819 126-2-199701150-00001

Minuchin, P. (1985). Families and individual development: Provocations from the field of family therapy. *Child Development, 56*(2), 289–302. doi: 10.2307/1129720

Spillman, B. C., & Pezzin, L. E. (2002). Potential and active family caregivers: Changing networks and the 'sandwich generation.' *Milbank Quarterly, 78*(3), 347–374. doi: 10.1111/1468-0009.00177

CHAPTER 3

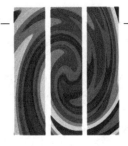

Assessing Families Traditionally and Creatively

TRADITIONAL ASSESSMENT METHODS

For many decades family counselors used assessment techniques designed for individuals rather than families. More recent research has focused on the development of valid measures for assessing family functioning versus individual issues. Olson (2000) developed a self-report instrument called the Family Adaptability and Cohesion Evaluation Scale (FACES). Based on what he termed the Circumplex Model, this inventory is based on three dimensions of marital and family systems: cohesion, flexibility, and communication. For this inventory, each family member is instructed to complete the instrument twice, indicating both perceptions of current family functioning as well as one's description of an ideal family. The discrepancy between the two sets of responses indicates how satisfied a family member is with the current family functioning. The greater the discrepancy between one's ideal family functioning and the perceptions of the present family situation, the higher the level of dissatisfaction.

The Clinical Rating Scale (CRS) was also developed by Olson in 1990 and is often used by clinicians as an instrument to assess family cohesion, flexibility, and communication as they observe them in clinical settings. This scale is solely from the clinician or researcher's perspective, rather than the self-report of the family members.

Another instrument for family assessment is the Family Assessment Measure (FAM). Based on the process model of family functioning, this inventory measures families on seven key dimensions: task accomplishment, role performance, communication, affective expression, involvement, control, values, and norms.

FACES

CRS

FAM

The FAM assesses these dimensions at three levels: within the whole family system, within various dyads, and in individual functioning (Skinner, Steinhauer, & Sitarenios, 2000).

Family counselors should consider a variety of qualitative methods in addition to the quantitative ones that are available. Quantitative measures may be limited in their ability to capture the subtle nuances of family functioning and in individual and group perceptions of the family and how the family functions as a unit. There are many types of qualitative family assessment techniques available for professionals to use for this purpose. One such technique is the genogram, an example of which is illustrated at the beginning of this book. A genogram is a 3-generation family tree, complete with names, birth and death dates, and other notations as desired. Genograms are useful in helping individuals and families detect and understand patterns that take place across generations, as well as cultural values and historical contexts of problems.

Genograms also provide individuals with insight on occupational choices and traditional familial and cultural expectations. For example, a family of physicians, military officers, or firefighters may have a tradition of following in one's parents' footsteps, thereby implying pressure for future generations to follow suit. A young person in that family who wants to pursue a career as an event planner, for example, may need to be prepared for some resistance to the idea of breaking out of the family occupational tradition. Other common patterns identified in genograms include divorce, health and medical issues, relationship patterns, gender role expectations, and geographical and psychological cutoffs.

Genograms are especially useful in families with a history of substance abuse. Not only are they helpful in providing insight for a family member struggling with addiction, but they also may prevent future problems for individuals armed with the knowledge of a predisposition to addiction. At our university there is a campuswide initiative to help students identify and attempt to change negative behaviors related to alcohol abuse. As a part of this initiative, students who have been charged with an alcohol-related violation on campus are required to meet with a faculty or staff member who helps them examine their behaviors and formulate a plan for change. Examining family history is an important part of this process. Often young people are not aware of their family history, particular around substance abuse, since it is often treated as a taboo topic of discussion. Assigning genograms for students as homework in between these sessions can help the students make more sense of why they might be struggling in their attempts to avoid alcohol abuse and help them formulate a clearer plan for behavior change.

Knowing one's family history helps to inform one's identity. Bowen's (1971, 1978) term *intergenerational transmission*, refers to the expectations, teachings, and influences passed down from generation to generation. These help make us who we are and help explain why we believe certain things and behave certain ways. However, not all people have access to the knowledge of their family history. In cases of adoption or abandonment, for example, the absence of a family history can leave a gaping hole in a person's quest for understanding the world and his or her place in it. A family counselor can use the development of a genogram to help clients formulate their own versions of their family histories. Working together to craft a genogram is an invaluable way to gather information, as well as to process the information that is gathered along the way.

Genograms can also serve as a tool for the elderly to recover and organize memories, as well as an assurance that one's family life span, and thereby one's impact on the world, extends into the past and well ahead into the future, rather than ending with one life span. The idea of one's family heritage prevailing can provide comfort to a person who is in the final years of his or her life and contemplating the impact of his or her mortality.

STOP AND THINK:

1. Looking at the Manning-Kelly genogram, what patterns do you notice?

2. How might you use the genogram in a session with Christina? With her family?

3. What cultural differences can you identify within the Manning-Kelly family?

4. How might these cultural differences impact the family as they try to blend into a new unit?

5. How might the cultural differences between the therapist and the family affect the helping process?

The Lifestyle Questionnaire

Another assessment technique is an exercise known as the Lifestyle Questionnaire (Kern, 1988). A popular tool among Adlerian therapists, the Lifestyle Questionnaire is for each individual family member to complete. It asks for the individual client's description of each family member, in order of birth, and for subjective descriptions of each family member, such as who is the smartest, who is the most easy-going, who is the loudest, who is a leader, and so on. The questionnaire also asks for the client's earliest memories, which typically involve family members and may provide insight about how the client views the world and his or her family, along with his or her position in the family/world. Other areas explored in the lifestyle assessment include childhood and recurring dreams, self-perceptions, pivotal transitions in one's development, and views of parents and their treatment of each child within the family constellation.

Extend Your Learning:

1. Visit the Alfred Adler Graduate School website at http://alfredadler .edu/sites/default/files/515_LifeStyle_Assessment_2011%20Final.pdf.

2. Complete the lifestyle questionnaire for yourself, focusing on your own family. What stands out to you in your responses? What surprises you? How do you think Christina would answer the questions you answered? What questions do you think will cause the most difficulty for her?

Family Sculpting

For those who prefer incorporating the creative arts into their work with families, family sculpting can be an effective way to determine how the family members view each other and their family as a whole. In this technique, the therapist instructs an individual family member to position, or "sculpt," people together in the way that they view the family. This requires some space for movement, as often individuals need to use some space to illustrate emotional or geographical distance between family members. A child who feels cut off by her parents may sculpt this by having her parents turn away from her and having substantial space in between them. Similarly, a mother who is having a hard time dealing with her youngest child growing into an adult might sculpt her family by showing herself holding onto the shirttail of her son, while he is turning away and trying to move forward. Props such as chairs or other objects may be used to symbolize position within families. For example, a daughter who feels overpowered by her mother might ask her mother to stand in a chair, towering over her, or a father who feels left out of his family might group his family members together facing away from him, showing the physical separation he feels. An adult child of an alcoholic may use an inflatable beer bottle or other alcohol-related object and place it in between family members, demonstrating the physical presence of a barrier between family members created by substance abuse. This physical representation of how each family member sees the family can provide insight and information for both the helping professional and the family members. In many cases, an important next step will include the family members providing a "sculpture" or some other representation of how they would like to see the family change. The following is a description of how Christina sculpted her family in the second session.

Christina's Family Sculpture. As instructed by the therapist, all of the family members stood up (Christina, Liz, Mark, Martin Jr., and Emma). Christina positioned herself standing in front of her family, partially facing them and partially turning away with one arm reaching out away from the family. She explained that this represented her desire to leave home but still wanting to remain connected to her family. She asked her mother to stand in the center of the group, with her arms outstretched toward Christina. Then she instructed her mother to make a pushing and pulling motion with her arms. This, she said, indicated the tension that she felt with her mother, from the pressure that her mother put on her (pushing) to be the perfect child and succeed in school and the pressure she felt from her mother to be a source of support for her mother's own emotional issues (pulling toward her). Then she asked her brother to stand beside their mother, facing outward, away from her. This was not surprising, since it seems that Martin Jr. had all but disengaged from the family entirely. He was a physical presence in the family but remained in his own world, not actively engaging with any of his family members. Christina asked her stepdad, Mark, to stand close to Liz and put his arm around her shoulders. She had him facing Christina, but with one arm reaching away, toward an invisible target, representing his biological children. Christina noted that she needed her father in the sculpture somehow, but since he was unable to attend that session, she decided to put a chair in the sculpture to represent him. She positioned the chair behind her, facing her, a little off to the side from her mother, Mark, and Martin Jr. She made note of how the chair was there to catch her if she fell. Finally, she brought Emma into the sculpture and asked her to stand in between Liz and Mark, holding onto to her mother's legs. This was an easy request as Emma usually clings to Liz.

The therapist in this session could have asked each family member to sculpt the family as they saw it, in turn. As you can imagine, this prompts reactions from each of the family members as they get a physical representation of how they are viewed by their family members. The therapist could then ask each family member how they would like to see the sculpture change. This can then lead to an establishment of goals for the family's therapy.

STOP AND THINK:

1. Note how Christina sees her family based on her family sculpture. What do you notice about her placement of each family member? Of herself in relation to them?

2. What do you think the other family members' reactions are to how she has sculpted them? How would you feel if you were Liz? Martin Jr.?

3. Which other family members would you like to see sculpt this family? What would you expect to see?

Extend Your Learning:

1. In class or in a small group, volunteers may sculpt their own families as they see them. Volunteers will need to choose members from the class to play the roles of their family members. They should position them as they see their family members (asking their permission before they touch them, of course). If you volunteer to do so, feel free to use props, such as chairs for people to stand on (to symbolize someone being on a pedestal, superior, or untouchable) or tables or desks as barriers between people. You can also have people stand in different parts of the room to symbolize space and distance between relatives. You may choose to put yourself physically in the sculpture or to ask someone else to play the role of you in the sculpture. Putting yourself in the sculpture allows for a more powerful experience of the emotions and nuances of the sculpture, while having someone else stand in allows you to walk around the sculpture and make sure it is displayed the way you want it to be.

Family Scripting

All families have patterns of interaction or scripts that they tend to follow. For example, one script may include the following each time the family gets together for a holiday meal: the mother scurries around trying to talk to everyone while she prepares the meal, inevitably forgetting a food item because she is too distracted by all the family interaction. Meanwhile, the dad and brothers retire to the family room to watch whatever sport event is on the TV, and the kids all run around, oblivious to the food preparation that's going on until it magically appears for them to devour. This pattern or "script" goes on year after year, with the roles rarely changing. For anyone to break away from this script, for example, if the mother suddenly declared that she was not going to participate in the meal preparation for this Thanksgiving and announced that the men needed to prepare the meal, everyone else in the family would be affected in some way. Either someone else would step into the mother's former role, or there would protest from other family members who have become accustomed to the pre-existing script.

Similar to Minuchin's Enactment Approach (Minuchin & Fishman, 1981), *family scripting* consists of therapists asking family members to identify the typical interaction patterns in order to define what a normal script is for that family. Once it has been identified, the therapist can ask each family member what purposes the current script serves, how it benefits certain family members, and how it may be detrimental to other family members. The therapist can then help the family discuss alternative scripts for use in making needed changes in the family.

STOP AND THINK:

1. What family scripts have you noticed in your family?

2. What functions do these scripts serve for individuals? For the whole family?

In the Manning-Kelly family case, during the third family therapy session, the therapist asked Liz to elaborate on why she was frustrated with Mark's level of engagement with others in the home. Liz then relayed the following script:

After we all get home I usually make dinner while Mark has a drink and reads the newspaper or watches TV. The kids are off in their rooms doing whatever they usually do—homework or on social media or texting their friends. We try hard to have dinner together every night—I think it's very important—though the kids never say much at the table. Mark opens a bottle of wine for me, I ask him about his day, and he gives me monosyllabic responses. He never asks me about my day or the kids about how they're doing or what they did at school. After dinner he disappears—in fact, they all do, except for Emma—and I do the dishes and then get to work on whatever case I'm working on after I put Emma to bed. Mark is in his study, having a drink and either on the phone or the computer. Christina and Marty have, once again, escaped to their rooms, and I usually fall asleep before Mark comes to bed.

STOP AND THINK:

1. What do you notice about Liz's script?

2. What do you think she wants from Mark?

3. How do you think Mark might describe their typical family evenings? What about Martin Jr.'s or Christina's perceptions?

Here the family therapist might ask Mark for his reactions to the scene Liz described, asking him what he thinks she wants from him. Mark may respond by relaying his own script of the evening activities and shed some light on the reasons he chooses to follow this pattern of interaction. The therapist might also invite the kids to insert their own interpretations and reactions to the script identified by Liz.

Family Play Therapy

"The family that plays together stays together" (unknown). A quick Internet search will show that this quote is very well-represented in organizations that promote frequent, playful family interactions. Related research reveals that families that make time to engage in leisure activities together actually do have more success in developing and maintaining positive relationships. Because play therapists have learned that children's play is a powerful medium for communication and understanding, the use of play in therapy with families has become increasingly more common (Bratton & Ray, 2000).

There are many benefits to using play as a therapeutic modality. An important one is that playing doesn't require talking. Many clients are not thrilled about being forced to talk to a stranger about their problems. Play provides an alternative to talking and, because it is a projective technique, often generates more insight than traditional talk therapy. Another benefit is that playing is pleasurable—having fun lightens the mood, decreases anger, and takes the pressure off being serious in therapy. Incorporating play therapy techniques into work with families may help break down barriers between individuals, improve communication, and increase the likelihood of more positive interactions taking place outside the counseling session. The family's full participation is crucial in these activities in order to get the most impact. The following are some examples of play therapy interventions.

Family Puppet Shows

Eliana Gil (2000) directs her family clients to choose from her impressive collection of puppets for a puppet show. She instructs the family members that they are to develop a story with the puppets that has a beginning, a middle, and an end, and then they perform it for her. As the family works together to create their puppet show, the family counselor can watch to see how the family interacts, what the major themes of the story are, and how they decide who does what. One example of a family puppet show is of a family in which the father was away on business a lot, and the mom was struggling to manage their children's behavior. As she watched this family select their puppets, she noticed that the father chose an alien puppet, while the mother chose a butterfly. The story that they performed depicted the alien as leaving earth frequently, while the butterfly was left alone to deal with the other animals' (children) rowdy behaviors. The alien indicated his annoyance that the animals were out of control and didn't want to hang around such wildness. The butterfly kept flying away when things got too tense. The therapist's intervention consisted of discussing with the family ways that the alien and the butterfly could work together to help the animals to calm down. After the alien agreed to spend more time on earth, and the butterfly agreed not to fly away, things in this family improved (Gil, 2000).

Family Build-A-House

Carla Sharp (2005) developed this technique in which families are instructed to build a house together out of Legos, Lincoln logs, blocks, or large cardboard bricks. In this exercise, the therapist looks for interaction patterns, such as who takes on the leadership roles, how decisions are made, and how the family communicates and solves problems. For example, are all family members working together, or does one person assume the lead? If a leader emerges, who is it? How is this person's leadership received? How are decisions made? Are issues handled democratically or does one person make the decision? The structure of the house is equally important. As the family builds the house, the counselor may ask, "What does the structure resemble"? Do individual family members have individual spaces or are all the spaces common areas? Are there boundaries between family members' spaces? Do the boundaries have openings (such as doorways or windows), or are they rigid boundaries? Does the structure look like a house, with internal walls separating bedrooms and other spaces, or does it appear to be lacking boundaries?

When the family therapist had the Manning-Kelly family participate in this activity, Martin Jr. was initially reluctant to participate, but with more prodding, ended up building his own little space separate from the rest of the family. Liz took the lead in building and making decisions about what the structure should look like, with Christina rebelling against each part of the structure her mother was trying to build by stealing blocks from her and changing the shape of the structure her mother was building. Although she built her room next to her mother's part of the house, she also built a wall (without doors) around her individual space, along with an escape hatch for her to use "when things get too intense" as she said. Emma followed whatever her mom did, occasionally getting distracted by the blocks and playing on her own for a bit. And, finally, Mark was a quiet participant, helping to put materials where others wanted them and including a room on the back of the house for himself, where no other family members spent time. It was interesting to see how the family worked together in this activity. Since this was not their first family play therapy activity, the atmosphere seemed more comfortable overall, compared to the awkwardness present at the first session. Liz seemed eager to participate in the building of the house, while Martin Jr. rolled his eyes the entire time. The therapist found Martin's eye rolling during the activity actually an improvement to the floor-gazing disengagement of the beginning of therapy. The therapist also saw Liz's eagerness as the possible representation of a wish to "build" a life together for her new family. Mark's involvement was also slightly more involved than in previous activities, and when he built his own space, the therapist reflected that he needed a space to call his own in this home and in this new family. At the end, the therapist asked each family member to share what they learned from doing this activity. When the family discussed the completed structure and the process itself, several conclusions were present and agreed upon by all family members:

1. Liz is the accepted leader of the family's "future" together.

2. Christina seems to want to remain close to her family, even though she keeps "walls" up and escapes from time to time.

3. Mark doesn't like to rock the boat and needs his own space for processing.

4. Martin Jr. seems to have cut himself off from the family altogether.

After discussing these conclusions, the therapist facilitated a discussion of what each family member would like this "house" to look like and from there was able to generate a list of goals for each family member:

1. Liz will be open about her wishes for the family but work on listening and being open to others' (especially Mark's) ideas about how the family should function. She will also pay attention to how much time and attention she devotes to Emma, as compared to the other children.

2. Christina will work on asking for what she needs (i.e., time, attention, understanding) from her family and recognize when she wants to escape.

3. Mark will work on communicating his opinions and desires to Liz and the rest of the family, despite his fear of conflict.

4. Martin Jr. will work on finding ways to share his life with his mom, sister, and stepdad, as well as showing more interest in their lives.

(Because Emma is so young, she didn't have individual goals.)

Although these goals are clear, and each family member agreed that they are what they would like to strive to achieve, the actual work is much harder than the establishment of goals.

Family Aquarium

The family aquarium (Gil, 2000) is a wonderful activity and a great way to make use of arts and crafts supplies if you have them. The family aquarium requires one poster board or large piece of construction paper colored either blue or white, several pieces of construction paper (one for each family member), glue, glitter, sequins, feathers, fabric, and any and all little craft pieces that may be glued to the poster board. Each family member is instructed to draw and cut out their own fish, symbolizing themselves as individuals. Next, the family is instructed to create a living environment together, such as an ocean, lake, or river, and place the individual fish in that living space. Once again, the therapist observes the process that takes place among the family members, assessing leadership roles, interaction, and problem-solving patterns, and methods of communication. Additionally, the final product can reveal some interesting data, such as the environment of the fish family: Does it include light, greenery, and sources of food? Is there danger present? If so, is anyone in the protector role of the smaller fish? Are the family members swimming in the same direction or facing different directions? Are they together or spread out? Are there places to hide or be left behind? As always, this activity should be processed with the family members after their project is complete, so they can draw their own conclusions about what they observed and experienced as well as those observations pointed out by the therapist.

A family counseling session with the Manning-Kelly family using this technique might have looked something like this:

> Christina's fish was gray and black, gothic, with some dark purple glitter precisely covering thin lines of glue.
>
> Liz, rather than use the crayons and paint provided, pulled her own fine point pen out of her purse and began drawing her fish. Her fish was plain white with a blue sequin as her eye. She added some pink feathers and a little sparkly crown on top. (Note: Christina said that this fish looked nothing like how her mom is and added that it should be wearing a business suit.)
>
> Mark used the crayons closest to him and colored his fish blue. His fish was smaller than Liz's and looked a little bit like a stingray as it had a long thin tail.
>
> Martin Jr.'s fish was smaller than Mark's, a black and yellow striped fish with a large dorsal fin.
>
> Emma's fish was pink and white, very similar to her mothers, but larger and more square-like, as she had some trouble with the scissors.

When it was time for them to build their aquarium, the family counselor provided them with a large piece of blue poster board. She instructed them to create a body of water for their fish to live together, noting that the body of water could be anything they wanted, that is, a pond, lake, ocean, river, or stream, and they could make it look however they wanted. The counselor explained that they might want to wait until they had decided where each family member should be before they glued their fish to the surface, just so they could make sure they were where they wanted them.

The family counselor watched as the family members stood around and looked at each other, waiting to see who would start the activity. Liz spoke up first, saying, "Emma, isn't there a fish tank at your school? How about if we make a fish tank?" Nods in response from the others followed. Liz placed hers in the middle.

Emma was next to mom, placing her fish touching her mother's fish's belly.

Emma grabbed some green pipe cleaners and yarn and placed it on the poster, saying it looked like what was in her class's fish tank at preschool.

Christina placed hers slightly higher up than her mother's and swimming in the opposite direction, almost colliding.

Mark was on the bottom swimming in the same direction as Liz but partially hidden by the green "kelp" that Emma placed on the board.

Martin Jr. placed his up near the top left corner and drew a hook, looking as though he was about to be caught by someone's fishing line. The counselor didn't know what this meant—it could have meant the presence of danger, or it could have been meant as a means of escape.

The therapist had them process the activity, asking what they noticed about their fish tank:

What do you notice about the environment?
What do you notice about each other's fish?
What do you notice about their placement in relation to each other?
What surprised you about the end product?

Family Play Genograms

An adaptation to the basic genogram activity, the family genogram provides an interactive way for the entire family to participate in the understanding of the family's genogram. The therapist provides a large sheet of poster board or newsprint for the family to draw their genogram, or a computer-generated image of the genogram may be provided. The family members are instructed to choose from a variety of miniatures provided by the therapist. Miniatures may include people, animals, mythical creatures, trees, plants, flowers, rocks, gems, household items such as dishes and kitchen utensils, furniture, and practically anything else imaginable. (For a comprehensive list of play therapy supplies, consult the list of reference sources in the For Further Study section.)

Each family member chooses a miniature to represent each member of the family, including himself or herself. Once the selections have been made, each family member places the miniatures on the appropriate spaces in the genogram. The therapist then instructs each person to describe what item they chose for each person and why. This activity can reveal some valuable information on how family members view themselves and each other in a family context. The fact that each person chooses an object for each family member will mean that several objects are representing each person, thus showing how different family members experience each other differently, as well as the similarities that may exist. Sometimes how one's family members view oneself can be in conflict with how one wishes to be viewed. In one case, a mother chose a baby to represent her 6-year-old son. Her son became very upset because he did not want to be viewed as a baby. The mother explained that because he was her youngest, she thought of him as her baby. When she saw how upset he was at this label, she was able to see possible implications of her wanting him to remain her "baby" and began to accept the fact that he was growing up.

CONCLUSION

In this chapter, we discussed several experiential methods of assessing families. It is important to have a comprehensive understanding of the family's circumstances before launching into a treatment plan. These assessment methods can serve as a starting point for beginning treatment with families but also serve the purpose of helping the families tell their stories and giving them a roadmap for improvement. The traditional methods of assessment are effective ways of getting valuable information on paper for the therapist to see and to help define problems faced by families. The creative methods also provide valuable information and allow for a departure from the typical, pencil-and-paper methods toward a more interactive and often enjoyable method of identifying family issues. Different types of assessment will yield different kinds of information. Drawing conclusions based on only one assessment method can lead to mistakes and misunderstandings with families. Therefore, it is important that family counselors and human service professionals employ multiple methods of assessment when working with families, rather than relying on one method alone. It is also crucial to keep in mind that any and all of these techniques may be used as interventions throughout the course of the counseling relationship as a way to check the family's progress, generate insight, or facilitate communication.

STOP AND THINK:

1. What method of assessment would you choose for assessing your own family? Why would you choose this method?

2. What method do you think would be the most effective to use with the Manning-Kelly family? Explain your choice.

Extend Your Learning:

1. Research quantitative family assessment techniques online. Outline advantages and disadvantages of each assessment measure you find, comparing them to the experiential techniques discussed in this chapter.

2. Interview a local family counselor about his or her preferred assessment methods. Find out which methods he or she finds most effective in working with families.

3. Find video clips online of family play techniques. Share in groups, and discuss your reactions to the techniques, what they appear to be assessing, and appropriate uses for each.

4. Find video clips online of families in play therapy sessions or demonstrations. Write a response discussing your reactions to the families in the sessions, what the play sessions seemed to reveal about them, and how you might use the techniques you saw in your own work with families.

REFERENCES

Bowen, M. (1971). The use of family theory in clinical practice. In Haley, J. (Ed.), *Changing families: A family therapy reader* (p. 159–192). New York, NY: Grune and Stratton.

Bowen, M. (1978). *Family therapy in a clinical practice.* New York: Jason Aronson.

Bratton, S., & Ray, D. (2000). What the research shows about play therapy. *International Journal of Play Therapy, 9(1),* 47–88.

Gil, E. (2000). *Family play therapy.* Fairfax, VA: Starbright Training Institute.

Kern, R. M. (1988). *The lifestyle questionnaire inventory (LSQI).* Unpublished manuscript, Georgia State University, Atlanta.

Minuchin, S., & Fishman, H. C. (1981). Enactment. In *Family Therapy Techniques* (p. 78–97). Cambridge, MA: Harvard University Press.

Olson, D. H. (2000). Circumplex model of marital and family systems. *Journal of Family Therapy, 22*(2), 144–167.

Sharp, C. (2005). *The Build-a-House Technique.* Kailua, HI: Self-published. Retrieved from http://carlasharp.com

Skinner, H., Steinhauer, P., & Sitarenios, G. (2000). Family Assessment Measure (FAM) and process model of family functioning. *Journal of Family Therapy, 22,* 190–210.

FOR FURTHER STUDY

Family Leisure and Family Functioning

Agate, J. R., Zabriskie, R. B., Agate, S. T., & Poff, R. (2009). Family leisure satisfaction and satisfaction with family life. *Journal of Leisure Research, 41*(2), p. 205–223.

Smith, K. M., Freeman, P. A., & Zabriskie, R. B. (2009). An examination of family communication within the core and balance model of family leisure functioning. *Family Relations, 58*(1), p. 79–90. doi: 10.1111/j.1741-3729.2008.00536.x

Zabriskie, R. B., & McCormick, B. P. (2003). Parent and child perspectives of family leisure involvement and satisfaction with family life. *Journal of Leisure Research, 35*(2), p. 163–189.

Family Play Therapy

Gil, E. (1994). *Play in family therapy.* New York, NY: Guilford Press.

Rotter, J. C., & Bush, M. V. (2000). Play and family therapy. *The Family Journal, 8*(2), p. 172–176. doi: 10.1177/1066480700082010

Genograms

Bowen, M. (1980). Key to the use of the genogram. In E. A. Carter & M. McGoldrick (Eds.), *The family life cycle: A framework for family therapy* (p. xxiii). New York, NY: Gardner.

Carter, E., & McGoldrick, M. (1985). *Genograms in family assessment.* New York, NY: W. W. Norton & Company.

Hardy, K. V., & Laszloffy, T. A. (1995). The cultural genogram: Key to training culturally competent family therapists. *Journal of Marital and Family Therapy, 21*(3), 227–237. doi: 10.1111/j.1752-0606.1995.tb00158.x

Jolly, W., Froom, J., & Rosen, M. G. (1980). The genogram. *The Journal of Family Practice 10*(2), 251–255.

McGoldrick, M., & Gerson, R. (1985). *Genograms in family assessment.* New York, NY: Norton.

Family Sculpting

Costa, L. (1991). Family sculpting in the training of marriage and family counselors. *Counselor Education & Supervision, 31*(2), 121–131. doi: 10.1002/j.1556-6978.1991.tb00150.x

Marchetti-Mercer, M. C., & Cleaver, G. (2000). Genograms and family sculpting: An aid to cross-cultural understanding in the training of psychology students in South Africa. *The Counseling Psychologist, 28*(1), 61–80. doi: 10.1177/0011000000281004

Simon, R. M. (2004). Sculpting the family. *Family Process, 11*(1), 49–57. doi: 10.1111/j.1545 5300.1972.00049.x

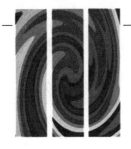

PART II

Theories of Family Counseling

CHAPTER 4

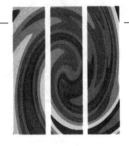

The Family Systems Approach to Family Counseling

Family functioning can be better understood if we take a closer look at the multiple systems at work in the daily lives of families. Systems are at work everywhere. Starting with the individual, our bodies are conglomerates of systems: circulatory system, skeletal system, muscular system, digestive system, nervous system, reproductive system, and so on. These systems affect each other in a variety of ways. For example, eating foods with a high amount of fat may have negative consequences for the circulatory and digestive systems.

Originally introduced in the 1970s, Urie Bronfenbrenner's (1994) Ecological Systems Theory describes how the systems that impact an individual interact with other systems in their lives. The cofounder of Head Start, a program aimed at increasing school readiness for at-risk preschoolers, Bronfenbrenner developed this model to show how children's environments, and interactions among the multiple systems within, impact their school performance. The Ecological System includes the following five interacting layers:

1. **Microsystem:** This layer includes interactions within the structures closest to the individual, including but not limited to, a person's family, friendships, school, teachers, and hobbies or afterschool activities.

2. **Mesosystem:** This system represents the many interactions and connections that may take place between more than one part of the microsystem. Examples include communication between the child's parents and the teachers,

connections between something that happens at home and a child's behavior in school, or vice versa.

Exosystem: This layer represents people and social settings that are more removed from the individual, but that nevertheless affect that person. For example if a mother's boss is making extra demands on her time, her child may be affected by her fatigue, mood, or lack of typical availability to help with homework or attend school events.

Macrosystem: This system represents the dominant values, morals, and traditions within a culture. A family's religious customs or other traditions will impact decisions and behaviors within the family, thereby spilling over into other areas of a child's life. For example, a family may hold a firm belief that children below a certain age should never wear makeup. This may impact the child if an upcoming dramatic performance involves makeup and her parents forbid it, resulting in her exclusion from the performance.

Chronosystem: The chronosystem includes events and transitions that occur over time. Individual and family developmental stages are included in this layer, as well as changing trends throughout society. Developmental changes can result in parents changing the rules and restrictions for their children as they get older or changing family structures due to births and marriages. Additionally, societal changes may impact the attitudes and functioning in families and their surrounding systems. For example, gay marriage is much more accepted, both legally and socially, than it was in the 20th century. This development has an impact on families and individuals as more same sex couples are getting legally married and having children. Parents and siblings of people in same sex relationships may respond differently to the knowledge of their child's or sibling's coming out because of these larger societal changes affecting their attitudes, thus having a ripple effect on relationships throughout the family. This societal trend, in turn, impacts schools and communities as children with same sex parents are becoming increasingly common.

Like a mobile, the family and its surrounding systems function like pieces within a structure of related parts. Each action or change affects others within the larger system. Below we discuss how systems theory applies in particular to families in counseling.

ORIGINS OF FAMILY COUNSELING

Family counseling arose from simultaneous discoveries by a number of psychiatrists along the east coast, including those at the Ackerman Institute and the Philadelphia Child Guidance Clinic, and the Mental Research Institute in California, where the anthropologist, Gregory Bateson, was influential. Bateson and his colleagues applied the concepts of biological systems theory described by Whitehead to human groups, especially the family (Bateson, 1972). Independently, psychiatrists began to notice that children with mental disorders improved in the hospital and then became symptomatic again after returning home. They speculated that something in the children's home environments must account for their regression and began to see hospitalized children with their families, sometimes hospitalizing the entire family. Independently and together, these pioneers of family counseling began to theorize about how the family functions and then experimented with whole-family interventions to change it. Murray Bowen (Chapter 5), Salvador Minuchin (Chapter 6), and both Carl Whitaker and Virginia Satir (Chapter 7) were part of the early family counseling movement.

Before we explore these three approaches to family counseling, it may be helpful to look at some of the family systems concepts from which they developed. Some of these concepts are quite complex. Like most people, you have probably thought of a family as a collection of individuals and cause-and-effect as linear in time. An example would be the operant conditioning premise that when parents reward a child's behavior after it happens, they encourage the child to repeat the behavior in the future, and, alternatively, when they consistently ignore the behavior, the child is less likely to repeat it in the future. The focus of operant conditioning is on the parent and the child as individuals and the reward and repetition or extinction of desired behavior as linear in time. While family counselors use behavioral techniques, behavioral family counseling views family dynamics as the source of reinforcement and extinction of behavior that serves a function within the family (Chapter 8).

FAMILY SYSTEMS AND FAMILY DYNAMICS

The concept of a family system changes the counselor's focus from the individual members of a family to the family as a group, or a whole. In other words, what do we notice about the collection of people we call a family, apart from who each individual is? One thing we notice is how members interact with one another. As we observe these interactions, we also notice that they repeat themselves over and over again, becoming patterns of interactions, or family dynamics, that can be predicted and, more importantly, changed when necessary.

Family members usually interact with each other regularly, and patterns to these interactions can be observed. These patterns repeat over and over again. For example, Christina said her mother frequently pressured her about going to college. Specifically, she said her mother made suggestions about what colleges she should consider applying to and what extracurricular activities she needed to be doing to make her application more attractive. She also said her mother had brought up the topic at least a couple of times a week since the beginning of Christina's sophomore year of high school. Christina responded to her mother by rolling her eyes and either telling her mother she did not know or care or by remaining silent. Liz, her mother, responded to Christina's behaviors by yelling at Christina that she was ruining her life and would regret her decision. Christina then yelled back that it was her life to ruin, not her mother's. The cycle of angry responses continued until either Christina stormed out of the room to her bedroom or, if her mother had come into her bedroom, pushed past her mother to get out of her room. Both Christina and her mother agreed that each of these arguments was the same in terms of who said and did what and in what order, although they had never thought about it until the counselor asked. In other words, Liz and Christina had a pattern to their interactions that repeated over and over again.

STOP AND THINK:

Describe one or more repetitive patterns between two members of your own family. How might these patterns impact the relationship between the two people in your example?

When other members of the Manning-Kelly family were present during an argument about college, they, too, became involved. When Mark was in the room, Liz told him to talk to Christina because she refused to listen to Liz. Then Christina would tell him he was not her father, and her father was fine with her decision about college. Mark sometimes told Christina not to talk to him and her mother "that way," to which Christina responded that it was none of his business.

If Martin Jr. was in the room, he glared at Christina and walked out of the room. Sometimes, Liz pointed out that Christina's behavior was upsetting her brother.

When Emma was in the room, she would begin to cry as her mother became visibly more upset with Christina. Sometimes, Liz shifted her attention from Christina to Emma. When this happened, Christina pointed out that Liz did not really care about her but only wanted to control her. Liz also sometimes said Christina was upsetting her sister.

Note that many of the behaviors described in the previous paragraph are reactions to what other family members did. For example, when Liz turned her attention to Emma, her argument with Christina shifted from being about college to being about whether Liz cared about Christina as much as she did about Emma. By starting to cry, Emma deflected Liz's attention from Christina to herself. And, this deflected the argument between Liz and Christina away from being about college, thus preventing them from resolving it.

Another way family members sometimes become involved is by attempting to stop an argument. When a particular family member repeatedly takes on the task of stopping arguments, he or she may be thought of as assuming the role of peacemaker, appeaser, or placator (see Virginia Satir, Chapter 7). Many mental health professionals fall into a pattern or role as peacemaker in their families and elsewhere.

Not all family dynamics are negative. Emma often played quietly while her siblings did homework and her mother prepared dinner. She brought her mother pictures she had drawn or called to her to go see something she had built or set up in her play area. Liz usually smiled and told Emma what a good job she had done, sometimes asking questions and encouraging Emma to answer them. As the family worked to change its negative dynamics, it was important for the family counselor to also support the positive dynamics. We will return to this topic in the section about first and second order change.

STOP AND THINK:

1. Describe one or more repetitive patterns involving more than two members of your own family.

2. What is your role in these patterns? Have you ever found yourself wanting or assuming the role of peacemaker?

3. If you described a positive pattern in your family, think of one that is not so positive as well. If you described a negative pattern in your family, think of a more positive one as well.

Family dynamics arise from these types of repetitive patterns of interactions among family members. Because family dynamics involve more than the individual members who are interacting, family counselors conceptualize the family system as greater than the sum of its parts. It is a holistic approach, shared by individual and family Gestalt counselors and by many physicians. The emphasis is on distinct facets, like individual family members, coming together into an integrated whole, in this case, the family. And, much like the distinct parts of an atom, members form an integrated whole while remaining in motion, changing and interacting in observable patterns of behavior. It is these observable patterns of behavior that comprise the family dynamics.

Family dynamics are complex. As we proceed through the remainder of the book, you will learn about a variety of ways in which observable patterns of behavior can be conceptualized and then changed. With each new example from the Manning-Kelly family and each new way of conceptualizing and treating it, think about the complexity of the family and its dynamics.

One conclusion that can be drawn from observing the Manning-Kelly family's dynamics during Liz and Christina's arguments about college is that no matter how many times the argument recurred and how many members became involved, nothing was resolved, nothing changed, and everyone felt increasingly upset and frustrated with Liz, Christina, and possibly themselves.

When asked what bothered her most about the arguments with her mother, Christina said it was that her mother brought up the subject over and over again, rather than that her mother was pressuring her to go to college. This distinction is important. The issue for Christina was not the content of the arguments (college applications) but rather her frustration that her mother did not stop pressuring her when she said she did not want to go to college the semester after graduating from high school. In other words, Christina was more frustrated by the repeated pattern of interactions within the family than by the specific content of those interactions. We might speculate that the family dynamics exemplified by these arguments would have been identical if Liz had been concerned about Christina's boyfriend or girlfriend or about how much she was or was not eating or exercising. The content, or topic, was far less relevant than how Christina and Liz were interacting with one another. And thus Christina and Liz's arguments about college provide an excellent example of why family counselors focus on changing the family's interactions, or dynamics, rather than the content of a particular argument.

At this point in counseling, a family counselor would not attempt to help Christina examine her motives for not wanting to go to college or her mother to examine her feelings about Christina's choice and call the work family counseling. If the family counselor were to do either, he or she would call it individual counseling with the family in the room. Similarly, a family counselor would not work with them separately to change behavior and call it family counseling. Rather, a family counselor would assume that by changing the family dynamics, counseling would allow Christina and Liz to resolve this and future arguments, as well as free Christina to think about what it is she wants to do after high school graduation and what she needs to do now, in her junior year, to ensure she achieves her goal. As you will see in Chapter 9, treating Christina's eating disorder and refusal to consider college as her next step after high school graduation as individual problems, rather than family problems, might have overlooked crucial information essential to both Christina and her family's mental health.

Family counselors view individual behaviors as comprehensible only within the context of the family system. As a result, a family counselor would intervene to change the family dynamics by disrupting the repetitive interactions among family members. The counselor would assume that unless the family dynamics, or patterns of interactions, changed, the family would not be able to find a solution and resolve the problems that brought them to counseling. As mentioned earlier, if Christina and Liz stopped fighting about college, perhaps Christina could think about what she wanted, rather than about whether or not her mother would stop talking to her about it. Similarly, changing the family dynamics might help Liz and Christina resolve other disagreements that arise as Christina is launched from the family (Chapter 2).

Family counselors, irrespective of which particular theory, or model, of family counseling they practice, believe that focusing on the family system, rather than individuals, and particularly the individual who has become the identified patient, provides a mechanism for changing the context in which the presenting problem occurred, thus preventing its recurrence or appearance in another family member. A family systems perspective focuses family counselors away from diagnosing psychopathology in an individual, therefore risking exactly what Liz expressed concern regarding, namely that being labeled as the sick family member would further entrench Christina's symptoms.

STOP AND THINK:

Think about a friend or family member of yours who has been diagnosed with a mental illness.

1. Was there anything in the way family members related to one another that might have contributed to your friend or family member's symptoms?

2. Was her or his family included in her or his treatment?

The emphasis of family counselors on identifying the family system, rather than individual psychopathology, as a contributor to an individual's distress has been criticized as overlooking diagnoses and treatments that might be effective. The authors do not believe that attention to family system contributions to the identified patient's distress or the presenting problem precludes effective diagnosis and treatment, including referring family members for individual counseling or medication assessment and management. When and how to refer clients who need services beyond the family counselor's scope of practice is addressed in Chapter 12.

FAMILY SUBSYSTEMS

All systems contain subsystems. Subsystems are parts, or units, of a system that form smaller systems of their own. Subsystems include individual family members; clusters of family members such as parents, spouses, siblings, sisters, or brothers; the nuclear family as part of a larger extended, multigenerational family including aunts and uncles, cousins, grandparents, and so on; and both the nuclear and extended family as part of larger work, school, neighborhood, spiritual, interest, economic, and political communities. Subsystems can be described with the same concepts used to describe family systems.

Most families contain generational subsystems, or groups of family members who were born into the same generation. As you will see in Chapter 6, Minuchin believed that maintaining a separation, or boundary, between generational subsystems is important for family functioning. However, he also believed that families work best when the boundaries (see below and in Chapter 6) between generations can be crossed. For example, it is fine for an older sibling to watch younger siblings on teacher workdays when parents cannot be at home. However, it is not all right for one parent to discuss her or his concerns about the other parent with a child. In single-parent families, a child may need to assume more parental responsibilities, and this is not by definition problematic. On the other hand, it may not be in that child's best interests to become the parent's confidante about financial worries or dating relationships.

Families include sibling subsystems, spousal and parental subsystems, grandparent subsystems, and gender subsystems, some of which are generational. Subsystems in the family do not change. For example, parents remain in the parental subsystem, and children remain in the sibling subsystem throughout their entire lives. Other subsystems form and reform for specific purposes. These are known as alliances and will be described in more detail in Chapter 6.

And finally, subsystems can form to exclude or oppose one or more family members. These are known as coalitions and will also be described in more detail in Chapter 6.

STOP AND THINK:

1. What subsystems exist in your family and of which are you a part?

2. In what ways is your nuclear family part of the larger system of your extended family and your community?

CIRCULAR CAUSATION AND FEEDBACK LOOPS

As noted in the introduction, we tend to think of causation as linear. In other words, something happens, and, as a result, something else happens. For example, an adolescent comes home after her or his curfew and is grounded, or an adult forgets an occasion that is important to another, and the other is hurt or angry.

Family counselors, on the other hand, view causation as circular. They ask not only about the action and reaction but also what happens next in a presumed sequence of events. Observed sequences tend to repeat and are viewed as part of the family's dynamics. In other words, family counselors examine how actions and reactions among family members reverberate throughout the family system.

When Liz and Christina argued about college, their reactions to each other not only influenced the other's subsequent behaviors but also influenced the behaviors of other family members, which then also impacted Liz and Christina's subsequent behavior. For example, as their arguments became more heated, Emma sometimes cried, and then her tears became part of the argument between her mother and half sister.

Circular patterns of interactions are conceptualized as feeding upon themselves. In this way, feedback loops are formed. Christina and Liz's arguments about college provide an excellent example. Once the anger began, each became angrier and angrier as she saw more and more of the other's persistence and anger and as other family members became involved. Family counseling theorists characterize such patterns as feedback loops. For the purposes of family counseling, you can think of them as cycles of behavior that become increasingly less functional and more disruptive.

As noted in the previous section of this chapter, what one family member does affects what other family members then do. And their behavior then affects what the first member, as well as other members of the family, do. This is a feedback loop. Note also that in feedback loops cause and effect are not unidirectional, or linear. Rather, causation loops back upon itself and so is circular.

STOP AND THINK:

1. What feedback loops occur among the members of your family?

2. What is your role in these feedback loops?

HOMEOSTASIS AND EQUILIBRIUM

Interestingly, patterns of interactions within families, while circular and sometimes escalating negatively, tend not to spin out of control. Family systems seek to maintain themselves in a balance that allows the family to stay together. This balance is referred to as the family's equilibrium. The process by which equilibrium is maintained is called homeostasis.

The process of maintaining homeostasis is similar to the thermostat on the heating or air conditioning system in your house, apartment, or dorm room. When the heat is set at 70 degrees, the temperature of your home is not consistently 70 degrees. The thermostat notes when the temperature rises above 70 degrees and shuts off the heat; then, when the temperature drops below 70 degrees, the thermostat turns the heat back on. So, in reality, the temperature in your home varies from slightly below to slightly above 70 degrees.

Similarly, in the Manning-Kelly family, Christina and Liz's arguments about college became increasingly heated as the feedback loop continued. This feedback loop involved each one's verbal and nonverbal communications further antagonizing the other, which then further antagonized the previous antagonizer. Other family members became involved, further escalating the feedback loops. However, at some point, the argument becomes so intense that the family system can be thought of as perceiving a threat to its stability, or equilibrium. When equilibrium was threatened, the family's homeostatic correction stopped the argument. Specifically, Christina stormed out of the room, effectively ending the argument before it became so heated that it undermined her relationship with her mother and disrupted the family equilibrium. Thus, Christina's departure provided a homeostatic mechanism that allowed the family to maintain its equilibrium.

The downside of homeostasis restoring equilibrium is that the argument ends before it is resolved. And because the argument remains unresolved, it will inevitably repeat itself. A family counselor can be helpful in preventing the family's homeostatic mechanism from disrupting Liz and Christina's efforts to resolve their argument while at the same time facilitating a new homeostatic correction to bring about more effective conflict resolution. According to family systems theory, when Christina and Liz learn to resolve their argument without undermining their relationship, the family dynamics, as well as the individual mental health of the family members, may improve.

STOP AND THINK:

1. Identify one or more feedback loop(s) in your family.

2. How and when does your family stop feedback loop(s) and return to a safer state of equilibrium? In other words, how would you define your family's homeostatic mechanisms?

FAMILY RULES

Family rules emerge from interactions, feedback loops, and homeostatic corrections to regain equilibrium. In some families, the rule is we do not cry; in families with this rule, feelings sometimes are not expressed, and children may not learn how to comfort themselves when they feel sad by observing how their parents comfort them. Other families do not allow anger, and so conflict is neither expressed nor resolved. In these families, children cannot learn from experience within the family to manage angry feelings. Family rules also govern homeostasis by specifying how high the temperature can go, for example, when Liz and Christina argue about college, before someone interrupts the process and returns the family to safety, or equilibrium.

Family rules are often not directly observable. They are conceptual and not written on a list and posted on the refrigerator. Rather, family counselors notice the consequences when the counselor or a family member breaks a family rule. As you will see in Chapter 6, there appears to be a family rule in the Manning-Kelly family that husbands stand up for wives when wives are under attack. When Liz's husband, Mark, failed to do so, Liz confronted him about this failure.

These family rules are not the same as the rules that are posted on the refrigerator or the understanding that you take your plate to the sink after a meal and put your homework in your backpack after you have finished it. The family rules that arise from family dynamics are usually unspoken, and family members are often unable to articulate them. Family counselors, however, do notice and talk about the family rules they observe. Having a family rule stated aloud allows the family to decide whether it is helpful to them, harmful to them, or needs adjusting.

STOP AND THINK:

1. What was tolerated, and what was not a subject of discussion in the family you grew up in?

2. Did you talk about money?

3. Did you talk about a grandparent's forgetfulness?

4. Were there other secrets in your family?

5. Who decided where you applied to college and what your major would be?

6. When and how were anger and sadness expressed?

FIRST AND SECOND ORDER CHANGE

Family counselors also talk about first and second order change. First order change involves a change in behavior. In general, first order change involves either doing more of the same or doing something as different as possible. For example, Liz and Christina attempted to resolve their conflict by doing more of the same, namely repeating their argument and each time escalating conflict until it reached a level where one or the other ended it. A counselor could suggest they each say what they want the other to hear and then repeat it back. This is a first order change, because the assumption is that they need to alter their argument, rather than the family dynamics, before it can be resolved. It is more of the same.

When asked what they have already done to address the presenting problem, most families will say they have done more of whatever is not working. For example, Liz might say she brought home books on how to choose a college after arguing with Christina about applying. Christina, on the other hand, wanted Liz to stop talking to her about college, which is doing the opposite of what they have been doing. Virtually all forms of first order change, whether doing more of the same thing that has not worked or doing the opposite of what has not worked, are doomed.

Second order change, on the other hand, involves a change in family rules. It is preferable to first order change, because when family rules change so do underlying assumptions. And when underlying assumptions change, it becomes far more difficult to recreate the patterns that created the problem in the first place.

One of many possible issues underlying the repetitive argument about college in the Manning-Kelly family may be a family rule about what decisions children can make for themselves and which decisions parents make for them. As adolescents approach high school graduation and the transition to adulthood, or launching (Chapter 2), these family rules need to adapt to the developmental needs of young adult children and families in the launching stage of family development.

When Christina entered high school, one of her friends transferred from public to private school, and Christina wanted to go to her friend's new school with her. Liz, Martin, and Mark all believe in the value of public education. They also wanted to use the family's financial resources to send Christina to the college of her choice, rather than the high school her friend's parents chose for their daughter. High school attendance is mandatory for children under 16 years of age in the state in which the Manning-Kelly family resides, parents can face legal charges when children are chronically truant, and Christina was 14 when she entered high school. So she had no choice but to go to the high school her parents insisted upon. Parents making school decisions for children who are not yet launching is developmentally appropriate for both the child as an individual and the family in the child-rearing stage of development.

However, Christina will be 18 years old when she graduates from high school. She will be a young adult, her family will be in the launching stage of family development, and college is not mandatory. Thus, the decision about who decides whether she goes to college immediately upon graduating from high school may be quite different than who made the decision about whether she went to a private high school.

Another example of second order change would involve altering the family rule that Emma's role is to provide the homeostatic mechanism that prevents the feedback loop in Liz and Christina's arguments about college from escalating out of control. Ignoring her would be a first order change, because it is the opposite of reinforcing her behavior by attending to it. However, changing the family rule that Emma's upset must be immediately handled by her mother is an example of second order change. Emma could then be encouraged and praised for either seeking comfort from her father, Mark, or for soothing herself with a comfort toy when Liz and Christina are arguing. The goal would be to change the rule that her upset must disrupt whatever is happening in the household and thus stop her from distracting Liz, further enraging Christina. Because the subject of the argument then shifts from Christina's choice about college to Liz prioritizing Emma over Christina, the possibility that they will resolve their conflict is in fact undermined by the family rule. Thus, this family counseling intervention would hopefully change Emma's behavior by changing a family rule, which is a second order change. And of course if the family's reaction to Emma's behavior and then the behavior itself changed, the possibility that Liz and Christina could learn to resolve their argument would increase.

STOP AND THINK:

1. Do you agree that the family rule that parents decide where children will go to school and when still applies as Christina plans what she will do after high school graduation? Why? Why not?

2. What has your family done that is more of the same or the opposite of what has not worked? Has that first order change been effective?

3. Has anything happened in your family to change its rules and bring about second order change? Describe what happened.

If a family counselor were able to help the Manning-Kelly family change the family rules that parents decide where and when young adult children go to college and Emma's upset must take priority over whatever else is happening in the family, the arguments between Christina and Liz might diminish noticeably. Liz does not need to be happy about Christina's choice or even pretend that she is. She also has the responsibility to provide guidance to her young adult daughter. However, while it may be reasonable for her to express her opinion and preference, it may no longer be an option for her to attempt to impose it upon Christina. A family rule that young adult children are allowed to make decisions about their next steps for themselves would thus help Liz view Christina's choice as something her daughter has a right to and view her own role as advisor, rather than enforcer. And if they stopped arguing about the family rule itself—who has the right to decide?—perhaps Christina would think more thoroughly about what she wants. As long as the family rule remains part of the debate, she appears stuck in defending her right to decide, rather than free to make a decision. And, changing family rules, rather than individual behaviors, is a second order change.

SECOND ORDER CYBERNETICS

Second order cybernetics is not the same as second order change. Second order cybernetics refers to the process by which the counselor becomes a part of the family system. It is an important concept because, while the counselor needs to become part of the family, he or she also needs to avoid supporting those family dynamics, family structures, and family rules that underlie the problem and that the rest of the family accepts. This is often a difficult balancing act. We address it further in Chapter 10.

FUNCTION OF THE PRESENTING PROBLEM IN THE FAMILY

Finally, family systems theory holds that symptoms of psychological distress, also known as the presenting problem, serve a purpose, or family function. The symptoms often help to maintain the family's equilibrium and are therefore essential to keeping the family together unless another way to maintain equilibrium can be found. For example, Christina's eating and cutting disorders brought the family to counseling so that other issues could be addressed. It is possible that were Liz not so focused on the college fights with Christina and on Emma's needs, she would pay more attention to the consequences of Mark's drinking and the distance and anger in their marriage. The risk, of course, is that if Christina's eating disorder resolved, she applied to college, and Emma became more independent, there would be no distraction, and Liz and Mark's relationship might become more openly problematic and perhaps even difficult to maintain. Should their marriage become tenuous, the family might have to endure another divorce. So Christina's eating and cutting disorders can be viewed as serving the family function of holding the family together.

While it is likely that no one is consciously thinking Christina needs to have problems to keep Mark and Liz's marriage intact, to the extent that Christina's symptoms distract Liz, they serve the family function of avoiding the risk of divorce. In other words, examining the family function of a symptom for the family is helpful to the family counselor as he or she assesses what the family needs. It is not something family counselors usually discuss with their clients, though they sometimes point out the symptom's function.

FAMILY RESILIENCY

Before assessing the Manning-Kelly family system, the concept of family resiliency is important to examine. The term refers to how families manage in order to cope with the inevitable stress they will face. People who work with families have been writing about and researching the area of family stress and coping since the 1960s. The early model (Hill, 1958) has been elaborated upon to include the stressor; its perceived severity to family members; the family's financial, emotional, and social resources for managing the impact of the stressor; and an outcome.

A stressor is any event that requires change within the family. There are life cycle stressors, such as the birth of a baby and death of a grandparent. Some stressors are internal to the family, such as marital conflict or a member with special needs. Others are external stressors, such as job loss, natural disasters, and being called to active military duty. Although researchers have often focused on single stressors, most families come to counseling with multiple stressors. For example, stressors impacting the nuclear Manning-Kelly family include Christina's grandmother Sally's husband's Alzheimer's disease, her stepfather Mark's parents' decline, her own mental health diagnoses, life cycle change as she prepares to be launched, Emma's special needs associated with her cerebral palsy diagnosis, marital distress between her mother and stepfather, her stepfather's drinking and its impact on the family, and managing both of her parents' blended families.

How the family views its stressors also impacts how it manages them. Some families view stress as a normal part of family life, something they as a collective can manage. Other families, however, view even the smallest disruption as a threat. Additionally, some families cope with stress in ways that produces more stress. For example, the multigenerational substance abuse issues in Christina's family were not considered problematic, despite being contributors, causes, or at least as aggravating factors for Sally's first husband's death, Christina's Uncle David's cut off from his son, and David's own metabolic disease. However, Emma's cerebral palsy has been assigned the meaning of being more debilitating than it is, as evidenced by her age-inappropriate level of dependence on her mother.

A family's resources for managing, or coping, with stress might include how it is viewed. It also includes the three broad categories of financial resources, emotional resources, and social resources. Christina's family clearly has the financial resources for Liz to have a job that allows her time to be with her children, despite the toll it has taken on her career. They also have the resources for the medical and mental health care they need. If they did not, they would be forced to wait in long lines for the limited resources available to low-income families.

Emotional resources include each individual's mental health and the family's rules for managing emotions. Are members of the family allowed to express their emotions? Is there a family rule that requires members to appear problem free? Is there a family myth that expressing strong feelings is dangerous and thus taboo? Or are feelings accepted among family members, and do children learn from their parents to soothe themselves when they are feeling something strongly? Finally, is there a history or presence of mental illness within the family? And if yes, do family dynamics support it?

Social resources are focused primarily on the family's social network, including friends, extended family members, neighbors, coworkers, and professionals. Research has consistently shown that, irrespective of the specific stressor, the presence of strong social networks is associated with a variety of positive outcomes. Similarly, the flexibility with which family members assign roles among family members and to outside support in times of stress is also associated with positive outcomes. When Christina's Aunt Barbara was in treatment for her cancer, she and her husband allowed their adult children, as well as other extended family members and friends, to assume roles they were unable to fulfill because of the demands of her illness and treatment.

Studies of outcome have included negative consequences, such as the impact of the stressor on family members' biomedical and mental health. More recently, the focus has shifted to positive outcomes, and these studies emphasize family resilience. We say a family is resilient, not because it is problem free, but because it is able to manage the stress without exhibiting symptoms associated with the distress of an inability to cope.

SYSTEMIC ASSESSMENT OF THE MANNING-KELLY FAMILY

What follows is an excerpt from a family counseling session with the Manning-Kelly family. In the Stop and Think section that follows the transcript, you will be asked to assess the Manning-Kelly family in terms of the various concepts described in this chapter.

FC: Liz, when I asked about extended family support, you mentioned that you and your sister are concerned about your mother's health as she cares for your stepfather. Tell me more about the demands on you and your family.

Liz:	Well, Mom has always liked things just so. And since Jim has been sick, he messes things up as fast as she can straighten them up. And of course he gets confused and isn't always his old pleasant self when she needs him to do something like take his medicine.

FC: So what have you and your sister tried to do?

Liz: Well, Barbara and I have talked about it, about getting her some help. And we've encouraged her to see her doctor and talk to him about it, but of course she thinks Jim's dementia should be private. And of course she says she's fine.

FC: And you and Barbara disagree?

Liz: Yes. She looks exhausted, and he can be pretty nasty. I think she's trying to hide how bad it's really gotten from the doctor.

FC: What is she afraid of?

Liz: Afraid? My mother's never been afraid of anything. But I don't think she wants anyone to tell her he needs to be put somewhere.

FC: She wants to care for him herself?

Liz: Well, yes. And she also cares a lot about appearances, always has.

FC: Tell me more about that. How has her caring about appearances affected you?

Liz: Hmm. I guess the main thing is that she wanted Barbara and me to look good, not gain weight, do our make-up correctly, wear nice clothes.

FC: Since you were teenagers?

Liz: Forever, about weight and clothes, not make-up of course.

FC: So her concerns were about physical appearance?

Liz: Yes, and she also wanted people to think she had everything under control, that we all did. She didn't like it when one of us was in conflict with a friend or didn't do well in a class or went through an awkward stage. And if we hadn't had a date to a school dance, oh dear. [Smiles, then looks thoughtful] And if we hadn't gotten into colleges she could tell her friends about or joined sororities, she would have been humiliated.

At this point, an individual counselor would have facilitated Liz's awareness of the similarities between what she described about her mother, Sally, and herself. However, Christina has been staring at her mother, and the family counselor decided to leave Liz with her thoughts, adding what Christina may have to say about how her grandmother's attitudes have filtered through the generations.

FC:	What do you think about what your mother has said, Christina?
Christina:	I don't think it's fair to Grandma Sally or Aunt Barbara. Neither of them is like her.
Liz:	You don't know what my mother and Barbara were like when we were growing up.
C:	Well, they're not like that now.
FC:	They, Christina? Who?
C:	My mom. She cares how she looks, she cares that I go to college so she can brag. [To Liz] Are you saying Grandma Sally cared how Aunt Barbara looked when she had her surgery and chemotherapy? That is low.
Liz:	[Tearful] Your aunt couldn't help having breast cancer.
C:	So what are you saying?
Liz:	That she expected us to control what we could: our weight, our life choices.
C:	And you've done a terrific job. [Nods toward Mark] You gave up Dad for that?
Liz:	Christina! You may not speak to Mark that way. Or me.
FC:	I've noticed we've gotten a long way from talking about your concern about your mother and how she's managing your stepfather's Alzheimer's, Liz. You had looked very thoughtful earlier, when you were talking about her concern about appearances. And I'm curious what happened.

STOP AND THINK:

1. What patterns of interaction, or family dynamics, did you notice?

2. Identify subsystems within the Manning-Kelly family.

3. Identify circular causation within the excerpt.

4. What feedback loops and homeostatic mechanisms did you notice? When was the family in equilibrium, and when was it not?

5. What family rules did you notice?

6. What might the family counselor consider in attempting to bring about second order change?

7. How might the family counselor have become part of the family system (second order cybernetics)?

8. What did you notice about the family function of the presenting problem of Christina's eating disorder?

CONCLUSION

With these concepts in mind, we will now turn to three schools of family counseling theory: Multigenerational Family Counseling (Chapter 5), Structural Family Counseling (Chapter 6), and Experiential Family Counseling (Chapter 7). We will end this section with a chapter describing several other approaches to family counseling: feminist family counseling, cognitive-behavioral family counseling, narrative family counseling, Adlerian family counseling, and integrative family counseling. These topics are ones about which our family counseling students have enjoyed learning. Although the list is not exhaustive of the scope of available approaches practiced by family counselors, Chapter 8 will provide an introduction to the breadth of approaches family counselors bring to their work with families.

REFERENCES

Bateson, G. (1972). *Steps to an ecology of mind.* New York, NY: Ballantine Books.

Bronfenbrenner, U. (1994). Ecological models of human development. In T. Husen & T. N. Postelthwaite (Eds.), *International encyclopedia of education*, 3, 2nd ed. Oxford, UK: Elsevier.

Hill, R. (1958). Generic features of families under stress. *Social Casework, 42*, 139–151.

FOR FURTHER STUDY

Alexander, J., & Parsons, B. V. (1982). *Functional family therapy*. Monterey, CA: Brooks/Cole.

Bowen, M. (1971). The use of family theory in clinical practice. In J. Haley (Ed.), *Changing families: A family therapy reader* (p. 159–192). New York, NY: Grune and Stratton.

Brown, J. (1999). Bowen family systems: Theory and practice: Illustration and critique. *Australian and New Zealand Journal of Family Therapy, 20*(2), 94–103. doi:10.1002/j.1467-8438.1999.tb00363.x

Crago, H. (2006). Bateson: What every schoolboy doesn't know. *ANZJFT Australian and New Zealand Journal of Family Therapy, 27*(3), iii–iv. doi:10.1002/j.1467-8438 .2006.tb00709.x

Davey, M., Duncan, T., Kissil, K., Davey, A., & Fish, L. S. (2011). Second-order change in marriage and family therapy: A web-based modified Delphi study. *American Journal of Family Therapy, 39*(2), 100–111. doi:10.1080/01926187.2010.530929

Gehart, D. (2010). *Mastering competencies in family therapy* (1st ed.). Belmont, CA: Brooks/Cole.

Gunner, A. C. (2006). Feedback loops in clinical practice: An integrative framework. *ANZJFT Australian and New Zealand Journal of Family Therapy, 27*(3), 143–152. doi:10.1002/j.1467-8438.2006.tb00712.x

Haley, J., & Hoffman, L. (1967). *Techniques of family therapy. Five leading therapists reveal their working styles, strategies, and approaches.* New York, NY: Basic Books.

Halpern, C. T., Harris, K. M., & Whitsel, E. A. (2014). Studying family transitions from a systems perspective: The role of biomarkers. In S. M. McHale, P. Amato, & A. Booth (Eds.), *Emerging methods in family research* (pp. 127–144). Cham, Switzerland: Springer International. doi:10.1007/978-3-319-01562-0_8

Hecker, L. L., Mims, G. A., & Boughner, S. R. (2015). General systems theory, cybernetics, and family therapy. In J. L. Wetchler, & L. L. Hecker (Eds.), *An introduction to marriage and family therapy* (2nd ed.) (pp. 43–64). New York, NY: Routledge/ Taylor & Francis Group.

Hoffman, L. (1981). *Foundations of family therapy. A conceptual framework for systems change.* New York, NY: Basic Books.

Hoffman, L. (1985). Beyond power and control: Toward a 'second order' family systems therapy. *Family Systems Medicine, 3*(4), 381–396. doi:10.1037/h0089674

Inger, I. B. (1993). A dialogic perspective for family therapy: The contributions of Martin Buber and Gregory Bateson. *Journal of Family Therapy, 15*(3), 293–314. doi:10.1111/j.1467-6427.1993.00760.x

Laing, R. D. (1972). *The politics of the family and other essays.* New York, NY: Random House.

Laszlo, E. (1972). *The systems view of the world.* New York, NY: George Braziller.

Lebow, J. (2014). *Couple and family therapy: An integrative map of the territory* (pp. 3–23). Washington, DC: American Psychological Association. doi:10.1037/14255-001

Liu, D., & Zhang, J. (2014). The application of case conceptualization in system family therapy. *Chinese Journal of Clinical Psychology, 22*(4), 746–748.

McCubbin, M., Balling, K., Possin, P., Frierdich, S., & Bryne, B. (2004). Family resiliency in childhood cancer. *Family Relations, 15*(2), 103–111.

Nichols, M. (1984). *Family therapy. Concepts and methods.* New York, NY: Gardner Press.

Rostosky, S. S., & Riggle, E. B. (2015). When the family rule is 'don't ask, don't tell'. In S. S. Rostosky, & E. B. Riggle (Eds.), *Happy together: Thriving as a same-sex couple in your family, workplace, and community* (pp. 30–38). Washington, DC: American Psychological Association.

Sexton, T. L., & Datchi, C. (2014). The development and evolution of family therapy research: Its impact on practice, current status, and future directions. *Family Process, 53*(3), 415–433. doi:10.1111/famp.12084

Stagoll, B. (2006). Gregory Bateson at 100. *ANZJFT Australian and New Zealand Journal of Family Therapy, 27*(3), 121–134. doi:10.1002/j.1467-8438.2006.tb00710.x

Stavrianopoulos, K., Faller, G., & Furrow, J. L. (2014). Emotionally focused family therapy: Facilitating change within a family system. *Journal of Couple & Relationship Therapy, 13*(1), 25–43. doi:10.1080/15332691.2014.865976

Watzlawick, P., Weakland, J., & Fisch, R. (1974). *Change. Principles of problem formation and problem resolution.* New York, NY: W. W. Norton & Company.

CHAPTER 5

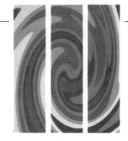

Multigenerational Family Counseling

One's family history is much more complex and extensive than what an individual may remember. In fact, the family history from before any of you were born can provide enormous insight into current issues and patterns of behavior. Now with resources like Ancestry.com available, information about our families' past is much more accessible. Still, even if you don't do an extensive search into your family background, you may find patterns of behavior and roles that have been predominant over the generations.

FAMILY BEHAVIOR PATTERNS

Think of an event (wedding, funeral, birthday, graduation, etc.) that would involve your entire extended family attending. What is the focus of the family members' attention during the event?

Is there food involved (there usually is), if so, who prepares it, and how is the food prepared? (i.e., Do all the family members work together as a large group, or are the meal preparation duties divided based on gender or some other distinction such as age or position in the family?)

When a decision must be made that affects the extended family (e.g., where to gather for this event, or what to do with a family inheritance), who makes the decision?

Is religion a part of your family dynamics or the focus of this event? How is this chosen?

Most likely your answers to these questions revealed some predictable patterns of behavior among your family members, for example, your dad and uncle always bet on sports and then argue over who owes money, or your grandmother always insists on taking numerous photos at each gathering, much to the irritation of those who don't want to stand still and wait for the flash on her camera to work. In many families, these patterns, and their predictability, are often comforting, familiar, and an important part of a family's group identity. In families facing domestic violence, substance abuse, or chronic illness, they may be troublesome and disturbing. Bowen's (1978) multigenerational family therapy emphasizes the importance of focusing on and learning from these patterns in order to shed light on current issues and problems. In this chapter, you will gain an introduction to the basic concepts of Bowen's multigenerational theory, including genograms, triangles, differentiation of self, emotional fusion, and cutoffs.

Bowen's multigenerational family therapy is an approach that focuses on the importance of examining families within the context of their overall family history, as well as the individuals within their families and the roles they play. Murray Bowen (1913-1990) was a psychiatrist who studied patients with schizophrenia. After discovering that all of his schizophrenic patients had troubled relationships with their mothers, he began to study the family unit and its interactions. Bowen's theory of multigenerational family counseling is based on empirical research in which he observed families who lived in a lab setting for up to 3 years (Kerr, 2000). Bowen believed that there is a difference between what people say they do and what they actually do. Therefore, the families he studied were observed 24 hours a day. The results of this in vivo observational research led to the main concepts of Bowenian Theory listed below:

1. Emotional Fusion and Differentiation of Self

2. Triangles

3. Nuclear Family Emotional Process

4. Family Projection Process

5. Cutoffs

6. Multigenerational Transmission Process

7. Sibling Position

8. Societal Emotional Process

The following sections describe these concepts, along with examples for application.

Emotional Fusion and Differentiation of Self

Central to Bowen's theory are the concepts of emotional fusion and differentiation of self. *Emotional fusion* refers to a sense of intense responsibility for others' responses to one's choices, to the point of putting one's own needs aside in favor of harmony. A person who is emotionally fused has a difficult time separating himself or herself from others' emotional responses and therefore is more reactive than proactive. An example of this was Christina's reliance on her mother's opinions before she weighed in with her own thoughts. She seemed to have learned over the years that in order to get her mother's attention, she needed to act out, and therefore, she tried to do so in the most effective way she knew how: by hurting herself. This was something her mother could not ignore. Emma, her younger sister, was also a likely candidate for being emotionally fused to her mother. Although it was still too early to know for sure how she would differentiate, since this usually happens during adolescence, Emma showed signs of emotional fusion in the way she frequently looked to her mother for cues, the ways she clung to her physically, and her lack of speaking with authority—she whispered most of the time, rather than talking outright, and generally talked to her mother in response to others, rather than addressing others specifically.

The opposite of emotional fusion, and the goal for individuals' healthy emotional functioning, is known as the *differentiation of self*. This process is marked by one's ability to distinguish one's own feelings and thoughts from those of family members and others, and therefore able to make individual choices easily without dependence on others' reactions. People who are highly differentiated are confident in their choices and decisions and are not plagued with worry about how others will react to their choices. If Christina had been differentiated, she would have had more confidence in her choice of not going to college and becoming a stay at home mom, and she would have been much less likely to cope with her severe anxiety by cutting and restricting her food intake. Likewise, Liz was so consumed with her image as a career woman, and being known as "able to do it all," that she had allowed some of her closest relationships to fall by the wayside in favor of keeping up appearances.

Triangles

Another concept central to Bowen's theory is the existence of triangles within family relationships. Relationships with significant others inevitably involve conflicts. These conflicts can be difficult to handle and anxiety can easily develop. When the stress between two people becomes intense, sometimes they recruit a third person to lessen the tension between them. This creates a triangular relationship with the person at the apex receiving the majority of the other two people's attention. Sometimes the triangulation is deliberate and focused on each person trying to get the third person to side with one of the members of the dyad. Other times it is less intentional and can include focusing on a child's behavior in school, or a parent's medical condition, in order to take the attention away from the underlying conflict between them. While triangulation may lessen the anxiety in the dyad and bring temporary relief to a tense situation, it does not attend to the underlying conflict, which may ultimately worsen if not addressed.

Several types of triangles exist, many of which are a part of typical family functioning. For example, a teenage daughter has found a prom dress she wants, but her mom has said it is too expensive. The daughter enlists her father's help, and they join forces to try and convince mom that the dress should be purchased. They may do this with some covert planning and scheming, such as the daughter being especially sweet to her mom and the father talking about his wife's prom dress and how important he remembers it was to her, but, in the end, no one is hurt. On the other hand, some triangles may be harmful, such as when two parents are arguing and each tries to get one of their children to side with them. Look at the following statements:

Mom to her child after an argument with her husband: "Can you believe how mean daddy was to me?", or

Dad to his child after the same argument: "Your mom is just unreasonable sometimes, don't you think?"

These situations pull a child into a triangle where they cannot win, they feel pressure to choose sides and may have anxiety and fears related to their parents' relationship.

A common triangle in families is known as the *Karpman triangle*. Also known as the *drama triangle*, this example has specific roles within the triangular structure: perpetrator, victim, and rescuer.

The perpetrator is the accused attacker, the victim is obviously the one allegedly being attacked, and the rescuer comes to the aid of the victim. A small example of this could easily take place in any home. Dad makes meatloaf for dinner, and his son Tommy comes to the table, starving after playing an intense soccer game, sees the meatloaf, and starts complaining: "Aw, come on, meatloaf? That's disgusting! Why can't we have real food, like pizza or macaroni and cheese?!! I'm not eating this!" Mom quickly comes to Dad's aid and tells Tommy, "Look, you're dad worked hard on this meal, and you're being ungrateful. If you don't like what he makes for dinner, then you should offer to help prepare the meals."

In this example, the child is the perpetrator, the dad is the victim, and the mom is clearly the rescuer. This is a relatively harmless example that can easily be resolved through good communication.

Problems may result from the Karpman triangle when the roles are static and repetitive. In particular, some family members may find difficulty in other relationships. Victims may remain in the victim role and tend to gravitate to those who are likely perpetrators, and rescuers seem to find themselves drawn to people who may be reluctant to defend themselves. For example, in the Manning-Kelly family, Christina remained in the victim role. According to Christina, her mother criticized her, her stepfather ignored her, her dad neglected her, and her friends were not supportive. She was the perpetual victim, and the others were perpetrators. Her rescuer depended on the situation: sometimes it was her stepmother, sometimes her boyfriend, and on rare occasions it was Martin Jr. In every case, however, the roles were always the same, with Christina attributing fault to others and failing to accept responsibility for the part she might have played in a conflict.

STOP AND THINK:

1. How do you think this repeated triangle affects Christina emotionally, socially, and academically? Discuss the positives and negatives of remaining in her chosen role.

2. What effects do you think this pattern might have on others in her family?

3. How do you think Christina's victim role might play out in her relationship with her boyfriend or in future relationships?

Extend Your Learning:

Look back at the Manning-Kelly genogram. What examples of triangles can you find? Are they functional or dysfunctional? Explain why.

Nuclear Family Emotional Process

The nuclear family is the center from which an individual views the rest of the world, and therefore serves as the barometer for how to interact with others. The way that the family copes with stress and manages individuals' differentiation may involve anxiety, conflict, closeness, and distance. For example, some people engaged in conflict argue and place blame on others. Others may distance themselves from other family members, struggle with other relationships, and avoid tense situations. Some individuals choose to take responsibility for the behavior of others in their family (e.g., an older sibling taking the blame for a younger sibling's behavior, or a wife taking responsibility for her husband's drinking). This is called reciprocity and may lead to overfunctioning or underfunctioning within a dyad (Vermont Center for Family Studies, n.d.). Bowen's theory holds that, when choosing a life partner, we tend to gravitate toward someone with a level of differentiation similar to our own. Therefore, if one person is highly fused to his or her family of origin, he or she may choose a partner who is equally fused to his or her own family and proceed to have children who are fused as well. The intensity of this fusion can grow, and as a family becomes more fused, the likelihood of resulting unstable relationships and anxiety is increased. Bowen believed that in particular, four basic relationship patterns could result from such intense fusion in nuclear families:

Marital Conflict. When the family's anxiety is primarily absorbed by the parents, problems in the marriage can result, in which the partners cycle in and out of emotional distance and intense closeness. Like a roller coaster, these positive and negative cycles can be equally intense and often go unresolved so that the patterns become chronic.

Dysfunction in One Spouse. The anxiety of the highly fused family members is absorbed by one parent, presenting as physical, mental, or emotional symptoms that may warrant treatment. These symptoms appear to serve the function of distracting the family's attention, a preferred alternative to openly dealing with the family conflict.

Impairment in One or More Children. A highly fused child who is having problems (emotional, psychological, physical, or educational, etc.), is often a welcome detour for parents from the anxiety present within their relationship. The more fused the child is, the more vulnerable the child is to developing symptoms. The child's anxiety and resulting symptoms will increase with any increase in the parents' anxiety. In some cases, parents may respond to the child's symptoms with even more anxiety, thus leading to chronic patterns of dysfunction (Goldenberg & Goldenberg, 2008).

Emotional Distance. Individuals may create distance between themselves and other family members to protect themselves from the tension and intensity of the relationships. While creating distance in the family may provide a welcomed break from the intense family tension and anxiety, it may also lead to isolation and lack of resolution.

Family Projection Process

Similar to the Freudian defense mechanism of the same name, projection occurs when attention and focus are given to one person or a group of persons in order to avoid the actual underlying conflict between two adults. Bowen believed that poorly differentiated, immature parents may target the least differentiated child in their family for the projection of their marital issues. Occurring as early as infancy, this process occurs as the parents triangulate the child into the couple's relationship. Kerr (1981) believed that the more the parents are dependent upon this projection process to stabilize their relationship, the more likely it is that their child will have significant emotional impairment. In turn, their child may become fused and emotionally reactive to his or her parents. This triangle is quite common and may seem to bring stability to the couple for a while. However, the tension between them has only been projected onto the child momentarily and will eventually return to the couple's relationship unless it is addressed directly (Bitter, 2014).

Cutoffs

Sometimes in families with intense emotional fusion, the tension becomes so much to bear that family members feel the need to disengage and separate themselves from a family member or subgroup. When this cutoff happens, it can happen in three ways:

1. Physically cutting off contact with the relatives by avoiding them or moving far away. Family members may still communicate by phone, e-mail, or other means but will rely on the geographical distance to make the communication "safe" and help them avoid conversations about emotions or any level of deep sharing.

2. Emotionally cutting them off while coexisting in the same area. This can happen between people living under the same roof, when one person refuses to engage other family members emotionally, refuses to let them in on any significant details of his or her life, yet remains in daily contact with only shallow exchanges.

3. A combination of a physical and emotional cutoff. This is when a family member will move away and cut off emotional contact as well,

sharing little if any parts of their lives and not seeing the family member at all for an extended period of time.

There are several reasons for cutting one's family off. It can be due to a fight over money or something material, or it can be in response to behavior related to addiction or abuse. Sometimes the cutoff is necessary in order for family members to protect themselves, emotionally, physically, or both. This is especially true for cases of physical and/or sexual abuse, where the family members need to separate themselves from the perpetrator in order to heal and move forward.

When cutoffs happen, there are usually deeply hurt feelings and a lot of repair that needs to be done if the relationship will ever resume. In the Manning-Kelly family, Uncle David and his son Carl had been estranged for many years. No one in the Manning-Kelly family had seen Carl for years, and no one talked about him either. It is unknown why the cutoff happened, but it remained a source of tension for this family, especially on occasions when Uncle David was present and Carl wasn't.

Family counselors generally work with families to help them find ways to address the cutoff, usually through first identifying the reasons for it, then attempting to reconnect with the estranged party, and having a candid conversation using "I messages."

An "I message" is a method of communicating in which a person takes responsibility for their own feelings and thoughts, rather than placing blame on someone else. For example: "When you didn't come to my wedding, *I* felt discounted and unimportant," instead of "You just didn't show up, and you knew I needed you there!" The first one allows the individual to own his or her feelings, rather than placing blame. This helps the other person feel less defensive and more open to understanding another's feelings. This conversation is often a necessary step to enable the families to move forward in rebuilding relationships with the cutoff person or people.

STOP AND THINK:

1. Think about the last conflict you experienced. Were "I messages" used? How did the people in the conflict react to how feelings were expressed?

2. Think about your response to someone blaming you for his or her unpleasant feelings. How do you respond?

3. Practice using "I messages" with others in your life. How do people react?

Multigenerational Transmission

The process of multigenerational transmission consists of various levels of individuation between parents and children. The combination of parents actively shaping their children's behavior, their children responding to their parents' moods and attitudes, and the parents influencing their children's behavior through their own inadvertent actions, often results in children's individuation levels being similar to that of their parents (Kerr, 2000).

Patterns in a couple with poor differentiation are usually marked by conflict and then pulling a child in to relieve the tension. Once this child grows up, becomes part of a couple, and starts a family, these patterns will usually continue. This is known as multigenerational transmission (Bitter, 2014)

The Manning-Kelly family had some very clear examples of multigenerational transmission. One was the emphasis on women in the family being thin, sometimes leading to eating disorders, most notably in Liz and Christina. Another example was the anxiety that seems to abound within intimate relationships in the Manning-Kelly family. Family members coped with the anxiety in a variety of positive and negative ways, but the anxiety remained a predictable trait transmitted from generation to generation.

STOP AND THINK:

Return to the Manning-Kelly and Jones genogram. What other multigenerational transmissions do you see?

Look at your own genogram. What multigenerational transmissions are there related to behavior, culture, religion, gender roles, money, education, careers, and so on?

Family Roles

Whether we realize it or not, we operate in relationships by assuming roles. Your role may be the super reasonable one who helps settle conflict and keeps the peace, the person that likes to stir the pot and see what trouble arises, or perhaps the person who stays on the periphery, quietly observing rather than entering directly into the main conversation or conflict taking place. Regardless of the roles we play, we all have a purpose in playing them and tend to remain in these roles as long as they serve us well. Common family roles include nurturer, matriarch or patriarch, trouble-maker, peace-keeper, people-pleaser, overachiever, follower, black sheep, prodigal child, perpetual victim, clown, and many others. A few of these roles are described below.

The Nurturer. The nurturer seems to always be caring for someone, whether that person wants to be taken care of or not. While nurturers may be taken advantage of by people who avoid the nurturer role and prefer to be taken care of, make no mistake, the nurturer enjoys his or her role and reaps some benefits from it. Even if they appear to be completely self-sacrificing, they still gain something from this position: martyrdom. No one can ever accuse them of being a slacker or not doing their part. And, this position of caretaker is a handy trump card for moments when they feel attacked by others (i.e., "How could you do this to me after all I have done for you?"). Additionally, this person may have difficulty letting go of the caretaker role—it is a part of his or her identity—and often has a hard time accepting help and care from others.

The Matriarch/Patriarch. This leader of the family is accustomed to making difficult decisions and being looked to for guidance, especially during difficult times. This person is usually an elder family member and commands respect from the rest of the family. Like the nurturer, this person may have difficulty allowing others to take the lead in situations. He or she expects to be consulted for advice and may feel responsibility for other family members' behavior and choices, as if their choices are a direct reflection of his or her leadership and therefore his or her character. Once again, this role is not without its perks. Having the respect of all the other family members certainly affords its own benefits. An obvious one is power as the chief decision maker and source of family guidance. Additionally, as the chief consultant of the family, the matriarch or patriarch is often privy to information about other family members before others are told. This knowledge gives him or her power over others, whether or not he or she chooses to exploit this power. This person can also claim stress and difficulties in his or her role as the decision maker, inciting sympathy from others, a benefit similar to what the nurturer may receive.

The Black Sheep. The black sheep is seen as the family screwup. This person is expected to fail and deviate from the family path to success. This person is frequently the focus of family energy, as family members bail him or her out of jail, pay off a debt, or take him or her in when he or she is homeless or jobless. This person often suffers from low self-esteem and difficulty with commitment due to a self-concept that is deemed unworthy. While it may be difficult to imagine this role having benefits, it actually does. For one, it is freeing to have everyone's expectations of you remain low. It means you don't have to try hard to please them. The bar is set low, so if you fail, no one expects anything different from you. If the black sheep does succeed at something positive, then it's usually chalked up as an anomaly or a fluke, so there's no pressure to continue to succeed. In contrast, those who succeed regularly have higher expectations and related pressure placed on them.

The Joker. There is usually one person in the family whose role is to ease the tension by making others laugh. Finding humor in otherwise somber and tense situations is this person's specialty. Other family members are often relieved when the joker's humor breaks the tension. Truly, this is an admirable trait. However, the joker may become annoying when he or she has trouble taking things seriously.

Role Shift. With the growth and changes that take place in every family, it is inevitable that some roles will change over time. The alcoholic gets treatment and is no longer the center of everyone's energy and frustration. The nurturer dies or becomes ill and dependent on others for care. Aging, marriage, having children, divorce, changing health, and distance can all affect the roles adopted by family members. When these roles within a family change, others must shift in order to maintain equilibrium. Imagine an addict who has been dependent on the nurturer in his family to clean up his mess and make excuses for him. The addict decides to get treatment and beats his addiction. Once he returns to the family, however, the nurturer still wants to take care of him. Because the addict is focusing on his own personal responsibility, he objects to the nurturer's coddling. Feeling lost and rejected, the nurturer turns to another family member to focus his or her caregiving. Sometimes these role shifts are resolved smoothly and family members move on, however, other times they may lead to conflict and estrangement.

STOP AND THINK:

1. What roles can you identify in your own family? What purposes do these roles serve?

2. What role shifts have you noticed as you have grown and your family has changed?

3. Now answer the same questions for the Manning-Kelly family. How do you think roles have shifted since Liz and Martin's divorce? What is Christina's role? How does this role benefit her? How might it benefit others in the family?

SIBLING POSITION

Bowen was also interested in how sibling relationships and one's position in the family could help us understand the roles individuals adopt in relationships. Walter Toman's (1976) view of sibling position aligned well with Bowen's ideas, so he incorporated it into his own theory.

Toman held that position determines how power is played out in relationships, and that one's experience with gender determines one's ability to get along with the opposite sex.

To examine these dynamics more closely, he focused on 10 power positions among siblings:

1. Oldest brother of brothers

2. Youngest brother of brothers

3. Oldest brother of sisters

4. Youngest brother of sisters

5. Male only child

6. The same 5 configurations for females in relation to sisters and brothers

Toman also believed that sibling position should be considered in marital relationships and might have an impact on marital satisfaction. For example, a couple coming from the positions of oldest son and youngest daughter are more likely to function well together, as the oldest is accustomed to taking charge of situations, and the youngest is comfortable with letting others lead. In contrast, a couple that consists of two firstborns, or two secondborns, or two middles, is more likely to have conflict because each person is likely to compete for the position he or she is most comfortable maintaining. Additionally, Toman noted that the divorce rate among couples comprised of two oldest adult children was higher than couples with other birth orders represented.

Bowen was especially interested in which sibling position was the most vulnerable to triangling with parents, particularly repeated patterns from previous generations. For example, a parent might identify more closely with the child who holds the same sibling position. For family counselors, it is important to recognize these patterns, discuss them with their client families, and work with the families to recognize and move beyond the limitations of their sibling positions. A more thorough discussion of birth order and sibling perceived position is described in Chapter 8.

Bowen's theory did not include information about ethnicity, race, culture, or other family structures, such as adoptive and foster families, and how these might influence sibling position. Blended families, in particular, are more common than in previous decades and therefore should be considered in the discussion of sibling position.

STOP AND THINK:

1. How might sibling position affect the marital relationships you have learned about in the Manning-Kelly family?

2. What sibling position would be the best fit as a romantic partner for Christina? For Martin Jr.? Why?

3. What sibling position do you think would be the best fit for you to have a romantic relationship with? Why?

SOCIETAL EMOTIONAL PROCESS

This last concept was Bowen's attempt to link his main theoretical concepts with a larger societal view, citing the evolutionary process of society as related to human behavior. The family cannot be studied in isolation of the culture and systems in which it functions. Factors such as religion, education, media, geography, community support, and health all affect human behavior within the family system. Additionally, all of these factors may change with time and advances in technology. For example, the ways in which people communicate today are very different from past decades. Texting, instant messaging, social media, and video chatting are all popular methods for people to make contact with others. While these advances in technology have permeated society and changed how people interact with one another, these methods have also changed the way families communicate, by helping families connect with one another much more easily and frequently, whether or not they live in close proximity to one another. News updates, photos, and jokes are easily and quickly shared with people around the globe, allowing family members to stay in touch. On the other hand, these electronic methods of communicating may allow one to communicate in ways they wouldn't in typical face-to-face contact. Pressing the "send" button to launch an angry message is much easier than confronting someone in person. Tone of voice, facial expressions, and context are often unclear in these messages, and therefore may contribute to more conflict or misunderstanding. Family counselors should work with families to examine how their communication patterns, as well as the above factors, influence family functioning.

Bowen noticed several parallels between family processes and processes happening within the larger society. He found in studying juveniles within the justice system that the patterns of their parents were repeating themselves within the structures of the justice system as well. For example, when a youth would act out, the parents would remove a privilege. This would be followed by the youth getting angry and acting out even more, which would then result in the parents getting angry and taking away more privileges. The youth gets disgusted with all the punishments and is therefore unaffected by them, continuing to act out, getting into legal trouble. The parents, feeling powerless, refer to the justice system, and the parental consequences are then replaced by those within the justice system. Once the justice system takes over, the cycle begins all over again, with the youth testing the boundaries, having consequences, getting angry, acting out more, and having harsher punishments. This same dance takes place until the officials within the justice system give up on the youth as well, labeling the youth as a delinquent, rather than a young person working on improving. The societal emotional process continues and loops back to the family, who may have given up all hope on the youth, and, protecting themselves, cut him off from the family.

GENOGRAMS

In addition to being valuable assessment tools (Chapter 3) genograms are also a key component of multigenerational family therapy and are therefore used throughout the therapeutic process, rather than solely as an assessment tool. Bowen believed that in order to understand an individual's problems, it is helpful to examine them within a three-generation context. At the heart of this concept is the genogram, which shows three generations of family members' names, ages, educational history, occupations, health and medical history (including addiction and substance abuse), marriage, divorce, death, and relationship dynamics between family members. Genograms may be developed simply with pencil and paper and drawn similar to a family tree, starting with the client (and siblings if applicable) at the bottom of the genogram and working upward with each previous generation. For those who like more precise and systematic genograms, McGoldrick (2008) has written extensively about the use of genograms and how to make them quite detailed, using a variety of symbols, including those for marriage, adoption, death, divorce, disease, suicide, miscarriages, abortions, stillbirths, and so on. She has also included some interesting genograms of famous families, including the Kennedys.

For the techies and those who don't like drawing freehand or using a ruler, there are websites and software available to create the genograms digitally. Regardless of how the genogram is made, it should have three generations present on the page and include all family members that the client considers part of his or her family.

The client develops the genogram, often assigned as homework, with guidance from the counselor. It may be necessary to consult with other family members or other sources for any necessary information unknown by the client. Once the genogram is complete, the counselor and client look at it together and discuss the patterns they notice. This can be a powerful experience for clients. The process of seeing a visual representation of one's family history, and the patterns within, may provide insight into current issues. For example, discovering that you are the first person in the history of your family to marry someone outside of your ethnicity, race, religion, or so on, may shed light on why your parents are having such a hard time with your choice of a life partner who is culturally different from you. Likewise, discovering a history of substance abuse in one's family may help caution a young person who is beginning to experiment with alcohol and drugs.

STOP AND THINK:

1. Take a look at the Manning-Kelly family genogram. What patterns do you notice right away? How might those patterns relate to what you know about Christina's issues?

2. What do you notice about gender roles within the Manning-Kelly family? How might those patterns impact Christina's choice to pursue marriage and start a family right after high school versus college and a career?

CONCLUSION

Bowen's theory of multigenerational family therapy focuses on patterns of behavior within the family system and how those patterns manifest themselves in a variety of ways. Understanding relationship patterns and roles that individuals play can provide insight for clients as they learn to focus on making changes in the self, rather than focusing on trying to change others. As family counselors-in-training, it is crucial to understand that reading a chapter about multigenerational counseling does not qualify one to go out and practice family counseling with real clients. It takes years of study, practice, and clinical supervision before one is adequately skilled at these approaches. In the meantime, here are some sources for you to consider if you are drawn to this theory as you develop your own personal theory of family counseling.

Extend Your Learning:

1. Create a family genogram that includes at least three generations before writing your family assessment or family reflective papers. If you don't have all the information, consult with other family members for help, or write questions about each relative that you don't know about. The family genogram should include both biological or adoptive parents as well as any stepparents; all their grandparents and their aunts and uncles and their families; and the student's siblings and their families, if they have them. It is helpful to include ages; dates of marriages, divorces, and deaths; occupations, including stay-at-home parent; and biomedical or mental health issues, including causes of death for deceased family members.

   If you don't have information about your birth parents or siblings, construct the genogram based on who you consider your family to be and with the information that you have. The genograms do not have to be solely based on biology. Behavioral and relational patterns occur in all relationships. Thus, people who have limited to no information about their birth families may still find constructing a genogram useful and learn more about their relationships with either their adoptive families or the people they have grown to consider family.

   In our experience, students find creating these genograms enjoyable and very informative. And, because genograms are clinical tools, we allow them flexibility about the medium they use. We also tell them that they can make a key for the genogram, explaining the details so that they don't have to fit lengthy diagnoses and multiple dates onto the genogram itself. Finally, we provide them with a list of symbols from McGoldrick's book to help inform what patterns or terms they may want to explore.

2. Family Reflection Paper: After completing your family genogram, write a 3 to 5 page reflective paper using the following prompts:

(a.) Looking at your genogram, how would you describe your family? Given what you know about your family, what did the genogram overlook or not capture about your family?

(b.) Looking at your genogram, what patterns do you notice in your family? Did these surprise you? Why, or why not?

(c.) How might you use the genogram as you move forward in your own personal, social, and academic development?

(d.) How might you use a genogram to assess and treat clients?

3. In class, divide into groups of 2, 3, or 4 to share your genograms. During this process, reflect on and discuss the following:

What patterns do you notice in your own genogram?

What surprised you?

What patterns do you notice about your classmate's genogram?

Did any of the patterns you noticed go previously unnoticed by your classmates?

What insights did your classmates have about your genogram?

How did this activity add to your learning about your family?

What new questions came from this activity?

4. Now that you have constructed and reflected upon your genogram, what will you do with the information you learned from your genogram? How does identifying the patterns affect your thoughts and feelings about your family? About other relationships? Will you discuss it with anyone else? How might this impact your life, future, or relationships with others?

REFERENCES

Bitter, J. (2014). *Theory and practice of family therapy and counseling.* Belmont, CA: Brooks/Cole.

Bowen, M. (1978). *Family therapy in clinical practice.* New York, NY and London, UK: Jason Aronson.

Goldenberg, H., & Goldenberg, I. (2008). *Family therapy: An overview.* Belmont, CA: Brooks/Cole.

Kerr, M. E. (1981). Family systems theory and therapy. In A. S. Gurman & D. P. Kniskern (Eds.), *Handbook of family therapy*. New York, NY: Brunner/Mazel.

Kerr, M. E. (2000). *A primer on Bowen theory*. The Bowen Center for the Study of the Family. Retrieved from http://www.thebowencenter.org

McGoldrick, M. (2008). *Genograms: Assessment and intervention*. New York, NY: Norton.

Toman, W. (1976). *Family constellation: Its effects on personality and social behavior*. New York: Springer.

Vermont Center for Family Studies. (n.d.). *Bowen family systems theory*. Retrieved from www.vermontcenterforfamilystudies.org

CHAPTER 6

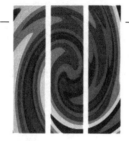

Structural Family Counseling

Structural Family Counseling is one of the oldest and most consistently used models of family counseling. The writers agree with Michael Nichols (1984) that, "The main reason for its success is that it describes families as having an underlying organization in terms that provide clear guidelines for diagnosis and treatment" (p. 469).

Salvador Minuchin, the founder of structural family therapy, contributed a number of concepts that family counselors use to understand how families function and to help the client families with whom they work (Minuchin, 1974; Minuchin Montalvo, Guerney, Rosman, & Schumer, 1967; Minuchin, Rosman, & Baker, 1978). Family counselors observe a tremendous number of interactions among family members. Careful observation helps them recognize repetitive patterns of interactions, or family dynamics. Minuchin's Structural Family Counseling further helps family counselors make sense of a family's dynamics by providing concepts that translate observed dynamics into descriptions of how the family is organized and the nature of its relationships, in other words, the family's structure.

Rather than beginning his career by conceptualizing and studying individuals and families, Minuchin's professional life began as a physician specializing in psychiatry. During the 1960s, he began working with children and adolescents identified as "delinquent." These children were primarily from low-income families and had come to the attention of the juvenile justice system. Minuchin began seeing these children with their families. Because the other early family counselors had been primarily concerned with theory and its application mostly to middle-income families, their techniques did not always apply to the families with whom Minuchin worked.

Minuchin's Structural Family Counseling arose as a method of intervention with low-income, multiproblem families. As he wrote about his work, however, the methods he used and the ways he thought about families were soon viewed by other family counselors as useful when working with families presenting with a variety of problems other than poverty and delinquency.

This chapter begins by exploring some of the family concepts that either originated in or were further developed for use in Structural Family Counseling. You will then read about some of the tools that make Structural Family Counseling unique. Finally, you will read about the application of the methods of Structural Family Counseling to the Manning-Kelly family.

STRUCTURAL FAMILY COUNSELING CONCEPTS

Structural Family Counseling arose from contemporaneous work by Minuchin and a number of his colleagues who were working with patients in psychiatric hospitals. Concepts developed by Murray Bowen (Chapter 5) are apparent in Minuchin's theory, especially the concepts of boundaries and triangulation. However, while Bowen approached these ideas from a psychodynamic and multigenerations perspective, Minuchin applied them to how the family is structured. These distinctions will become more obvious as we describe Minuchin's Structural Family Counseling theory.

STOP AND THINK:

As you read this chapter, notice the similarities and differences between Minuchin and Bowen's (Chapter 5) theories and approaches to family counseling. In your notebook, write down these similarities and differences as you notice them.

Three concepts are crucial to Structural Family Counseling as described by Minuchin. These are boundaries and their impact on relationships (generational, permeability, diffuse/rigid boundaries continuum, enmeshed/disengaged relationships continuum); triangles and other alliances and coalitions; and hierarchies. Understanding these concepts will allow us to more clearly understand how and why Structural Family Counseling interventions change families in the way that they do.

Boundaries

Minuchin viewed boundaries as a reflection of family rules for managing physical and psychological distance among members, between groups or subsystems of family members, and between the family as a whole and both extended family and nonfamily systems. In other words, through repeated interactions, families develop rules about closeness and distance at all levels within and outside the family system.

STOP AND THINK:

Think about your own family and the families of your friends growing up.

1. Were you able to run in and out of any of their apartments or houses to eat a snack or use the bathroom?

2. Were there other homes you wouldn't go into without being invited?

3. Are there both public spaces and private spaces in your own family's home, or can visitors go anywhere?

4. Do family members close and/or lock the doors of bedrooms? When and why?

5. Are there times children know not to disturb their parents?

6. If siblings argue, do parents intervene or let their children "work it out" themselves?

7. Is it all right to talk about your family to people who are not family members?

8. Are there topics of conversation that aren't talked about between parents and children, or would one of your parents complain to you, for example, about the other's behavior or about money?

9. Do family members tell each other everything that happens to them?

10. Do you tell one of your siblings or one of your parents more than you tell other family members?

11. Do family members believe each other's lives are private and only provide information on a need-to-know basis?

12. Did your parents help you with homework? If yes, how old were you when they stopped? Do you continue to talk about your classes and assignments?

13. Can you think of other questions that might reflect family rules about closeness and distance?

The answers to these questions reveal information about the rules governing distance and closeness within your family. These rules can differ dramatically in different families. Additionally, how a family defines boundaries is influenced by the family's cultural identity. For example, in some cultures, an elder speaks for all family members, whereas in a family of western European descent one family member speaking for others would be considered a sign of diffuse boundaries and enmeshed relationships (see below). Family counselors therefore attend to a client family's culture and its general assumptions about rules governing relationship boundaries to fully understand and avoid pathologizing an individual family's boundaries.

Minuchin's theoretical perspective on boundaries reflected his absorption into Western culture. As you read about them, remember that they are not universal. In other words, what is considered dysfunctional in some cultures may be viewed as functional in others. Although the purpose of this text is to introduce you to the general concepts that underlie family counseling, the writers encourage you to familiarize yourself with cultural differences in their application as you proceed in your studies of family counseling.

Relationships are defined by the boundaries between and among family members. When these boundaries are so easily crossed that members have difficulty knowing where one member stops and the other begins, the boundary is labeled diffuse. One of the typical ways a family counselor can recognize a family with diffuse boundaries is when one member speaks for other members of the family, although as previously mentioned, this is specific to the dominant culture in the United States.

The relationships among family members and within and between subsystems in families with diffuse boundaries are enmeshed. When relationships are enmeshed, the boundaries are so unclear, or diffuse, that members do not develop individual identities. It is difficult for families with diffuse boundaries and enmeshed relationships to allow children to explore relationships outside the family with peers or other adult role models. Sometimes it is even difficult for young adult children from enmeshed families to leave home during the launching stage of the family life cycle.

It may also be difficult for enmeshed families to differentiate appropriate roles for parents and children. Do you know someone who says she's her mother's best or only friend? Even as a young adult, it is difficult for someone in the child subsystem to be friends with someone in the parent subsystem. Would you really want to hear about your parents' concern about their sexual relationship? Probably not, and yet best friends sometimes share such concerns for emotional support.

When the roles and behaviors of parents and children are not clearly differentiated, families often experience the kinds of problems that bring them to counseling. This statement, like all that follow, is specific to the dominant culture in the United States and cannot be assumed to be universal.

Enmeshed relationships are different than close relationships. People who are close to each other care deeply about each other and each allows the other to see who she or he really is. People who are enmeshed don't see that they are separate and fail to recognize aspects of the other that are not identical to self. So you might say a close friend puts up with more hurtful behavior from her boyfriend than you would; if you were in an enmeshed relationship with her, you might not even notice that she isn't just like you and instead focus only on his hurtful behavior and how you would handle it. The risk, of course, is that your friend would feel that you were not listening to her and instead might be angry that you were deflecting the conversation from her problem to talking about yourself. The problem then becomes not his hurtful behavior but your failure to see her as separate from yourself. Additionally, if you told her to dump him and she didn't, then you might be angry that she did not listen to you.

Alternatively, when boundaries are virtually impossible to cross, they are labeled *rigid*. The relationships arising in the presence of rigid boundaries are termed *disengaged*. Families with rigid boundaries, like families with diffuse boundaries, do not provide children with a sense of self. In families with rigid boundaries, there is not sufficient connection for children to learn who they are by seeing how parents and siblings respond to them. In families with diffuse boundaries, on the other hand, identities of members are not distinct, and children do not learn who they are apart from other family members.

Families with disengaged relationships do not often present voluntarily for counseling. They more frequently come to the attention of juvenile authorities and so are more likely to be seen for court-mandated services.

Diffuse and rigid boundaries and the resulting enmeshed and disengaged relationships may be thought of as two ends of a continuum. As one moves inward from the ends, boundaries become clear and relationships flexible. Minuchin considered clear boundaries and flexible relationships to be especially important between generations, as they allow parents and children to be close without confusing who is responsible for what.

There is great variation among families with clear boundaries. Some are very close, spend lots of time together, talk often when they cannot be together, and hold a strong family identity. Others are not as close, spend less time together, talk less frequently, and do not hold a strong family identity. Yet members of these families know they can rely on one another and are loved by the other members of their families. As closeness and distance within families approach either end of the continuum, however, the characteristics of boundaries and relationships may become problematic for family members and for the family as a whole.

There is no clear line of demarcation between each type of boundary. However, as a family counselor, you can recognize how the boundaries and relationships are either facilitating or impeding family functioning. Minuchin believed that when boundaries fall at either extreme of the continuum, they impede the adaptability of the family and its members to stress, exacerbate symptoms within the family, and require intervention by a family counselor to achieve more balance, clarity, and flexibility.

In her book, *Schopenhauer's Porcupines: Intimacy and Its Dilemmas*, Deborah Anna Luepnitz (2002) described the parable for which the book is named. When it is very cold, porcupines begin to huddle closer together for warmth. However, when they become close enough to be pricked by one another's quills, the porcupines move apart to avoid pain until they are so cold that they once again shift direction and move closer together. At the extreme ends of this process, the porcupines are either uncomfortably cold or uncomfortably irritated by each other's quills. Finding a balance somewhere in the middle allows them to attain warmth without pain. There is not a perfect balance point, and each group of porcupines will move closer together and further apart until it finds its own. What's important is not where the balance point is but that the porcupines in the group are neither uncomfortably cold nor uncomfortably pricked. The porcupines also provide an excellent example of homeostasis (Chapter 4).

Coalitions and Triangles

The concepts of coalitions and triangles are credited to Murray Bowen but are also central to the practice of Structural Family Counseling. According to Bowen, dyadic and triadic relationships, or those that occur between two or three family members, are the essential building blocks of family dynamics. However, when tension and anxiety build in a dyad, the dyad becomes unstable and the tension and anxiety can be defused by triangulation, the process of bringing in a third person. When this happens, the family remains in equilibrium, but the stress in the dyad is not resolved. Paradoxically, the presence of the triangle actually interferes with resolution of the issue that created the instability and anxiety in the dyad in the first place. Most commonly, dysfunctional triangles involve both parents and a child.

Minuchin also believed that, when flexible or fluid through time, triangles are a normal part of family life. From his perspective, it is only when they cross generations and become rigid, or fixed through time, that they become dysfunctional. To address dysfunctional triangles, Minuchin recommended strengthening the boundary between the parental and child subsystems. This restructures the family, hence the name, Structural Family Counseling.

In any group, including families, members form alliances with one another for various purposes involving mutual benefit. Alliances fulfill family needs in a way that is beneficial to all family members. Alliances can involve any two or more family members. When an alliance occurs among three family members, it is also referred to as a triad.

Christina's cousins, Paul and Patricia, formed an alliance to help their father with the demands of their mother's cancer treatments. While the time they devoted to this endeavor may have detracted from the time they spent with their partners, everyone agreed that their alliance to care for a sick parent was important, temporary, and worth the time it took.

By contrast, coalitions are negative alliances between any two or more family members. Most commonly, they are two or more people either excluding or pitting themselves against another family member. When a coalition occurs among three family members, it is called a triangle. This distinction is important, because a triangle involves bringing a third person into a distressed dyad and thus puts great pressure on that person, while the same pressure is spread among several people and focused on the excluded family member in larger coalitions.

The person who is triangulated into a distressed dyad or excluded from a coalition often is the one who exhibits symptoms and brings the family to counseling. In other words, that person often becomes the identified patient. While coalitions and triangles often keep the family system in equilibrium, they do so at the expense of individuals and, thus, ultimately to the family as a whole.

Christina's stepfather, Mark, described his first wife as alienating his children from him. It appears the family developed a coalition among his first wife, Shoshana, their two children, Jason and Ashley, and Shoshana's parents that excluded Mark. Shoshana would make plans for the children with her parents and not tell Mark, then laugh at him while telling the children that he forgot to attend. This pattern repeated over and over again, creating a family dynamic that included a coalition among Shoshana, her parents, and the children that excluded Mark. The children could not have left the coalition, even if it made them uncomfortable, because the parents' conflict would have left them no option other than to form a new coalition with Mark against Shoshana. Declining to participate in the coalition was not an option for Jason and Ashley, because neutrality would have forced Mark and Shoshana to address the problems in their relationship, risked dissolution of the marriage, and left the children feeling at least partially responsible. When Jason left home for college, the coalition fell apart and, rather than resolving their issues or forming a triangle with Ashley, Mark and Shoshana divorced.

Triads are fundamental units of communication within families. They are inevitable. If they are shifting and flexible, they generally do not cause problems. However, when they become rigid and inflexible and when they involve two or more members forming a coalition against a third, they can be problematic.

Christina's stepmother, Daniella, taught her to cook. This alliance between Christina and Daniella was flexible, in that Martin or one of the younger children could join if they wanted to, and temporary, in that it only involved an activity in which they shared an interest. At other times, Christina had conversations with her father, Martin, that Daniella did not participate in, sometimes because she wanted to give them father-daughter time and other times because she was busy doing other things.

Alternatively, a triangle shifts attention away from the true problem onto secondary symptoms. It is also a coalition, with consequences for a single child. Christina's stepfather, Mark, and his first wife, Shoshana's, children, Jason and Ashley, could talk and complain about their parents' behavior, and each could validate the other's discomfort. By contrast, when there is only one person who deflects the tension from the dyad, that person has to display very obvious symptoms in order to create enough distraction. Emma, Mark and Liz's daughter, exemplifies the presence of a triangle. Her dependence on Liz exceeds the needs of her disability, and excluding Mark is unnecessary. Her excessive dependence has left Emma less mature than she could be and may inevitably create issues for her with peers and a concomitant diminishing of her self-esteem, already threatened by her motor differences.

Similarly, Christina and Liz triangulated other family members into their distressed relationship. Christina brought her Aunt Barbara, her stepmother, Daniella, and her father into her fights with Liz about postgraduation plans. Liz brought in Mark and Emma. Martin Jr. avoided triangulation, but that avoidance brought its own toll of distancing him from the family. And while Christina's eating disorder may have been a multigenerational effect (see Chapter 5), she may also have been triangulated into her mother's distressed relationship with Mark, her on-going fights with Liz distracting them from their marital problems.

As the result of a triangle, the third person, who is usually a child, may exhibit physical, emotional, or behavioral symptoms that can be quite severe. Minuchin and his colleagues did a study of children with diabetes. They sat the children behind a one-way mirror and let them observe their parents interacting. They simultaneously monitored the children's blood sugar. The results indicated that when the parents argued, the children's blood sugar was more likely to spike than when they observed their parents interacting without conflict. Since elevated blood sugar can cause both acute symptoms and long-term problems, the child's blood sugar spikes required adult attention. Minuchin and his colleagues concluded that this phenomenon indicated the presence of a triangle in which the child's diabetic symptoms disrupted parental distress, stopping it from escalating and also leaving it unresolved.

Sometimes the presence of a third person brings the other two together for a common purpose, as when parents need to care for a diabetic child exhibiting acute symptoms of the disease. Other times, as when Christina and Liz argue, the child engages only one of the parents to the exclusion of the other, which also stops the escalating instability in the dyad and attendant anxiety. In every example of a triangle described in this section, a child has become part of the parental subsystem. According to Structural Family Counseling theory, in each of these examples, the family needs to be restructured so the child returns to the child subsystem and the parents can address the distress in the parental subsystem. With clear boundaries between the generations, the child can interact with and be close to both parents without becoming part of the parents' relationship with each other.

As you can see, the most common triangles involve two parents and a child and result from the distress in the parents' relationship. Such triangles usually result in the dyadic distress remaining unaddressed and unresolved and the child developing a symptom that either brings the parents together to help or provides a rationale for one of the parents becoming overly involved with the child to the exclusion of the other parent. In either case, the parents are distracted from their couple problems. As a result, the tension between them doesn't escalate to the point of divorce. However, because of the distraction provided by the child's symptoms, the parents' problems also remain unresolved.

STOP AND THINK:

1. Take a moment to reflect on the difference between the triangle involving Christina and Liz that excludes Mark and the triad involving Christina and Daniella that excludes Martin.

2. Now identify an alliance and a triad in your own family. Are either of these also a coalition or a triangle?

Liz and Christina formed a triangle that excluded Mark when they repeatedly fought about Christina's future. This repetitive, unresolved argument between them appeared to be stressful for other family members, who either withdrew (Martin Jr.), made minimal efforts to help (Mark), or attempted to deflect Liz's attention (Emma). Christina and Liz's fights had created a rigid boundary around them that no one, including Mark, Liz's husband and Christina's stepfather, could cross. It thus placed Christina in the midst of the marital subsystem. And Christina's presence in the marital subsystem both masked and prevented resolution of the distress between Liz and Mark.

Alternatively, Christina and Daniella formed a triad with Martin when Daniella gave Christina cooking lessons. Martin elected to exclude himself, rather than being prevented from participating. Christina and Daniella cooking together only applied to one activity and did not arise from distress in Daniella and Martin's marriage. The boundary around them when they were cooking remained clear and could be easily crossed if Martin or one of the other children wanted to be in the kitchen with them.

Structural Family Counseling focuses the family away from the identified patient, strengthens the boundary around the parental subsystem, and addresses the distress in the parents' dyadic relationship with the intention of resolving, rather than deflecting it. With a more functional structure, specifically a clear boundary between the parental and child subsystems, the identified patient's symptoms will be alleviated, and the parents will be positioned to acknowledge, address, and ultimately resolve the distress in their dyadic relationship.

Hierarchies

Structural Family Counseling aims at strengthening hierarchies. Hierarchies involve generational boundaries that are assumed to lead to more functional family dynamics.

Clear boundaries between generations lead to parents assuming parental responsibilities and children not stepping into parenting roles, while both generations continue to interact with one another. They do not preclude children taking on age-appropriate responsibilities and decision making. Older siblings can babysit younger siblings without becoming primary caretakers and disciplinarians. Similarly, children and parents can enjoy close relationships without the children taking care of their parents' emotional needs. Family counseling interventions aimed at strengthening generational hierarchies are yet another way of framing the need to get the identified patient out of the parents' relationship.

Minuchin once compared the role of the family counselor to that of a grand-parent, teaching parents how to parent and helping them teach children how to be children. As you read about the techniques of Structural Family Counseling, consider your thoughts about that statement.

Clear generational boundaries were apparent in Christina's father's family. He and his wife, Daniella, took responsibility for caring for their two young children, his stepson, and his two older children. As previously mentioned, Daniella was teaching Christina to cook, and Christina admired Daniella to the point that she told her mother she wanted to be like Daniella. Martin's mother, Roxanne, expressed her views that Martin should have been providing more religious experiences for his children. She then stood back and allowed Martin to decide how he wanted to parent his children, not commenting on areas in which she either agreed with his parenting or found less important than religion.

Similarly, Martin talked to Liz when he needed to communicate about Christina or Martin Jr. When he needed to alter the visitation schedule, he called or e-mailed Liz, rather than asking Christina or Martin Jr. to let their mother know. This kept them free of any potential conflict and from being triangulated into the negotiation between him and their mother.

STOP AND THINK:

Do the hierarchies in your family involve clear boundaries between gene-rations? How?

STRUCTURAL FAMILY COUNSELING

Structural Family Counseling is based on the concepts already described in this chapter. Structural family counselors focus on increasing individual and rela-tionship health by restructuring the family. Restructuring is aimed at boundar-ies, hierarchies, coalitions, and triangles. Structural family counselors assume that any change in the family structure will reverberate throughout the family system, and, as it does, individual and relationship health will improve.

Structural family counselors engage every family member in the processes of assessment and intervention. They ask each member how they view the pre-senting problem and to explain specifics about what happens throughout the family when it surfaces.

Structural Family Counseling requires an active counselor who is willing to question the family's assumptions about themselves, help them increase their repertoire of ways to interact, and use what is happening in the room to enact the dysfunctional family dynamics and suggest alternatives to change them. Structural family counselors do this bearing in mind the need to restructure the family in order to change it.

Questioning Family Assumptions

Families, like individuals, tend to make the assumption that what they think and feel and how they behave is safe and good because it is familiar. Christina's half sister, Emma, had a central nervous system disorder that affected her movement and the clarity of her speech. The family seemed to accept the assumption that Liz therefore needed to focus the bulk of her attention on Emma, often to the exclusion of her husband, Mark, and her two older children. And, although her repetitive argument with Christina about posthigh-school plans engaged her with her older daughter, the family appeared to assume that nothing else would or even should distract her from Emma.

It was up to the family counselor to question assumptions like these. A consultation with Emma's pediatrician revealed that although she was scheduled for regular appointments for speech and occupational therapy that intruded on play and social time, Emma was able to function as independently as any other 4-year-old. She walked independently, was able to feed and bathe herself, and had exhibited no cognitive deficits. Yet within her family, she was treated as though this was untrue. Being treated as more disabled and dependent than she was interfered with Emma's social and emotional development. Simultaneously, Liz's involvement with Emma created distance from her husband, Mark, and her older children, neither of whom appeared happy and both of whom had displayed identifiable symptoms of emotional distress.

Enactments

Enactments are a technique frequently used by Structural Family Counselors. Enactments allow the family to practice corrective interactions which, once experienced in the counselor's office, can be recreated and practiced at home.

The first step in an enactment involves the structural family counselor observing the sequences of interactions within the family and using these observations to map the family boundaries, coalitions, and hierarchies. This process is called tracking. It can occur while the counselor establishes a therapeutic relationship with the family and asks questions about the presenting problem and how it plays out in the family dynamics.

The second step in an enactment involves the structural family counselor inviting the family to enact their dynamics. If the family was complaining about the arguments between Christina and Liz, the counselor could invite them to talk about Christina's postgraduation plans in the office. Family members may have become self-conscious, and the counselor could encourage them by asking questions about what they thought was happening and what usually happened next. The counselor could also ask other family members what they did while Liz and Christina argued and what they thought about the argument.

The structural family counselor then moves the family into the third step of the enactment, which involves the family counselor redirecting behaviors to clarify boundaries and hierarchies, thereby disrupting coalitions and triangles. To repeat, structural family counselors assume that changes in the family's structure will change the dynamics and thus the mental health of the family members and the functionality of their relationships with one another.

Redirecting during an enactment may include asking family members to move around the room and sometimes even moving office furniture. Redirecting may also involve orchestrating the conversation, asking a silent member to talk to a particular family member, or interrupting a family member who is talking. Such redirection enhances the repertoire of interactions among family members and allows a shift in structure and dynamics.

We will now turn to the application of Structural Family Counseling to the Manning-Kelly family. The following section demonstrates how enactments work, using excerpts from the Manning-Kelly family's counseling.

USING STRUCTURAL FAMILY COUNSELING WITH THE MANNING-KELLY FAMILY

After the Manning-Kelly family sat down in the family counselor's office, she introduced herself and said hello to each family member, thanking them for taking the time to come in that day. Because Liz had called her to arrange the appointment, the family counselor decided not to begin the conversation by addressing her. She also did not want to begin by talking to Christina, as that might communicate to the family that she agreed with their assumption that the identified patient was the problem. She also avoided beginning with Martin Jr. or Emma, because siblings are often more helpful after their parents and the identified patient have described what goes on in the family.

Mark, Christina's stepfather, was the logical family member with whom to begin the conversation. Like many women who initiate family counseling, Liz had warned the family counselor that he might not want to be involved. If the identified patient's father or stepfather doesn't want to be in counseling, then part of the family counselor's job in the first session is to engage him in the process to maximize the possibility that the family will continue counseling.

FC: I want to thank you all for coming in today. I know how difficult it is to coordinate schedules, and I also think it's important that you're all here. As you all know, I spoke to Liz briefly on the phone. So, Mark, I'd like to start by asking you what is going on.

The family counselor did not identify the problem as Christina's. A nonspecific question that addresses "the problem" or "what is going on" avoids the counselor falling into the trap of agreeing that the problem resides within the identified patient, rather than with the family. Questions like this one allow family members to define the problem that brought them to counseling in a variety of ways. It also conveys that the family counselor doesn't see the problem as residing solely in the identified patient, even if the family members do.

Mark: Well, I'm not sure exactly why you wanted me here. I understand Christina's doctor is worried about her weight, and Liz has always been concerned about weight and health. But I don't see weight as a problem for either of them.

At this point, it was very tempting to ask Mark about how Liz's concerns about weight and health affect their relationship and the family. But a structural family counselor would remain focused on identifying patterns of interactions, or dynamics, among family members in order to identify and then change the family structure.

FC: And what do you think about their worry?

Again, the family counselor's goal was to avoid labeling the problem as being about Christina's weight or even the possibility that an eating disorder is a multigenerational phenomenon in this family.

Mark: I think Liz looks fine. And Christina's just being a teenage girl. My daughter worried about her weight when she was in high school, too.

At this point, it was also tempting to ask about his daughter. However, counselors cannot focus on everything at once, and the purpose continued to be to learn about the family's structure.

FC: So it isn't much of a problem for you.

Mark: No.

FC: What happens when Liz or Christina worries about weight?

Mark: I'm not sure what you mean.

FC: Well, do they talk about their weight? Argue with you when you tell them they look fine? Do they insist others eat the way they're eating? Things like that.

Mark: No. Well, Liz sometimes goes on diets and won't eat what the rest of the family is eating, and she doesn't believe me when I tell her she looks fine. But the arguments are mostly about college.

This is not surprising. The issue in families is very rarely limited to the problem that brought them to counseling. In reality, it may have taken longer for the argument that exemplifies the dysfunctional impact of the family structure to emerge. For illustrative purposes, the process was foreshortened here.

FC: Christina and college?

Mark: Yes.

FC: Tell me about that.

Mark: Liz could tell you more about it. [Pause]

FC: OK, but at some point I'd like to hear your take on it. Liz?

Liz: I'm not sure what this has to do with Christina's alleged eating disorder?

Family structure, like all aspects of its dynamics, serves to maintain the family's homeostasis. Shifting the conversation from Christina's doctor's concerns to what was happening in the family may disrupt the family's equilibrium and thus be perceived as a threat by family members. It is safe to assume, as the family counselor did, that Liz's refusal to talk about the family apart from Christina's problem was a homeostatic mechanism.

FC: Neither do I, at this point. But I suspect what goes on in the family affects everyone in the family. So I'd like to hear more about you and Christina and college.

While not wishing a confrontation with Liz, focusing on the presenting problem and the identified patient only serves to maintain the family's equilibrium, preventing any meaningful, second-order change from happening (Chapter 4).

Liz: [Pause] Well, as you know, Christina is a junior in high school and needs to apply to college in the fall. [Christina sighed loudly, rolled her eyes, and looked at the floor while Liz ignored her.] Most of her friends used their spring breaks to visit colleges, and Christina refused. [She glared at Christina.]

Christina: [Glaring at her mother] They didn't all. [At this point, Emma began pulling on Liz's sleeve and holding the paper on which she had been coloring so Liz could see it.]

FC: Mark, is this what happens at home?

Mark: Usually they start arguing with each other.

FC: So Emma doesn't distract Liz at home?

Mark: No. Well, not until after it's been going on awhile.

FC: Liz and Christina's argument?

Mark: Yeah.

Already, there was a pattern emerging. Liz made a statement about how Christina was not doing what she expected of her, adding the pressure that all her friends were doing what Christina refused to do, Christina contradicted her, and Emma interrupted the argument. The expression on Mark's face suggested he had not put the pieces together prior to that moment. Note also that Mark and Martin Jr. were observers of the argument, at least up to this point.

FC: Do you ever try to stop the fight?

Mark: Every now and then. Mostly when I'm tired.

FC: What do you do when you get involved?

While it would have been interesting to hear about Mark's internal processes, the structural family counselor remained focused on identifying dynamics that would provide information about the family structure.

Mark:	I tell Liz to let it go. Probably not the right thing to do. [Smiles, but not with his eyes] But they get nowhere talking about it, and she doesn't need to get all stressed out.
FC:	I'm sorry, Liz gets stressed out when they argue? Or Christina? Or both?
Mark:	Well, I guess Christina must get stressed out, too. But I was thinking about Liz.

It would have been very tempting to ask what happened between Mark and Liz when she was stressed. However, identifying interactions among all family members remained the counselor's goal. And family systems, in an attempt to maintain equilibrium, will distract the family counselor from attempts to change the family dynamics.

FC:	[To Martin Jr.] What do you do when your mom and sister argue?
MJ:	Nothing.
FC:	Do you watch?
MJ:	Mostly if I'm there I leave.
FC:	Where do you go?

The other option would have been to address the word *mostly* and ask what happened when he didn't leave. In retrospect, finding out about each separately would have been a good idea.

MJ:	My room or out if it's [during the] day. I guess sometimes I tell Christina there's no point trying to convince Mom. Later, when we're talking.
FC:	So when you talk to Christina about it, that happens later, not while Christina and your mom are arguing?
MJ:	Yes.

We now have a preliminary picture of the family structure. Note that we have almost no information about the content of the argument itself or whether it has any impact on Christina's relationship to food. As structural family counselors, those are secondary to determining the family structure. To review, the theory states that changing the structure will lead to other changes within the family and its members.

What we see is that Mark and Liz are not aligned in a parental subsystem. This may be because Mark is the stepfather and they agreed not to parent each other's children. However, a structural family counselor would focus on the structure of the marital subsystem within the larger family system.

The observed structure of the Manning-Kelly family lacks a strong parental subsystem with clear boundaries around it, leading to several important questions. Was there distance and tension between Mark and Liz that the argument with Christina masks? This would be one triangle. Was Emma serving as a surrogate parent to distract and thus stop, though not resolve, the fight between her mother and stepsister when Mark remained disengaged from it? That would be a second triangle. Was she also part of a triangle with Mark and Liz, as Christina was? Did Martin Jr.'s distance serve as a mechanism that kept him from becoming part of a triangle or coalition within the family? And finally, that he talked to Christina alone about anything suggests the presence of a sibling subsystem clearly differentiated from the parents.

FC: [Continuing to address Martin Jr.] What do you think about what's happening between your mom and sister?

MJ: [Smiling] I don't really know.

FC: [Smiling also] OK, I'm going to let you off the hook for now. But I think you're probably a very good observer, and I'm going to ask for your help after I've talked to your mom and sister.

MJ: [Nods]

FC: Christina, you haven't had a chance to talk. And the rest of us have been talking about you especially and sometimes also your mom as though neither of you were here. I'd like to hear from you what goes on at home, but first I'd like to ask your mom to finish her description, if that's all right with you.

C: [Nodding] Fine.

FC: Great. Liz, I think I interrupted you earlier, and I would like to hear about what's going on about Christina and college.

Liz: I don't know what else to say. Christina has got to decide where she wants to apply. Time is running out.

FC: It sounds as though you're feeling some urgency about Christina's college decision.

Liz:	Of course I am. I care about her [Christina snorts], and it's nearing the end of her junior year. And I don't understand why she isn't feeling the time slipping away.
FC:	And how are your concerns playing out between the two of you?

Once again, the counselor avoided identifying Christina as the identified patient with the wording of her question.

Liz:	Well, Christina seems determined to ruin her life. She refuses to talk to me about college, to even think about college. She says she doesn't need to go [Changes to a sing-song voice] because she wants to be a housewife like Daniella and Barbara.
FC:	And Daniella and Barbara are?
Liz:	My ex's wife [Note she doesn't say Christina's stepmother] and my sister [Again, not her aunt]. It's ridiculous. [Voice rising in pitch and volume] She's limiting herself so much, and I don't want to see her dependent on some man to survive.
FC:	So what do you do to help her understand that?

While being empathetic, structural family counselors do not address the feeling level of family life as part of their intervention. Liz's intentions appear positive; however, the intervention would be on the family structure, rather than the content of Liz's concerns and Christina's resistance to them.

Liz:	She's got to think about college, plan some visits for the summer, begin thinking about her application essays. [Looks at Christina] At least talk to the college counselor at school.
FC:	And you tell her this?
Liz:	Yes.
FC:	And what happens?

This is tracking sequences of behavior.

Liz:	She's defiant and disrespectful.
FC:	How does she show you defiance and disrespect?

These words have meaning for Liz, but there is no way for the counselor to know what the particular meaning is. So once again, the focus returns to sequences of interactions, rather than detouring into meanings.

Liz: She refuses to do any of it. She says she doesn't need to go to college because she wants to be a housewife. [To Christina] Barbara went to college.

FC: [Turning to Christina] You've decided you don't want to go to college?

C: Yes. I mean, no.

FC: [Smiling] No to college or no to decided?

C: No to college.

FC: And you've decided to be a housewife and stay-at-home mom like your aunt and stepmother?

Liz identified these two women in terms of their relationship to herself. When talking to Christina, the counselor intentionally defined them in terms of their relationship to her.

C: I want to be a stay-at-home mother, like Aunt Barbara and Daniella.

FC: Oh, you want to be at home full-time while your children are growing up.

C: Yes. [Glaring at her mother] I think it's better for children.

FC: And you don't like that your mother works outside the home?

C: I don't care what she does. I want to be home with my children.

FC: And that's a perfectly fine choice, one many women make when they can afford to. Help me understand how it's connected to whether or not you go to college.

C: I just don't see why I should waste 4 more years in school when I don't want to use it to get a job afterward. I might as well start my life now, start working.

FC: OK, so your life now is working, not having children?

C: Well not yet, no.

FC: And so your mother says you need to make college decisions because the next step in your life is college, and you don't see any reason to because the next step in your life is work. And the two of you argue about what the next step in your life is. Then what happens?

A structural family counselor would stick to questions about family dynamics and the structure they portray. Changing those, rather than individual thinking, feeling, or behavior, is the goal. The assumption, as discussed earlier, is that changing family structure changes individual functioning. And so, while the counselor questions the assumption that they're really talking about being a housewife and not working outside the home while raising children, the sequence of interactions, rather than the assumptions they make, are the focus of her questions.

C: She gets mad and yells at me and tells me I'm throwing away my life on some man.

FC: And then what happens?

C: I tell her what I do with my life's none of her business. It's my life, not hers.

FC: I see. So you're arguing about who is in charge of your life?

C: Yes! That's exactly it.

Liz: [Angrily, to the counselor] This is ridiculous. Of course it's her life. But she's obviously not mature enough to make reasonable decisions, and she's going to regret what she's doing. As her mother, I'm responsible for guiding and protecting her from herself.

The counselor could have allowed herself to become defensive and responded to Liz's anger. Doing so, however, would have disrupted the sequencing of the family dynamics, so she decided to return to Liz's frustration with her later.

With respect to the family structure, it appears that Liz recognized the formation of an alliance between the counselor and Christina and, perhaps anxious that it would become a coalition against her, turned her anger on the counselor to disrupt her conversation with Christina. If that is the case, then likely something similar happens at home whenever an alliance forms. In keeping with structural family counseling, the counselor decided to explore that possibility.

FC: Mark, when do you get involved?

Mark: As I've said, these fights can happen in Christina's room.

FC: And you're not there? Where are you?

Mark: I don't know. Somewhere in the house.

FC: Does Christina call her mother into her room, or does Liz initiate the conversations?

Mark: Well, you'd have to ask them.

FC: So Liz doesn't tell you she's going to talk to Christina about her future?

Mark: No.

FC: What about the times you're there when they argue?

Mark: Well, they usually start arguing somewhere else in the house, where I happen to be.

FC: And what do you do?

Mark: I try to let them work it out, but then if it's going nowhere, I might explain to Liz that if she leaves her alone, she'll come around.

FC: And then?

Mark: She gets mad at me for interfering.

FC: Liz gets mad? Or Christina?

Mark: Liz.

FC: How does she show you she's mad?

Mark: Well, she says it's none of my business, or I didn't do such a great job with my own daughter.

An experiential family counselor (Chapter 7) would have empathized with how Mark might feel when Liz brings up his daughter. A structural family counselor would remain focused on the family structure as distinct from members' emotions about each other.

FC: And Martin Jr.? Do you ever get involved?

MJ: I just leave.

FC: You get out of there.

MJ: [Nods]

FC: Can't help your sister?

MJ: Not when she and Mom are going at it.

FC: Do you and Christina ever talk about college when your mom's not around?

MJ: Not really. But sometimes we talk.

FC: [Turning to Liz] So Liz, I'd like you to talk to Christina about college. Maybe trade places with Martin Jr. so you can sit next to her.

This was the invitation to an enactment.

Liz: Now?

FC: Yes.

When Liz got up, Emma followed her to where Martin Jr. had been sitting, while he got up and moved to the couch. Emma stood next to Liz after she sat down, on the other side from Christina.

Liz: You want me to start?

FC: Yes, please.

Liz: [To Christina] I don't understand why you don't want to go to college. Most girls your age look forward to living in a dorm, decorating their room, making new friends, taking more interesting classes than they could in high school.

C: [Not looking at her mother] It's a waste of time. I've already told you that.

Liz: How can you know before you try it?

C: [Looking at her mother] Because I'm not like you. That's what you would do if you were me.

Liz: Because it's the smart thing to do.

C: No. You'd do it because it's the perfect thing to do. You want to be the perfect mom with the perfect family and the perfect job and the perfect life.

Liz:	And you are so angry, Christina, that you'll ruin yours thinking it'll hurt me. What did I ever do to you that was so awful? I took care of you and your brother, worked, and raised you after the divorce, created a lovely home for you and made sure you had all the things you needed, that you wouldn't suffer because your father and I were divorced.
C:	[To the floor] It's all about her, always.
FC:	[After a pause] Is this where it ends at home?
Liz:	She always turns it back on me and then refuses to talk about it.
FC:	Mark? Where are you at this point?
Mark:	Sometimes I'm not even there. Liz'll go into Christina's room, and I hear them yelling and then a door slam.
FC:	And when you're there?
Mark:	Well, I figure this is between the two of them.
Liz:	Do you have any thoughts about it?
Mark:	Well, yeah, I think Christina is smart and would do well in college. And I also think this is between her and her mother.
FC:	Liz, what would you like Mark to do?
Liz:	I'd like a little support. And a little fathering. It's not like he met her yesterday.
FC:	I'd like to come back to what goes on between you and Mark. But first I'd like to go back to the argument you were having with Christina. Let's have Liz and Mark on the couch, and Martin Jr. and Christina back where you started.

This is to more clearly define the parental subsystem as separate from the child subsystem.

FC:	Emma, would you like to sit with your brother and sister? I can pull a chair over there for you? [Emma shakes her head and holds onto Liz's arm]
FC:	Ok, maybe another time. [Turning to Liz and Mark] Liz, now start the conversation again with Christina about college. Start with, "Mark and I would like to talk to you about planning some college visits this summer."

This is where the enactment began to become an intervention to change the family system. Placing the parents together and, ideally, the three siblings together, changed the boundaries and hierarchy within the family. Instead of Mark and Martin Jr. being observers who remained relatively uninvolved, Mark was physically moved into a coparenting role with Liz. This conveyed nonverbal and relationship messages about the two of them as parents, whether he said anything or not.

Similarly, positioning Christina with her siblings conveyed both a structural and hierarchical change that would theoretically reverberate throughout the family. Ideally, Emma would have gone to sit with them, removing her from a triangle with Mark and Liz. Her refusal to leave Liz's side is a good example of how a counselor cannot change a family in one session.

Finally, Christina does have a biological father with whom she interacts frequently. When assessing the family, the counselor would either ask about him and his role in the family structure or, preferably, invite him and his second wife to a session.

The family counselor chose to invite Martin and his wife, Daniella, to a session. Below is an excerpt from that session. The family counselor also asked a colleague to join her as a cocounselor for the session because of the number of people in the room.

Inviting a cocounselor or counselor in the role of consultant to work with a family was common practice for many years. However, with changes in the way mental health is funded, it is no longer economically feasible for most families to work with two counselors. To illustrate structural family counseling, however, we included a second counselor when Christina's entire nuclear family was present.

FC: Welcome. I'm glad you are all here together. I think it will help me get a better sense of the family as it is now and also learn more about your history as a family than seeing each nuclear family separately would have. And, as I mentioned when I suggested a session with all of us, I've asked my colleague, Family Counselor 2, to join us because, with so many people, two pairs of eyes and ears will be very helpful. So we're all on the same page, last time, everyone who was here had a chance to talk about how they understand the reason you're here. So I'd like to begin by giving you, Martin and Daniella, a chance to talk. But first, FC 2, is there anything you'd like to add?

FC 2:   [Making eye contact around the room] I only want to say how nice it is to meet all of you.

FC 1:   Martin, would you like to start?

Martin: Why we're here, right? [FC 1 nods] To tell you the truth, I'm not sure why we're here. You said it might help Christina, and of course I'll do anything to help my daughter. [Looking at Liz] But I'll tell you, when she's with us, she seems fine to me.

Liz: [Sighs, purses her lips, and shakes her head]

FC 1:   [Nods] Daniella?

Daniella: I agree with Martin. Christina is a lovely young woman, and we've never seen any evidence of her having problems. When she's with us, she's outgoing and cooperative and fantastic with her younger sister and brothers. She does her homework and seems happy to be part of whatever the family is doing. So when she told us about this, that she was going to counseling, we wondered why.

FC 1:   I see.

FC 2:   [To FC 1] It sounds to me as though Christina is a different person at her dad and Daniella's than she is at home with her mom and Mark. I wonder what accounts for that.

C: [Mumbles] It's easier there.

Liz: Of course it's easier there. You don't live there.

C: They're my family, too.

Martin: Liz, let her talk.

Notice the triangle, with Christina and her father, Martin, teaming up in a coalition against Liz.

Liz: [To Mark] Are you going to just sit there and let him talk to me that way?

Mark: He's her father.

Remember that Mark not only had nothing to say while Liz and Christina argued in the first session, he also reported keeping out of their arguments at home.

FC 1:	Martin, have you and Liz talked about the doctor's concerns about Christina?
Martin:	Liz told me about them, yes, and they sound very serious. But as I said, we don't see any evidence of problems when Christina is with us.
Liz:	Of course not!
FC 1:	[Ignoring Liz and continuing to address Martin] What do you make of that?
Martin:	Well, I think Liz is a wonderful mother. But she has her hands full with Emma and her work, and things seem a bit out of control over there.

Notice he did not mention Mark. Has he also noticed how uninvolved Mark is? Or, is he challenging Liz's ability to mother effectively, as her verbal and nonverbal responses to his statements suggest?

Liz:	Could we get through 5 minutes without you criticizing me?
Martin:	I'm not criticizing you, Liz. You're a wonderful mother. It seems, though, that things are a bit out of control at your house, at least with Christina.

Notice the triangle with Christina brought into what appears to be unresolved tension between Martin and Liz. She appears to be the identified patient in both her mother's marriages.

Liz:	And things are always so controlled at yours?
Martin:	[Maintaining a calm voice tone in the face of Liz's challenge] Why do you hear everything I say as critical of you?
Liz:	Uh, because you've always criticized me? You're the most critical person I know.
FC 2:	Somebody may have mentioned this last time, but I'm curious why Martin and Liz aren't sharing custody of Christina and Martin Jr.
FC 1:	Martin? Liz?

Martin:	When we first separated, Liz suggested it would be easier on the children if they lived at one of our homes and visited the other. And I thought she might be right.
FC 2:	And now?
Martin:	I'm not sure. But Christina is about to graduate from high school and Martin Jr. isn't far behind. There doesn't seem to be much point in revisiting our custody arrangement.
Liz:	Seriously Martin?
FC 2:	[To Martin] I'm curious what you were thinking when you said things seem a bit out of control at their mother's.
Martin:	It's an observation.
FC 2:	I'm unclear what you've observed.
Martin:	Just that the doctor is worried about Christina's health, and Liz has told me she's concerned about Christina's attitude about college.
FC 2:	The doctor and Liz are worried about Christina. What about you?
Martin:	Not really. She's a bit thin, but she seems healthy enough to me.
Daniella:	Honey.
Martin:	What?
Daniella:	[to FC 2] He tries not to, but he worries a lot.
Martin:	Daniella.
FC 2:	[To Martin] You don't want anyone to know you're worried?
Martin:	I agree with Liz that all this fuss isn't good for Christina.
FC 2:	I see.

The exchange revealed quite a bit about the dynamics between Martin and Liz and between each of them and their new spouses. It is especially noteworthy that Daniella sat near Martin, leaned toward him, and occasionally interjected information he was not including, even risking his displeasure when she revealed he worried about Christina. Mark, on the other hand, sat across the room from Liz, did not follow the conversation with his eyes, and said nothing unless someone directly asked him. He specifically declined to engage with Liz when she attempted to include him.

FC 1:   Perhaps this is a good time to ask about the family's history. Liz and Martin, you've been divorced for 8 years?

It would be a mistake for the counselors to fall into a discussion with the parents about whether or not the doctor's concerns are valid.

Liz and Martin: [Both nod]

FC 1:   What happened?

Martin: Pretty much what you saw here just now. We're both strong willed and want other people to agree with us. And after awhile it seemed as though I couldn't say anything without being accused of criticizing her.

FC 1:   Liz?

Liz: That about sums it up, although I would add that I couldn't say anything without *being* criticized by him. He acts like it's all in my head—he's so sane and I'm so out of control—but he lets people know when he's displeased in a very indirect and hostile way.

FC 1:   Uh-huh.

It is now clear that control was an issue between Martin and Liz. This exchange was also an example of how a counselor cannot address everything that arises during a session and must make choices. In this case, the counselor decided to stick to the topic at hand and not digress into an attempt to resolve the marital issues that remained between Liz and Martin. However, as you will see, it is important that she heard about them. Additionally, family counselors can always return to a topic of importance at a later time.

FC 2:   Mark, let's get you involved. When did you and Liz begin seeing each other?

Mark: Right after my separation, in 2004.

FC 2:   So a couple of years after Liz's?

Mark: Uh-huh.

FC 2:	And how soon did you meet Christina and Martin Jr.?
Mark:	Almost right away.
FC 2:	And what happened in your first marriage?
Mark:	Her parents moved here right after the kids were born, and the three of them kind of pushed me out of the family.
FC 2:	Your first wife and her parents?
Mark:	Yes.
FC 2:	And how did you react to that?
Mark:	Well, I was supporting everyone and Shoshana, my ex, was home with the kids. She didn't go back to work until they were older. And there were three of them and one of me. I don't know. What would you have done?
FC 2:	Sounds like you weren't sure what to do?
Mark:	I didn't have much choice. You seem to think I had a choice.
FC 2:	And how did the marriage end?

Being structural family counselors, both chose to ignore the emotional tone of Mark's responses and focused on the family structure.

Mark:	She told me that she felt alone in the marriage.
FC 2:	And then?
Mark:	And then I left.
FC 2:	How old were your children?
Mark:	They were 16 and 18 when we split up. Our son had just left for college.
FC 2:	And did you share custody of your younger child?
Mark:	My daughter? No. She told me she'd fight me for custody, and I wasn't that close to my kids by then anyway.
FC 2:	Are you closer to your children now?
Mark:	Not really. Jason's away at school, and Ashley moved back home after college.

FC 2:	Do you see them?
Mark:	Maybe once or twice a year. Jason stays with his mother when he's in town, and they're both busy with friends.
FC 2:	I see. And how old were Christina and Martin Jr. when you started living with their mother?
Mark:	Well, we didn't live together until we got married. But I was there a lot from the beginning.
FC 2:	So your relationship with Liz began in 2004, and Martin Jr. and Christina are 14 and 17 now. They must have been about eight and 11 when you first met them?
Mark:	Mm-hm.
FC 2:	And Daniella, when did you and Martin begin your relationship?
Daniella:	[Smiling] I think it was about a year after Martin and Liz split up, in 2003. Christina must have been 10 and Martin Jr. seven. They were so cute, and I remember thinking how lucky I was to have met a man who loved his children so much and was good to my son and also wanted us to have more children together.
FC 2:	So you and Martin have other children, also?
Daniella:	Yes, a boy and a girl, two and four And as I said, I have an older son who's 11 now.
FC 1:	Martin Jr.? Christina? I'd like to hear from the two of you also. What was it like when your parents split up and then meeting your stepparents and stepsiblings?
MJ:	[Shrugs] It was fine. I don't know Mark that well, but he's OK. My brother Jamal is really cool.
FC 2:	I'm sorry, I don't know all your brothers' and sisters' names. Which one is Jamal?
MJ:	He's the 11-year-old.
FC 2:	I see. Thanks. And he lives with you and Martin, Daniella?
Daniella:	Yes.
FC 1:	Christina?

C:	Yeah, the little kids are all right.
FC 1:	And what about your stepparents?
C:	Daniella is wonderful. She takes care of everyone. And I like hanging out with her and my dad.
FC 1:	[After a pause] Anything else you'd like to add about your family?
C:	No, not really.
FC 1:	Liz?
Liz:	I don't see where you're going with all this. We told you a lot of it last time. We're here because the doctor was worried about Christina, and I didn't want to be accused of neglecting her, and then you pretty much insisted the entire family come in last time and even more of the family this time. Are we going to bring my parents and Martin's in next time? And my sister and her family the next? I don't notice that more people here is changing anything.
FC 1:	So you're pretty frustrated with how long it's taking us to learn about your family. Tell me what you'd like to see change.
Liz:	I already told you. [To FC 2] Didn't she tell you? We're worried that Christina won't consider going to college, and we think the doctor is overreacting.
Daniella:	She is awfully thin.
Liz:	Stay out of this, Daniella.
Martin:	Liz!
Liz:	[Glaring at Martin] As I was saying, if there is a problem at all, it's that Christina won't even consider going to college. And talking about all the divorces isn't going to change that.
Daniella:	Martin, it's time to say something.
Martin:	No, no.
Daniella:	If you don't, I will.
Martin:	[To Liz] Look, I've always thought you were a fantastic mother. But I don't like the way you're talking to Christina here.

Liz:	You don't like the way I'm talking to Christina here? I'm trying to help her, which is more than anyone else in this room seems to be doing.
C:	[Tears running down her cheeks] Mom, please.
Liz:	This is between your father and me. [To FC 1] The children should not be here for this. I don't know what you're doing, but I do know it's hurting my daughter.
FC 1:	I suspect that Christina and Martin Jr. haven't heard anything that surprised them. Although I wonder whether they knew you're as isolated as you are?
Liz:	Isolated?
FC 1:	Yes.
Liz:	I don't know what you're talking about.
FC 1:	You turn to Mark for help, and he tells you Christina is your kid. You turn to Martin with your concerns about Christina going to college, and Martin tells you he's concerned about how you talk to her. Christina talks about how close she is to Daniella, and both she and Martin Jr. say they hardly know Mark even though he's your husband and has been in their lives for 6 years. Daniella stands up for Martin and he for her. Who stands up for you? And who do you feel close to? I don't see that there's anyone in this family who is there for you, who will listen to your worries. I would feel very lonely and besieged if I were in your position.
Liz:	Oh.
FC 1:	And I think part of what we need to work on is getting the pressure off Christina and Martin Jr. and maybe Emma, too, to be in the middle of what's going on among their parents. And to do that, we need to work on a way for you and Martin to put what tore you apart in the past so you can work together as parents now and for Mark to stand up for you when you need him.

Notice how the family counselor got Liz's attention through empathizing with her isolation before suggesting her hypothesis, or assessment, that the problem was lack of resolution of Liz and Martin's marital issues. By doing so, she also began to move from taking a history and observing dynamics to assessing the family and suggesting a goal. She was talking about restructuring the family to strengthen the generational boundaries between parents and children, allowing parents to resolve their conflict and freeing Christina from the role of identified patient. Family counselors need to establish trust, often through empathy and tolerating the clients' intensely negative feelings, before clients can hear an assessment that may be unwelcome. And with families, the assessment inevitably concludes that the problem does not reside with the identified patient but rather with the family as a system.

STOP AND THINK:

1. What might it be like to be Liz during the session?

2. If you were one of the family counselors in this session, what other avenues might you have explored as the family brought up new topics tangential to the goal of the session?

3. What are the differences between the sessions with and without Christina's father and stepmother?

CONCLUSION

In this chapter we explored the concepts of structural family counseling, as well as the methods used by structural family counselors. Then we applied them to the Manning-Kelly family.

Structural family counseling elaborated upon the concepts of boundaries and triangles while adding the importance of hierarchies to family functioning. The practice of structural family counseling includes questioning family assumptions, tracking family dynamics, and inviting the family to an enactment during which the counselor can facilitate interactions that change the family's structure. Structural family counselors believe that changing the family structure leads to both changes in family functioning and the mental health of family members.

The Manning-Kelly and Jones families sessions contain examples of the important concepts of structural family counseling. Excerpts from family counseling sessions with the family illustrate the tools used by structural family counselors to facilitate change.

> ## STOP AND THINK:
>
> 1. What have you learned about the Manning-Kelly and Jones families in this chapter?
>
> 2. What assumptions have you made about the Manning-Kelly and Jones families?
>
> 3. How do you distinguish what you know from what you assume?
>
> 4. What else do you need to know about these families in order to practice structural family counseling with them?

In the next two chapters, as in the previous one, we examine theories and methods of family counseling and demonstrate their use with the Manning-Kelly and Jones families. As you read about these theories and methods, note the similarities and differences to structural family counseling.

Extend Your Learning:

1. In small groups, role play an enactment of an interaction you imagine would take place between Christina and Liz or another subgroup of the families discussed in this book. Have observers comment on the structures and boundaries they see in place.

2. Watch the film, *Silver Linings Playbook* (2013). In a written assignment or in a group discussion, note the boundaries and family structures you see in that family. Are these boundaries clear, rigid, or diffuse? How do the boundaries appear to affect family functioning? Which boundaries need to be changed in your opinion? Why? What alliances, coalitions, or examples of triangulation do you see? What might an enactment look like in this family? Are there any examples of enmeshed or disengaged relationships in this family? Explain.

REFERENCES

Luepnitz, D. A. (2002). *Schopenhauer's porcupines: Intimacy and its dilemmas*. New York, NY: Basic Books.

Minuchin, S. (1974). *Families and family therapy*. Cambridge, MA: Harvard University Press.

Minuchin, S., Montalvo, B., Guerney, G., Rosman, B., & Schumer, F. (1967). *Families of the slums*. New York, NY: Basic Books.

Minuchin, S., Rosman, B. L., & Baker, L. (1978). *Psychosomatic families. Anorexia nervosa in context*. Cambridge, MA: Harvard University Press.

Nichols, M. (1984). *Family therapy. Concepts and methods*. New York, NY: Gardner Press.

Russell, D. O., De, N. R., Tucker, C., Cooper, B., Lawrence, J., Quick, M., & Entertainment One (Firm). (2013). *Silver linings playbook*. United States: Eone Entertainment.

FOR FURTHER STUDY

Gehart, D. (2010). *Mastering competencies in family therapy* (1st ed.). Belmont CA: Brooks/Cole.

Lum, D. (2007). *Culturally competent practice. A framework for understanding diverse groups and justice issues* (3rd ed.). CA: Brooks/Cole.

CHAPTER 7

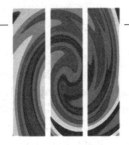

Experiential Family Counseling

In this chapter, we describe two approaches to experiential family counseling. Carl Whitaker has been credited for founding the experiential family counseling model. Although he was trained as a psychiatrist, he worked almost exclusively with families. His colleague, Gus Napier, has described the model as experiential symbolic therapy. Some writers (Gehart, 2010; Nichols, 1984) include Virginia Satir as an experiential family counselor, because she also based her family growth model on experiencing the emotional layer of family functioning.

WHAT IS EXPERIENTIAL COUNSELING?

Experiential Family Counseling refers to the family's experience of being in counseling, as well as the family counselor's experience of working with the family. In a 2009 interview, Whitaker's long-time colleague and protégé, Gus Napier, explained the concept.

> Our assumption is that psychotherapy is a kind of italicized experience in that it's heightened. It provides a slice of experience that the client may not have experienced, which is more honest and more caring, with insights, etc., that they haven't had, and the assumption is that these incidents that occur in the psychotherapy experience—in the room itself—have a kind of symbolic importance The therapist is symbolic, often of a parent or some family-like authority figure, and what we try to provide is a slice of something that's missing from the family's life. . . . It's like a slice of a pie that goes deep but not broad. (Aponte, 2009, p. 1)

As you can see, the focus is on what is termed the here-and-now, what is happening in the room among the counselor and the family members. By helping family members experience what they are describing happens outside of counseling, experiential family counselors increase the family's awareness and options for how to handle its challenges.

Focusing on the moment is a very powerful tool, one shared by several schools of family counseling and by mindfulness meditation. By drawing the attention of family members to what is happening and how they are experiencing it, the counselor blocks people's tendency to think about rather than fully live their lives. It draws family members' attention to their interactions and especially how these interactions may be preventing the change they say they want. It also forces the family counselor to be fully present, aware of her or his own reactions to the family and its members, and to use these reactions and her or his experience of being with the family as the basis of her or his interventions with the family.

EXPERIENCING THE EMOTIONAL LAYER OF THE FAMILY

Kantor and Lehr (1974) described families as operating on three levels, usually preferring one. The three levels are power, affect (emotion), and meaning. Experiential family counselors recognize that when clients recognize and acknowledge their feelings as they experience them in the moment and the meaning those feelings lead them to ascribe to their experiences, the result can be very powerful and change the way clients view their lives and behave.

Experiential Family Counseling targets the emotional layer of behavior and cognition. In other words, people experience their lives emotionally and their thoughts about their lives, or cognitions, and the attendant ascribed meanings, are heavily influenced by those feelings. While many people pay attention to what they think and do, people often overlook what is happening in the present moment as well as how they feel in the present moment. Sometimes people review their feelings when thinking about a particular incident after it is finished. Reviewing feelings is very different than experiencing them as they are happening.

STOP AND THINK:

1. Think about something that happened to you recently, whether with your family or people at work or school. What do you remember about what you thought and did? Do you remember your emotions as the situation played out?

2. Now observe yourself over the next couple of days, paying atten-
    tion to whether you are experiencing your emotions as well as your
    thoughts and behaviors as you go about your life. You can begin by
    noticing the food you are eating, a walk across campus, and how you
    greet each new day. What did you notice?

Experiential individual counselors often ask clients to begin to change by
noticing, rather than thinking or pressuring themselves to do something differently. Because the focus of Experiential Family Counseling is on individuals as
well as the family system, Experiential Family Counselors can do exactly the
same thing with themselves and the families with whom they work.

Experiential Family Counselors rely on the emotional layer of experience in
their interventions with the family. They use warmth, empathy, and themselves
to create emotional connections with family members. They also share their
experience of being with the family.

Christina said she wanted more life experience before going to college, she
and her mother continued to argue about whether she needed to be looking at
colleges during her junior year of high school, and her primary care physician
was concerned about her weight loss and cutting behaviors. After describing
her view that the problem was not her weight and the scars were from sports
injuries, Christina talked about pressure from her mother to go to college right
after she graduated from high school.

Christina:	I know she thinks going to college right away is important, but it's not what I want. And it's my life.
Family Counselor:	I'd be so aggravated if no one heard me but my doctor.
C:	I'm not aggravated.
FC:	Tell me what it's like for you not to be heard.

There are three points to underscore in this brief interchange. First, the
family counselor attended to her own experience of listening to Christina's
words as well as her voice tone, body language, and other nonverbal communications as she described her view of the problem and then used them
empathetically as part of her feedback. Christina did not endorse that she felt
aggravated. Whether she experienced aggravation and was not comfortable
with it, experienced it and overlooked it, or was more sad than frustrated by
her mother is unclear. The family counselor then asked Christina to describe

her own emotional experience, hoping it would help Christina experience her emotions, rather than continuing to repeat the behavior of resisting her mother and her thought that her mother was exerting too much pressure, possibly by restricting food intake and cutting herself as well as by arguing with her mother.

The second point to note is that the family counselor could have easily substituted the word *lonely* or *sad* for *aggravated*. All three are likely true, and the purpose of the counselor's statement is to help the client focus on the emotional layer of her experience, not to accurately guess what was true for Christina. Any emotion that indicates empathetic listening and that genuinely reflects how the counselor experienced the events Christina described will do.

The third point to note is that the family counselor indicated her knowledge that the doctor had heard Christina's distress as manifested in her restrictive eating and cutting behaviors. Christina did not question the counselor's assumption, in part because she could not address both aspects of the counselor's sentence at once and opted for the statement of feeling. This is what usually happens in situations when an experiential family counselor delivers an assumption along with a statement about emotions. Subtly, she alerted Christina that she saw a connection between Christina's arguments with Liz and her self-harming behaviors. She will likely revisit this more directly with Christina at another time.

The next transcript looks at what the family counselor might have done had Christina opted to question the family counselor's assumption.

C: My doctor doesn't know anything about this.

FC: Well, your mother doesn't hear your wish to work after high school, and you don't talk to your friends about it. So I'm not sure anyone heard you until the doctor noticed you're hurting yourself. That's usually a sign someone is hurting inside, as well.

At this point, some clients might argue that they're not hurting themselves. The empathy the family counselor had expressed in her words, voice tone, and body language, which included leaning forward toward Christina, would be difficult to resist, and thus many clients would not argue about whether they are engaged in self-harming behaviors.

Whitaker wrote about gently perturbing the family system and referred to his work as the therapy of the absurd. He used gentle confrontation and both symbolism and hyperbole to force families to examine themselves, even as they resisted his suggestions.

Some students of Experiential Family Counseling express concern about clients becoming frustrated and angry at counselors who directly challenge them. While anger at the counselor happens, it is also part of the experience of being with a counselor who is willing to be present and share a client's experience. And client frustration, when it arises, can be successfully addressed as part of the here-and-now experience. The Experiential Family Counselor would be empathetic with the client's anger at him or her, facilitate resolution by acknowledging his or her own role, and not allow the client to avoid talking about his or her self-harming behaviors because of frustration with the family counselor.

Note that this exchange, as well as what followed, occurred with the entire family present. Everyone in the family needed to hear how the family counselor views the presenting problem. They particularly needed to hear her insight that the arguments about college, which involved everyone in the family, were connected to the self-harming behaviors that brought them to family counseling and reflected Christina's frustrated need to be heard and respected as a young adult.

THE FAMILY SYSTEM

Unlike Structural Family Counseling and some of the other models you will learn about in Chapter 8, Experiential Family Counseling combines attention to both individual family members and the family system. Experiential Family Counselors do not assume that changing the family system will change the mental health of its members. Alternatively, however, a change in one member is likely to reverberate throughout the family system, perhaps creating change in other members and in the family as a whole.

This is not to say that Experiential Family Counselors ignore the role of the family system, either in their assessment/diagnosis or in their interventions. Experiential Family Counselors, like Structural and Multigenerational Family Counselors, believe that facilitating clear boundaries within and around the family promotes healthy individual and family functioning. At the same time, they believe in generational boundaries and intergenerational mandates. Intergenerational mandates can be thought of as a combination of the concepts of hierarchies in Structural Family Counseling and the intergenerational transmissions in Multigenerational Family Counseling. Like Structural Family Counselors, Experiential Family Counselors also believe that flexibility in the roles members assume within the family and flexible alliances and triangles among members are essential to healthy family functioning.

With the exception of role flexibility, all of these concepts have been described in previous chapters. Roles are expectations for behavior. When a family member assumes a role, she or he also assumes the expectation that she or he will fulfill the tasks and responsibilities associated with that role. When family members can assume multiple roles, as needed, the family is more flexible and thus able to adapt to stress, including stress brought about by life cycle changes and the presenting problem. When Barbara was diagnosed with cancer, role flexibility in her family allowed her husband, adult children, Liz, and friends to assume some of her roles during her treatment.

> **STOP AND THINK:**
>
> 1. Think about your own family. Who is responsible for earning money? Who is responsible for the instrumental and emotional tasks (cleaning, cooking, nurturing children, etc.) that keep the home and family functioning well? Who is/was responsible for child rearing? Who is responsible for maintaining relationships with friends and extended family members? Who is responsible for caretaking when someone is sick?
>
> 2. Have the expectations for who assumes which roles changed over the years? How? And how has it changed during difficult times?

An Experiential Family Counselor beginning to work with the Manning-Kelly family would posit that Christina's self-harming behaviors put her at risk and reflect an identifiable individual distress. The authors, like most family counselors, prefer to avoid attributing psychopathology to the identified patient. Identifying sources and consequences of Christina's emotional distress avoids aligning with the family's view of her as the problem. Like Behavioral Family Counselors, Experiential Family Counselors also believe that referring to the symptoms and behaviors of concern as Christina's psychopathology would only serve to further entrench her role as identified patient.

The Experiential Family Counselor would also look for family dynamics that may be associated with Christina's self-harming behavior. Reviewing the brief counseling session transcript earlier in this chapter, the family counselor speculated that Christina's self-harming behaviors arose as a way to be heard in a family where she was ignored in two obvious ways. First, her mother, Liz, had said her younger daughter needed care due to her age and disability, while Christina was almost grown. The counselor has observed behavior in sessions that supports Liz's statements and Christina's accusation (Chapter 6) that Emma was more important to Liz. So it may have been safe to imagine that Liz's attention may have been focused on Emma to the virtual exclusion of her older children, at least some of the time.

Christina's preference for her first step after high school has also been largely ignored by Liz. While Liz was reactive to Christina's refusal to look at colleges during her junior year in high school, their arguments suggested that

Liz's goal was for Christina to agree with what Liz thought was the right thing to do, rather than to listen to Christina's view and reconcile their disagreement through negotiation.

STOP AND THINK:

1. Have you ever argued with someone who was focused solely on convincing you and wasn't listening to what you were saying?

2. Has the argument resolved? If yes, how? If no, what happened?

Mark, like Christina, appeared to be engaged in self-harming behavior. Specifically, he was drinking a lot. His drinking behavior could have arisen in a number of ways. First, it may have been associated with increased distance in his marriage to Liz following Emma's birth. It also could have developed as Liz's conflict with Christina increased. Third, his drinking behavior may have preceded these events, pushed Liz away from him, and thus contributed to her increasing involvement with one or more of her children. Finally, it could have been a long-term problem for him, perhaps a coping mechanism when he was angry or hurt. Whatever its origins, the result of his drinking was that he was fairly disengaged from the family.

Martin Jr., Christina's younger brother from Liz's first marriage, was also disengaged from the family. He kept to himself when home and said he preferred to be with friends. An Experiential Family Counselor might hypothesize that whether members withdrew into self-harm, kept to themselves and their lives outside the family, or became overinvolved with another family member, the family as a whole was disconnected, and all these behaviors can be viewed as attempts to be heard by the others. Changing the family system might draw its members back together. However, Mark would still have a dysfunctional relationship with alcohol, Christina would still struggle with restrictive eating and cutting, Emma may have balked at diminished attention from her mother, and Martin Jr. may have continued to feel more distant from his family than did his friends from theirs. So an Experiential Family Counselor would not stop with changing the family system but would also work with the individual members and their struggles.

EXPERIENTIAL FAMILY COUNSELING INTERVENTIONS

Experiential Family Counseling interventions are simultaneously simple and complex. Experiential Family Counselors emphasize emotional logic, process, and the meaning inherent in family system interactions. And because attention is focused on the here-and-now emotional layer of the experiences of individuals and the family dynamics, techniques arise from the experience of the counselor when with the family. Thus, the techniques of Experiential Family Counseling sometimes look very similar to those used by family counselors who hold other theoretical perspectives. Yet the underpinning of the family counselor's choice of intervention remains her or his experience with the family in the moment. Remaining aware, empathetic, and fully present in the moment comprise the difficult tasks of Experiential Family Counseling for the family counselor.

The best way to demonstrate Experiential Family Counseling is to give you the pseudoexperience of being with the Manning-Kelly and Jones family by reading a transcript of a hypothetical session with them. Before turning to the transcript, however, you will read about the specific contributions of Whitaker and Satir to the field of Experiential Family Counseling.

Carl Whitaker's Symbolic Experiential Family Counseling

Whitaker began to write about Experiential Family Counseling in the mid-1950s. His theoretical approach to family counseling arose in contrast to the multitude of theories about both individual and family counseling being promoted at the time. Nichols (1984) says of Whitaker:

> Whitaker says that therapists who base their work on theory are likely to substitute dispassionate observation for caring, and goes on to imply that theory is a refuge from the anxiety-provoking experience of sharing a family's life stress. Instead of having the courage to just "be" with the family and help them grapple with their problems, theoretically-inclined clinicians use theory to create distance in the name of objectivity. (p. 264)

While these were inflammatory sentiments, Whitaker's point was that clients are best served by a counselor who can allow herself or himself to fully experience her or his clients' pain. This is not an easy task, and counselors who are fully present and empathetic in the moment need a repertoire of self-care to be sure they do not become traumatized by their experiences at work. Yet being fully present and empathetic with clients in the moment is essential to the practice of Experiential Family Counseling.

Whitaker's method of intervention has been called both experiential symbolic therapy and therapy of the absurd. Experiential Family Counselors gently perturb the family system, using compassion, playfulness, and humor to guide the family members toward new options for relating to themselves and each other. Experiential Family Counselors also use their experience of being with the family to guide their interventions. Experiential Family Counselors truly *practice* being counselors. Experiential Family Counseling is a perspective that includes the counselor's own growth as she or he obtains more and more experience doing Experiential Family Counseling.

When Christina's stepfather, Mark, talked about his view that he was failing as a husband and father when there was conflict in the family, Whitaker, had he been the Manning-Kelly's family counselor, might have started tossing a soft Frisbee back and forth with Martin Jr. as he asked Mark what it was like to go home from work wondering whether Christina and Liz would argue and speculating that he'd want to run away. At some point, he might also toss the Frisbee to Mark. Throughout the Frisbee throwing, there would be no change in Whitaker's empathy or responsiveness to Mark. The message? Mark and Martin Jr. both experience ineffectiveness when with the family and distance themselves from their feelings and from other family members. The Frisbee would engage them while the Experiential Family Counselor talked about how engaging with the family feels like a worse option than withdrawal to them. At the same time, the other family members would watch, hear, and experience the impact of the message. In the best case scenario, Emma would leave Liz's side and want to join the Frisbee game.

STOP AND THINK:

1. Did you follow the logic of the previous example? Did it seem absurd to you?

2. Can you imagine yourself engaging in a game of Frisbee while telling someone how you view their situation and behavior or while hearing about your own?

Napier, whose quote opened this chapter, wrote that marital choices are attempts to fix what was wrong with each partner's relationship with their own parents. He believed that after 7 years, couples give up being one another's counselors and either give up on the marriage or adapt to the reality that a spouse cannot change one's past. In either event, the couple's children sometimes become part of this process and may exhibit symptoms as a result. Along these lines, a glance at the Manning-Kelly genogram reveals that Liz gave up on her first marriage and divorced Martin the same year her father, Bill, died.

Virginia Satir's Family Growth Model

Satir's growth model of experiential family counseling focuses on communication as well as emotion. She emphasized emotional warmth to foster positive self-esteem in family members and positive communications within the family. She believed that the experiential family counselor's role was to provide the family with the experience of emotional warmth in communication and direct them toward expressing emotional warmth when interacting with each other.

Her work also had a family systems foundation. She believed that when families were in crisis, a positive feedback loop occurred in which change engendered more change with resulting discomfort and attempts to regain the former status quo, or equilibrium. Family crises therefore present the possibility of new meanings and patterns of interaction for the family, with new dynamics forming as the family system reorganizes around a new equilibrium. Facilitated by a warm and caring Experiential Family Counselor who prevents the family from returning to its previous equilibrium, the family is able to reorganize in a way that promotes family members' self-actualization and positive communication.

Not all families present for counseling in crisis. Sometimes the crisis has passed, and the family is unhappy with how they managed or resolved it. Other times, families experience distress without crisis. Satir believed that when a family is not in crisis or has already reorganized in a way that does not promote members' self-actualization and positive communications, a therapeutic intervention could be used to precipitate the chaos inherent in all crises and that is necessary for change.

Satir did not intend that Experiential Family Counselors would intentionally create problems for families. Her definition of crisis involved sufficient change to destabilize the family's equilibrium. In that sense, the birth of a baby creates a family crisis, as does a young adult child moving out of the family household. Within Experiential Family Counseling, any intervention that causes the family to experience each other and their dynamics differently has the potential to disrupt the family equilibrium sufficiently to precipitate the crisis and allow for the change Satir described.

One of the many techniques Satir used involved inviting the family to recall and then enact a situation in which members were frustrated with one another. She would then ask them to imagine what other family members felt at the time, in other words, to attempt to empathize with them. And finally, she would ask the family to reenact the situation accounting for how the others felt. An example with the Manning-Kelly family would involve Liz and Christina's arguments about college as the frustrating situation, or crisis. She would then ask each family member what they imagined every other family member was feeling during one of Liz and Christina's arguments, even those who were not directly involved in the argument itself. Finally, she would ask the participants to reenact the situation from the perspective of how the others felt.

FC: Christina, when your mother insisted just now that you plan a summer college tour, what do you think she was feeling?

C: I don't know.

FC: If you knew, what might it be?

C: I don't know. I guess she seems scared.

FC: Scared.

C: Yeah, like something bad is going to happen if I don't do what she wants. [Previously, Christina had thought their arguments were about her mother trying to control her, rather than her mother's fear or worry about her.]

FC: Liz, how do you think Christina felt when she said she wanted some life experience before college?

Liz: Honestly? I think she wants to defy me. I don't know why she's so angry at me, but that's what I think it is.

FC: Uh-huh. So that's what you think. When Christina talks, what do you imagine she is feeling?

Liz: Defiance?

C: Seriously, Mom? You think I'm going to throw my life away just to hurt you?

FC: Liz, what do you suppose Christina is feeling right now?

L: Now?

FC: Yes.

Liz was experiencing difficulty empathizing with her daughter. After the family counselor's interventions with Liz, she was able to see that Christina's wishes were at least somewhat independent of her relationship with her mother and say that Christina wanted to experience life as an employed adult for awhile before likely going to college. She then could disagree, saying Christina would have years of employment opportunity after college but only one chance to be 18 years old and transitioning to college with her peers.

Both Christina and Liz were also asked to imagine how Mark, Martin Jr., and Emma felt when their arguments occurred, and Mark and Martin Jr. talked about how they thought Christina and Liz felt. The family was then able to reenact the argument with the addition of a greater ability to listen to one another. It should be noted, however, that all this did not occur in a single counseling session.

Satir focused on nurturance, as well as empathy, within the family. She posited that the fundamental unit of individual and family development was what she termed the *survival triad*. A survival triad involves two parents and an infant, the infant's survival being dependent upon the parents' nurturing. She believed the nurturing one receives as an infant within the survival triad determines the stance one takes in communication throughout life.

While the survival triad was fundamental to her contribution of the concept of communication stances within the family, the concept assumes that the two biological parents and only those two people must be present for an infant to receive sufficient nurturance. In the 60 years since Satir's Growth Model arose in the middle of the last century, a number of shifts in family structure have occurred and been recognized as sufficient for nurturing infants. The ability of the care-taking adult(s) to nurture an infant and their consistent presence determine an infant's later communication stance far more than the biological connection between the adults and the infant or how many adults are in the home.

A communication stance can be understood as an approach to communication in intimate family relationships at times of distress. Each stance includes the family member's orientation to, or consideration of, self, others, and the context in which the communication occurs.

When an infant is sufficiently nurtured within the survival triad, she or he develops what Satir termed a *congruent stance*. A congruent stance involves consideration of self, others, and the context in which the communication occurs. Individuals who assume a congruent stance are versatile, able to tolerate conflict, and express themselves in a way that considers everyone's feelings as well as the situation. A congruent communicator thus expresses what needs to be communicated with empathy.

When nurturance within the survival triad is less than needed, infants develop one of four defensive stances. All four defensive stances are aimed at avoiding conflict, in contrast to the congruent stance in which conflict can be tolerated and may even be viewed as a means to resolve problems that arise.

The first defensive stance is the Blamer. The Blamer attends to self and the context in which communication occurs, but does not attend to the feelings of others. The Blamer does not display empathy in her or his communications with other family members at times of distress, though she or he may be empathetic in less stressful situations or toward nonfamily members.

A second defensive stance is the Placater. The Placater attends to other family members and to the context in which communication occurs, while ignoring herself or himself. Placaters would prefer that conflict was avoided, irrespective of the cost to their own health and well-being. The family member who bears the symptoms of distress, in other words, the identified patient is often a Placater. By ignoring herself or himself, the Placater also ignores the toll of placating on her or him.

The third defensive stance is the Super Reasonable stance. This stance involves attention to the context in which communication occurs while simultaneously ignoring the subjective needs of oneself and other family members. Super Reasonable family members appear rational, critical, and powerful. Yet they lack emotional logic and flee into the Super Reasonable stance because they cannot tolerate conflict.

The fourth and final defensive stance is Irrelevant, also known as the Distractor. The Distractor ignores self, other family members, and the context in which communication occurs. The family member who assumes the Distractor stance may develop symptoms that distract other family members from conflict. Other times, the Distractor is either the family clown or is physically or emotionally disengaged from what goes on within the family.

Our description of the Manning-Kelly and Jones families to this point does not include clear examples of defensive stances, although everyone appears to assume one. From what we have seen so far, we can hypothesize that Liz was a Blamer. Notice that she had difficulty empathizing with Christina when the family counselor asked her what Christina was feeling. Liz appeared to attend to her own anxiety and to the context in which communication occurred by only bringing up the subject of college when the family was home alone. She did not, for example, start arguing with Christina at a holiday gathering at her sister Barbara's house when someone asked Christina about her college plans. She may have, however, thought about it and brought the subject up as soon as the family got home. While Liz did not actively avoid conflict, she waited to talk to Christina about college until she was anxious and upset and could not contain her feelings any longer, in other words, without consideration of the impact of how she expressed herself at those times or the possibility that Christina would be more willing to talk about college if Liz brought the subject up when she was not already upset and in a more empathetic way.

Christina may have been a Placater. While she was willing to argue with Liz, she was also the one who ended the argument at a certain, probably predictable (at least to an observer who was not a family member) point. Christina was the one who left the room, even pushing past her mother to leave her own room when the argument occurred there. Christina was also attentive to others. She easily empathized with her mother when asked by the family counselor. However, although she sometimes sounded all about herself, she was acting in. In other words, she was turning whatever distress she felt inward and hurting herself through her eating and cutting behaviors. This indicated she was not attending to her own needs, becoming symptomatic instead.

Although Mark had not talked much, and his verbal interactions at home have not been thoroughly described up to this point, there was other evidence that he was Super Reasonable. It later emerged that when he did get involved, either at home or in sessions, his statements sounded very logical, with minimal emotion and the expectation that because he was the family member who made rational sense, others needed to listen to him. His attention was to context, specifically seeking to stop the arguments between Liz and Christina. However, he was not attentive to himself or to any of the other family members. Liz and Christina found his efforts annoying and intrusive, which he could not understand. Mark ignored his own frustration with his wife and stepdaughter, not questioning his role as the rational member of the family. Like Christina, his inability to attend to self was associated with acting in behavior and symptom development, namely his use of alcohol.

Both Martin Jr. and Emma appeared to be Distractors. Martin Jr. made himself irrelevant by isolating himself when he was home and by planning to be out of the house as much as possible. Emma was more dependent on her mother than the typical 4-year-old child, which appeared to be because of both her cerebral palsy and the family dynamics. She may have distracted from the argument by insisting on her mother's attention, perhaps through a tantrum, calling for help, crying, or finding other ways to trigger Liz's concern about her. When this happened, it of course confirmed to Christina that Emma was more important to their mother than she was. In any case, neither Emma nor Martin Jr. appeared to be attending empathetically to themselves or others or to the context of the communication.

In summary, Virginia Satir believed that the Experiential Family Counselor's most important goal was to alleviate lack of validation and intimacy within families. To achieve this goal, Experiential Family Counselors help family members assume congruent stances, teach them to empathize with one another, and encourage or amplify enough crisis that it becomes possible to alter the family system in such a way that members are forced to change. In essence, Experiential Family Counselors guide families toward these goals of empathy, validation, and congruent communication. Because her work was oriented to the emotional layer of family dynamics and involved experiences in the here-and-now of the family counselor's office, she is viewed as an Experiential Family Counseling theorist in addition to her contributions to the field of family communication.

USING EXPERIENTIAL FAMILY COUNSELING WITH THE MANNING-KELLY FAMILY

Following is a transcript from the same hypothetical first session with the Manning-Kelly family that you read about in the previous two chapters. As you read, note the differences in the family counselor's approaches, the differences in the information she obtains using the various theoretical approaches, and how family members behave differently in response to her approach.

After the Manning-Kelly family sat down in the family counselor's office, she introduced herself and said hello to each family member, thanking them for taking the time to come to the session. As she would have using any family counseling approach, the family counselor decided not to begin the conversation by addressing Liz because she was the one who had called to arrange the appointment. As an experiential family counselor, she also decided not to begin by talking to Christina, as that might communicate to the family that she agreed with their assumption that Christina was the problem, or identified patient. She also avoided beginning with Martin Jr. or Emma, because siblings are often more helpful after their parents and the identified patient have talked.

Mark, Christina's stepfather, was the logical family member with whom to begin the conversation. Like many women who initiate family counseling, Liz had warned the family counselor that he might not want to be involved. If the identified patient's father or stepfather doesn't want to be in counseling, then part of the family counselor's job in the first session is to engage him in the process.

FC: I'm glad you're all here today. I know most people aren't fall-
           ing all over themselves to go to counseling. Anyone excited to
           be here?

Note that she went right to the emotional layer, acknowledging what she assumed to be true and using humor to convey the absurdity of wanting to go to counseling.

FC: Mark, tell me what it's like to be part of this family.

Mark: Oh, I don't know. I think we're like most families. Well,
           most—what do you call them—blended families?

FC: Yes, blended families. I've never lived in a blended family, so tell me what life in a typical blended family is like.

Even though the family counselor has worked with blended families in the past, she wanted Mark to talk about what it was like for him to live in a blended family. Because his previous answers had been general and vague, she decided to engage him as her guide to blended family life experience.

Mark: Well, Liz and I are very happy. We have a good marriage. But of course, we've been parents since before we got married.

FC: Not like your first marriages?

Mark: No.

FC: Tell me about the parenting.

Mark: Well, we decided we'd each let the other take the lead in parenting the children from our first marriages. My kids never lived with us, but they visited every other weekend until they went to college and then some during vacations. It's the reverse with her children. Christina and Martin Jr. go to their dad's every other weekend and holidays.

FC: So you defer to Liz about parenting them? You're the family observer?

Mark: No. Well, with parenting Christina and Martin Jr., yes, I guess you could say that I am.

FC: Can you describe a time recently when Christina or Martin Jr. needed parenting, and you deferred to Liz?

Mark: Well, yes. When Liz encourages Christina to think about college.

FC: OK, so Liz encourages Christina to think about college, and you defer to her. Can you tell me more about what happens when Liz encourages her and how Christina responds?

Although at this point the family counselor does not know anything about Liz and Christina's arguments about college, if the topic popped into Mark's head, she could assume it may be important.

Mark: Well, Liz tells Christina it's time to think about which colleges she wants to visit and apply to, and Christina says she doesn't want to yet.

Christina rolled her eyes, and Liz sighed and looked away from Mark at this point.

FC: So Liz and Christina, you don't seem too happy with Mark's description. What's he not talking about?

Note that the family counselor was again making an assumption and acting on it before being certain her assumption was correct. Experiential family counselors often invite clients to tell them they are mistaken. Among other things, the approach encourages clients to think and to challenge the counselor respectfully. The experiential family counselor can then accept the client's disagreement, rather than becoming defensive about her position.

Liz: He makes it sound so benign. [To Mark] She screams at me, she's disrespectful, she doesn't care about her life.

Mark: [Tenses his mouth and looks away] OK, then, you describe it.

FC: Mark, what's it like for you when Liz is angry with you? Or with Christina?

Mark: It's fine. She's got a full plate, with Emma's challenges, and two teenaged kids, and her work. She's got to let off some steam, and I don't think she's really angry at me.

Here is an example of what Virginia Satir described as the super reasonable stance in family communication.

FC: So it doesn't bother you. And do you ever want to snap back at her?

Liz: Him?

Mark: Sometimes I tell Liz to lay off.

FC: How are you right now, with me asking questions and Liz angry at you?

Mark: I'm fine.

FC: Really? I don't think the world would end if you told Liz her anger bothers you. And I know it would be all right with me if you said my questions bother you. Because it's our first session, though, I'll leave you alone for now. [To Liz] Liz, what was it like to listen to Mark describe what happens at home?

Liz: [Shakes her head] He's immune to everything. Did you hear him list those things on my plate? Emma's his daughter, too. And Christina and Martin Jr. are his stepchildren. He's known them for 6 years and lived with them for 4. You'd think they were strangers the way he talks about them.

FC: I did. And I get the sense you heard more than the words.

Liz: Oh my God! Nothing phases him. He goes to work, he comes home, but does he get involved in the life of the family? No. I feel like it's all on me, and that's fine, I'm used to that, but that he doesn't care, he doesn't even get what it's like, he doesn't even want to know.

Note that Liz is talking about what Mark was doing.

FC: And you feel so alone.

And so the family counselor brought the conversation back to Liz.

Liz: Yes, I do. And I don't know how to get through to Christina, how to help her plan her future.

FC: And you want someone to be there with you, to help you even?

Liz: [Plaintive] I want a husband. You know what I mean?

FC: Yes, I think so, but probably all I know is what I'd mean if I said that. What do you want to be sure I know?

Note the limits of empathy acknowledged by the family counselor. Even as experiential family counselors make assumptions about people's feelings, they avoid the presumption that empathy is sufficient to fully understand another person's experience.

Liz: That I'm so worried about Christina. That I don't know what to do to stop her from throwing away her life, and I think I should. What kind of parent am I, if I can't help my daughter?

FC: A loving parent who wants some help. Christina, what's it like for you to listen to your mom?

Christina: [Shrugs] I don't know.

FC:	Scared? Sad? I want to reassure her, but I'm not her daughter. Tell me about being her daughter.
C:	She's so sure she's right. Well, not here, but at home. She tells me I'm going to ruin my whole life if I get a job after high school instead of going to college. It's like, if I want to live my own life and stop going to school for awhile I've ruined her life.
FC:	I'm confused about whose life you're ruining.
C:	[Looking puzzled] Hers. Her perfect little life. Not mine.
Liz:	Yes, yours. I'm worried about you.
C:	Well, it sounds like it's all about you.
FC:	At home it sounds like it's all about her? What about now?
C:	No. At home it sounds like it's all about her. But not here.
FC:	How's it different here.
C:	Well, I'm not mad at her, and I'm always mad at her when she starts talking about college. This is so weird.
FC:	I know. What else is different here?
C:	I want to talk to her, and at home I always want her to go away.

Liz had been crying through this exchange between Christina and the family counselor, and Emma was patting her knee much harder than appeared comforting.

FC:	Emma, it looks like you don't like to see your mom cry. There's a doll and some stuffed animals on that shelf in the corner. Maybe your brother can help you pick one and pat its tears away. Martin Jr., would you help her?
Martin Jr.:	Sure. [He reaches out to take Emma's hand, and she pulls it away, starts shaking her head, and begins to cry.]
Liz:	[To Emma] It's OK, Sweetie. You can stay here with me. [To Martin Jr.] Thanks, MJ.

[Martin Jr. returns to his seat. Throughout this exchange, Mark sits quietly, sometimes watching and other times looking out the window.]

FC: Martin Jr., who takes care of people in this family?

MJ: Mom takes care of Emma. I'm not sure anyone else needs taking care of.

FC: Oh, I think everyone needs taking care of. Teenagers and grown-ups don't need the same kind of help children do, of course. Who has your back?

MJ: My friends do. My dad, when I'm there. Sometimes Christina.

FC: And who has Christina's back?

MJ: I'm not sure. Same as for me, I guess.

FC: Christina?

C: Yeah, he's right. [Still looking puzzled] Mom, who has your back? [Liz ignores the question.]

FC: [After a pause] Just the question I would have asked, Christina. [Christina smiles a little.] I think you have her back.

C: Me?

FC: Yeah. You brought her to counseling.

C: Me?

FC: Yes. You. If you hadn't starved and cut yourself and worried your doctor, she wouldn't be here. And if you went to college, who'd take care of her? This doesn't look like a family you'd want to leave her with.

C: Oh.

Mark: What?

Liz: I don't need my daughter to take care of me. I'm her mom.

FC: Seems to me you all need to be there for each other. And yet no one knows quite how. Mark, I think you take care of Liz by leaving her alone to do what she needs to do. And Emma takes care of her by needing her attention. And now Christina is taking care of her by refusing to do what she needs to do next for her own life. Martin Jr., I'm not sure how you take care of your mom, but I suspect you do, maybe by not needing anything from her. And Liz, you take care of Christina by urging her to do what you think is best for her and ignoring what she's been doing to her body. And you take care of Mark and Martin Jr. by letting them go off on their own. I think you and Mark need to learn to parent your children together, and Christina and Martin Jr. and Emma need to learn how to be taken care of as grown-ups, which they'll soon be.

STOP AND THINK:

1. What are the differences you noticed between the session using Experiential Family Counseling and those using Structural Family Counseling and Multigenerational Family Counseling?

2. What were your reactions as you read this transcript?

You may have noticed that the experiential family counselor addressed feelings without ever asking, "How are you feeling?" Rather, her questions were directed toward empathizing with the family members while gently perturbing the system. She was confrontative about Mark's passivity, Emma's dependence on Liz, and Christina's symptoms. The family counselor confronted in a noncombative manner, indicating she empathized with the family members' situations. We tend to think of confrontation as combative, and this transcript demonstrates they need not be the same. The experiential family counselor showed the members of the Manning-Kelly family different ways of interacting when she asked Martin Jr. to take over for Liz with Emma, suggested Mark might have unexpressed emotions that could be expressed safely, and hypothesized that Christina's symptoms and refusal to go to college after high school were methods of caring for her mother.

The experiential family counseling session was very different than either the structural or multigenerational family counseling sessions. The family counselor asked about current experiences during the session and attended to the experience of each family member. She did not get into questions about patterns of family interactions, structure, or intergenerational phenomena. She also talked about herself more than either of the other two family counselors.

CONCLUSION

We have found that students are rarely neutral in their reactions to Experiential Family Counseling. Some are very attracted to the possibility of exploring themselves as counselors. Others find the ideas and interventions practiced by experiential family counselors to be uncomfortable and unstructured. If you find yourself in either one of these categories, ask yourself what you liked and what made you uncomfortable as you read the transcript.

STOP AND THINK:

1. What is your experience as a member of your family? Ask yourself the question, what is it like for me to be part of my family? Your answer need not be the same as that of any other family member or of anyone outside your family looking in on it.

2. What have you learned about the Manning-Kelly and Jones families in this chapter?

3. What do you assume about the Manning-Kelly and Jones families?

4. How do you distinguish what you know from what you assume?

5. What else do you need to know about these families in order to practice Experiential Family Counseling with them?

In this chapter, you learned about the principles of Experiential Family Counseling. You also saw examples of this theoretical approach in practice. You may have found yourself discomforted by the directness of the family counselor or the prospect of fully experiencing the here-and-now with a distressed family. Experiential Family Counseling forces the family counselor to examine her or his own experience and reactions and to use them to guide interventions. At the same time, an experiential family counselor must be careful to use her or his reactions to the family and its members in an empathetic way that facilitates their awareness, increases options, and provides a safe context in which change within the family and its members can occur. Experiential Family Counseling thus requires a high level of self-awareness from the family counselor, as well as a strong sense of the ethics of using oneself as a counseling tool. We will explore ethics further in Chapter 11.

Before we turn to issues in family counseling that transcend theoretical approaches, we will present a brief overview of some of the other major theories of family counseling. Continue to notice which approach makes most sense to you when you think about families.

Extend Your Learning:

1. In class, have several students role play another scenario, either imagined happening within the Manning-Kelly family, or from a fictional example, such as a family from a recent popular film or television program, or an example from pop culture, like the Kardashians. Students should identify one student as the family counselor and invite the family members to discuss their perceptions of the dominant issues that have brought them to counseling. As the session progresses, the instructor should interject with "time-outs" during which the student observers are asked to comment on the here-and-now processes they see happening in front of them. What processes should the family counselor pay attention to? Why? What stances are present in this family? How might these stances be confronted by the family counselor? The role-play can resume once the class has decided how the family counselor should proceed.

REFERENCES

Aponte, R. (2009). Augustus Napier on experiential family therapy. *Psychotherapy .net*. Retrieved from http://www.psychotherapy.net/interview/augustus-napier# section-experiential-family-therapy

Gehart, D. (2010). *Mastering competencies in family therapy: A practical approach to theory and clinical case documentation.* Pacific Grove, CA: Brooks/Cole.

Kantor, D., & Lehr, W. (1974). *Inside the family. Toward a theory of family process.* San Francisco, CA: Jossey-Bass.

Nichols, M. (1984). *Family therapy. Concepts and methods.* New York, NY: Gardner Press.

FOR FURTHER STUDY

Banmen, J., & Maki-Banmen, K. (2014). What has become of Virginia Satir's therapy model since she left us in 1988? *Journal of Family Psychotherapy, 25*(2), 117–131. doi:10.1080/08975353.2014.909706

Connell, G., Mitten, T., & Bumberry, W. (1999). *Reshaping family relationships: The symbolic therapy of Carl Whitaker.* Philadelphia, PA: Brunner/Mazel.

Hale-Haniff, M. (2013). Virginia Satir's growth model: Therapy as intra- and interpersonal communication. In A. Rambo, C. West, A. Schooley, & T. V. Boyd, (Eds.),

Family therapy review: Contrasting contemporary models (pp. 54–57). New York, NY: Routledge/Taylor & Francis Group.

Haley, J., & Hoffman, L. (1967). *Techniques of family therapy. Five leading therapists reveal their working styles, strategies, and approaches.* New York, NY: Basic Books.

Hoisington, L. A. (2012). Family paradigms and human emotions. *Dissertation Abstracts International, 72,* 4302.

Kane, C. M. (1994). Family making: A Satir approach to treating the H. family. *The Family Journal, 2*(3), 256–258. doi:10.1177/1066480794023013

Martin, A. (2011). Symbolic-experiential family therapy. In L. Metcalf (Ed.), *Marriage and family therapy: A practice-oriented approach* (pp. 147–173). New York, NY: Springer.

Napier, A. Y. (1999). Experiential approaches to creating the intimate marriage. In J. Carlson, & L. Sperry (Eds.), *The intimate couple* (pp. 298–327). Philadelphia, PA: Brunner/Mazel.

Napier, A. Y., & Whitaker, C. A. (1978). *The family crucible. The intense experience of family therapy.* New York, NY: Harper & Row.

Neill, J. R., & Knishern, D. P. (Eds.). (1982). *From psyche to system. The evolving therapy of Carl Whitaker.* New York, NY: Guilford Press.

Pereira, J. K. (2014). Can we play too? Experiential techniques for family therapists to actively include children in sessions. *The Family Journal, 22*(4), 390–396. doi:10.1177/1066480714533639

Sanders, P. (2013). The 'family' of person-centered and experiential therapies. In M. Cooper, M. O'Hara, P. F. Schmid, & A. C. Bohart, (Eds.), *The handbook of person-centred psychotherapy and counselling* (2nd ed.) (pp. 46–65). New York, NY: Palgrave Macmillan.

Satir, V., Stachowiak, J., & Taschman, H. A. (1975). *Helping families to change.* New York, NY: Jason Aronson.

Whitaker, C. (1989). *Midnight musings of a family therapist.* New York, NY: W. W. Norton & Company.

Whitaker, C. A., & Bumberry, W. M. (1988). *Dancing with the family. A symbolic-experiential approach.* New York, NY: Brunner/Mazel.

White, S. L. (1978). Family therapy according to the Cambridge model. *Journal Of Marriage and Family Counseling, 4*(2), 91–100. doi:10.1111/j.1752-0606.1978 .tb00516.x

Wulff, D. (2013). Using family therapy à la Carl Whitaker. In A. Rambo, C. West, A. Schooley, & T. V. Boyd, (Eds.), *Family therapy review: Contrasting contemporary models* (pp. 51–53). New York, NY: Routledge/Taylor & Francis.

Yalom, I. (2003). *The gift of therapy: An open letter to a new generation of therapists and their patients.* New York, NY: Harper.

CHAPTER 8

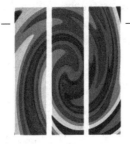

Other Approaches
to Family Counseling

You have read detailed descriptions of three major theories of family counseling in Chapters 5, 6, and 7. These are classical theories developed by
pioneers in the field. As a student of family counseling, your knowledge of
them will form a foundation for how you choose to practice. You have also
learned the general principles of family systems theory (Chapter 4). Family
systems theory informed not only the early practitioners of family counseling
but also more current practitioners and theorists.

In this chapter, we will explore four additional theories of family counseling, though in less detail. Some of these approaches were originally developed
as theories for working with individuals and then adapted to working with
families. As you read about these approaches, keep in mind that these theories
have taken years of research and development in order to gain acceptance in
the helping professions. As such, aspiring family counselors (and counselors
in other fields as well) should expect to take several years developing their own
theoretical orientations. It is important for students to realize that reading one
section of a chapter on a theory does not qualify one to practice that approach.
Being competent in a theoretical approach requires substantial study, practice,
and supervision. As you read, pay close attention to these approaches and compare them to the ones you read in the previous chapters. See which ones seem
to resonate the most with you, and imagine which ones you would be willing
to read and learn more about.

We have chosen these four theoretical approaches based on our experience of student interest in them. They are Adlerian family counseling, which
includes attention to birth order; cognitive-behavioral family counseling, including

rational emotive behavioral therapy (REBT), Hutchins's (1979) thinking-feeling-acting (TFA) model, and reality therapy; postmodern family counseling, which includes narrative family counseling and feminist family counseling; and finally integrative family counseling, because many practitioners find that several theories can be used in a complementary way to inform our work with families.

ADLERIAN FAMILY COUNSELING

Alfred Adler's emphasis on birth order and family constellations helps us understand how our position in our families influences our interactions with others. Adler also believed that all of our behaviors are goal-directed and therefore serve a purpose for each of us. This concept is known as teleology. Even those who appear to live the lives of martyrs are still served in personal ways by being the martyr. What may appear to be self-sacrificing isn't necessarily self-sacrificing at all. Being a martyr brings lots of adoration and praise:

"My how self-sacrificing you are!!!"

"How could anyone ever be mean to you, when you do so much for so many?!!!"

"How could your children be so ungrateful after all you have done for them?!"

Examining our behaviors and how they serve us, plus looking more closely at the possible goals for others' behavior, may provide a clue for improving relationships.

Rudolf Dreikurs (1947) took Adler's teleology a step further when he wrote about the four goals of misbehavior. Even children have goals in mind when they misbehave, though the goals may not totally be in their consciousness. They still have an end they are moving toward and choose behaviors they think will get them there. Understanding this can be very liberating for parents who are scratching their heads trying to get their children to behave.

It is crucial for parents to pay attention to their own feelings when their children misbehave. If parents can identify their child's emotions, they will have clues as to what their child's goal is for acting out and then can respond accordingly. The following section discusses children's goals for misbehavior, along with the corresponding parental emotion (see Table 8.1).

Table 8.1   Dreikurs's Four Goals of Misbehavior

Child's Behavioral Goal	Parent's Emotional Response
Attention	Annoyance
Power	Anger
Revenge	Hurt
Display of Inadequacy	Pity

SOURCE: Adapted from Dreikurs, R. (1947). The four goals of the maladjusted child. *Nervous Child, 6*, 321-328.

The Four Goals of Misbehavior

The table above shows how a parent's emotional response to a child's behavior can provide clues about the child's behavioral goal.

Attention. Think about the child who immediately starts tugging on mom's arm the minute mom gets on the phone. No matter how many times the mom holds up her hand and politely asks her daughter to wait, the child continues to tug on her arm, "Mommy, mommy, mommy, mommy, mommy!"

The mother finally tells the person she's talking to that she'll have to talk later, and then, annoyed, puts the phone down, saying to her daughter, "What is it?! What do you want?!"

"I don't know," the child responds.

This happens a thousand times in multiple households, and most of the time there is absolutely no urgent reason for the interrupted phone call. The child simply wanted the mom's attention. The mom was annoyed at the interruption, and then she gave the child her attention, however negative it may have been. This can become a cycle if parents don't recognize it and address it. Dreikurs recommended that parents give children attention for positive behaviors, rather than negative ones. For example, in the case above, the mom could have taken a moment before making her call and commented on her daughter's drawing, saying something like, "I like how you're experimenting with different colors. I can tell you're really concentrating on making it exactly the way you want it." This would have given her daughter positive attention, thus reinforcing her daughter's current behavior.

Power. Parents often find themselves in power struggles with their children. These can be some of the most infuriating moments between parents and their children. For an example of power as a goal for misbehavior, we turn to Mark and his daughter, Ashley, from the Manning-Kelly family. Ashley is 22 and has finished college, so the main current issue is that she needs to find a job and move back out of the house. This is not a power struggle, nor is it a major problem for the family. However, when Ashley was younger, there were some serious behavioral problems. Ashley started acting out most noticeably when she was about 8 years old. She refused to do her homework, wouldn't bathe or brush her teeth, and screamed hysterically, sometimes becoming violent with her parents when they tried to take her to school each morning. They spent day after day, and week after week, negotiating with Ashley, "If you go to school, I'll buy you ice cream this afternoon," or "Just go for the first half of the school day, and I'll check you out at lunch." Nothing worked. Teachers called home almost daily. Ashley would cry in class, refusing to do any of her work, and would ask to call home every few minutes complaining of a stomachache or some other malady. Miraculously, when her parents came and took her home, she would recover and feel well enough to play in her room or watch television. Mark would become furious with Ashley, taking away her toys or restricting her television time.

The problem was that Ashley already had all of the power. Even though Mark could take away toys or privileges, he still could not make Ashley go to school, unless he physically carried her in the building, kicking and screaming, only to get a phone call from the school shortly thereafter. Because her parents had negotiated with Ashley about school, they were giving her the power to refuse. She knew that she could either say "no" or just throw a fit and she would be whisked away from the school carpool line.

Dreikurs cautions parents about engaging in power struggles. If you bring yourself down to the same level as a child, you are surrendering your power and authority. Parents should refuse to engage in a power struggle with their children. For Ashley, school should never have been optional. Sure, parents can give children choices. In fact, giving children choices about less significant things in their lives will help them feel more powerful and less likely to try to engage their parents in power struggles about larger issues. Children live in a world where so much of is out of their control. Having some decision-making power helps them feel more in control of their surroundings. Still, parents should be careful not to give their children too much power. When they relinquish their control over to a child, giving them decision-making power about larger family issues, it may backfire, resulting in anxiety for the child. He or she may feel as though his or her parents are no longer capable of making decisions and therefore not capable of keeping him or her safe. The key is to find a balance. Parents can easily give their children choices about things that don't impact the rest of the family negatively or suspend family functioning. Rather than give Ashley choices about how much school she could attend, her parents could have given her choices about what she would wear to school (e.g., Do you want to wear your green shirt or your red shirt?) or whether she would buy lunch or take her lunch. School is not optional. If Mark and Daniella had refused to enter the power struggle with Ashley from the beginning, she would have quickly realized that her behaviors would not get her what she wanted.

Revenge. This one is easy to recognize. Although there are lots of ways children can get revenge on their parents, there is one that immediately comes to mind. What is the one worst thing a child can say to her parents? Altogether now: "I hate you!!!" Yep, many of us have been there. Many people have said it to their own parents. Parents who have been on both sides of that sentence can honestly say it hurts. Yes, children can hurt their parents. Most of the time they aren't trying to hurt them, but when they choose this sentence, hurting their parents is usually their goal. They are hurt or angry at their parents about something and they want to hurt them back.

Dreikurs recommends that parents try to remember this goal and keep it in mind when they are hurt by this statement. The best way to respond to "I hate you" is to say, "I know, but I love you," and say nothing else. Don't get sucked into the revenge cycle. It just takes you to a dark place from which it is difficult to recover.

Display of Inadequacy. Often students are surprised that any child would purposely want to appear inadequate. Still, if you think about it, being inadequate at something lets you off the hook and lowers everyone's expectations. Here's an example. These days it is very easy to buy shoes that don't require tying laces. As a result, children are learning to tie their shoes at later stages, and some older children still don't know how to tie their shoes because they can easily find slip-ons or shoes in any size with Velcro closures. So, the 10-year-old child, whose parents are committed to teaching him how to tie his shoe, might not be terribly excited about mastering this skill. As his parents show him the way they learned to tie their shoes, and he tries and fails the first few times, he looks at his parents helplessly and says, "See? I just can't do it. Please don't make me try it anymore. It's humiliating."

What emotion do you feel as a result of what he just said? You feel sorry for him, right? No one wants his or her child to be humiliated. Still, if his parents cave and let him off the hook at this point, he will be that much farther away from learning what really is an important skill to have. Even though displaying inadequacy is his goal, and he wants to get out of the difficult skill instruction, he still doesn't feel good about the fact that he, as a 10 year old, doesn't know how to tie his own shoe. Therefore, how his parents respond to this display of inadequacy is crucial. If they let him off the hook, he will learn that his parents don't have confidence in him either.

Dreikurs recommends that similar to power struggle situations, parents simply refuse to go down this road with their children. Simply ignore the display of inadequacy and don't give up on your child. "I know it's hard, but keep trying. You'll get it." Then walk away and allow the child to struggle. Nothing good comes easily. Think about it: the accomplishments that you are most proud of—were they easy? Of course not! There are tremendous potential gains from struggling. Persevering through a struggle proves to ourselves that we can be successful. "I did it!" "I made it through!" "I never thought I'd be able to do it, but I did." These are the statements we want our children to be able to say.

Birth Order

Adler was perhaps the first researcher known for his emphasis on birth order position and family constellation. As a psychodynamic theorist who studied with Freud, Adler also believed that a child's view of the world, and his or her place in it, is developed by the age of 5. Because of this view, Adler placed a lot of emphasis on a person's birth order or at least their perceived birth order. Whether you are the firstborn, youngest, middle child, twin, or only child, you learned and developed a way of interacting with others based on your position in the family. Adler believed that because of this adaptation, many people tend to develop patterns of behavior based on their position in the family. Here are some examples of birth order positions and their common behavioral patterns.

Firstborns. Firstborns have the position of being the one on whom parents place their highest expectations, toughest rules, and highest anxiety. After being the center of their parents' universe, firstborns are dethroned by the parents' subsequent children, and, in many cases, become the substitute parents for the other children. Because of this, firstborns are typically leaders, over-achievers, and take charge of situations. It is usually easy to identify firstborns in class because they are the ones who ask about assignments well in advance, are always in class on time, and well-prepared. In group work, the firstborns are usually the ones who take on the leadership role.

Middle-borns. Middle children are typically good negotiators, avoid conflict, and tend to get along well with others. Being stuck in between the oldest and youngest siblings, middle-borns are frequently dragged along to their older siblings' events and forfeit attention in favor of their younger siblings, and they will often pursue interests different from their siblings.

Youngest. The last-borns, or youngest children, are accustomed to being the center of attention, because they have never had to share their spotlight with a younger child. Parents frequently refer to their youngest child as "the baby" even when he or she is fully grown. This label can carry on into adulthood, and in some cases, serve as a barrier to adult functioning. Many last-borns are accustomed to having things done for them, rather than being independent. Once they reach adulthood, if this pattern has not been broken, it may be difficult for them to transition into doing things for themselves. It also may interfere with self-confidence, because the ability to do things independently is often the birthplace of self-confidence.

COGNITIVE BEHAVIORAL THERAPY

Similar to cognitive behavioral therapy (CBT) with individuals, CBT with families involves paying attention to our inner dialogues (monologues) or what our thoughts are as well as the feelings that accompany those thoughts. David Hutchins (1979) developed the TFA Model (see Figure 8.1), helping individuals separate their thoughts (T), feelings (F), and actions (A). When seen in a diagram, one can easily see if a person responds to a situation with more thoughts, more feelings, or more actions. Additionally, the TFA model helps us see how the thoughts, feelings, and actions work together or against each other. For example, if a teenage son walked in on his mother dancing to a song on the radio and said to her, "Wow, mom, you really shouldn't dance in public," the mother might think to herself, "My son is embarrassed by me. He doesn't want to be seen with me in public." This kind of thinking could lead to her own fears and doubts related to her son's love for her or her feeling unworthy. It could also lead to her own discomfort in public, resulting in refusal to accept an invitation to a party where dancing would be in order.

Now, think about the previous example, and see if you can identify where the mother's reaction seems to lie on the TFA model triangle (see Figure 8.1). The dark Xs show where a person's responses would fall when asked if, during the event, she was more focused on thinking, feeling, or acting or some combination of those. We start this process by looking at the mother's thoughts: Was she thinking? Was she feeling? Or was she somewhere in between? (Remember

Figure 8.1   TFA Triangles

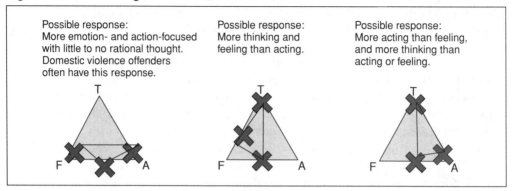

what she said to herself in the example.) Now onto the feelings associated with her thoughts. Was she angry? Embarrassed? Irritated? Or was she more in "thinking mode" than focused on her feelings? Finally we look at her actions. Was she acting—meaning did she do anything? If so, what did she do? Or was she thinking or feeling more than she was acting?

Now that you have identified them, let's identify which thoughts were (rational) helpful to her and which ones were not helpful (irrational). First of all, her son's comment does not define her. What do we know about it? All we know is what he said, we don't know what he meant, how he felt when he said it, or what his intentions were. We also know that he is a teenager, and must take that into account, knowing that most teenagers are embarrassed by their parents, regardless of how cool or coordinated they might be. This mother could be a prima ballerina and still embarrass her son when dancing in public. Therefore, how she reacts to his comment is up to her.

When using the TFA model, the goal is to arrive at a more unilateral triangle, where thoughts are lined up with feelings (rational), and actions are appropriate and acceptable responses to thoughts and feelings. Unfortunately, many of us are focused more on one or two portions of the triangle rather than having an even distribution.

Hutchins (1979) also described how domestic violence perpetrators that he worked with had triangles that were high on the feeling/acting portions, with little attention to the thinking portion. This shows a lack of understanding of how the perpetrators got to the aggression that led to their incarceration. They didn't realize that thoughts, such as "how dare she disagree with me!" or "If she doesn't do what I ask, then she doesn't respect me" or "If I don't hear from her, then she must be screwing around," led to anger, which led quickly to violent behavior. Being able to catch these thoughts and dispute them, followed by replacing them with rational thoughts, helped these prisoners learn how to recognize triggers and avoid future violent outbursts.

Rational replacement thoughts:

Irrational:	How dare she disagree with me!
Rational:	I don't like it when she disagrees with me, but she is her own person and not everyone agrees, so maybe it is okay if her opinion is different from mine. It doesn't mean she doesn't respect me.
Irrational:	If she doesn't do what I ask, then she doesn't respect me.
Rational:	I don't like it when she doesn't do what I ask, but she probably has a good reason for it, so I should listen to her. It also doesn't mean she doesn't respect me. It could mean a lot of different things.
Irrational:	If I don't hear from her, then she must be screwing around.
Rational:	I would rather hear from her regularly, because hearing from her makes me feel good. But when I don't hear from her it doesn't mean she's cheating. It could just mean she's busy with work, or her family, or her hobbies. Maybe it even means she's doing something for me. The more I trust her, the more I'm showing her respect and that will only strengthen our relationship.

Understanding our feelings, thoughts, and actions can also help us understand how we are coming across to others, as well as how others may intend for us to receive their words. For example, in the Manning-Kelly family, Liz might not have realized how her attention to Emma was perceived by Christina, or her lack of concern about Christina's eating disorder, for that matter. She might have thought she was communicating warmth, love, and support to her entire family by spending so much time and attention with Emma and by not being overly concerned about Christina's issues. She might have thought that by downplaying the eating disorder, she was helping Christina by not contributing to her anxiety. What she didn't realize was that to Christina, she came across as aloof and uncaring, with all of her time and attention devoted to others, namely Emma.

STOP AND THINK:

1. Looking at the TFA triangles in Figure 8.1, which one do you think best fits the response the mother had to her son on p. 176?

2. What type of TFA triangle best fits Christina's response to her mother's pushing her to go to college?

3. Think of other examples of TFA triangles in Christina's family. Compare them to TFA triangles of your own or your family members.

REALITY THERAPY

William Glasser's (1998) Control Theory, the basis for Reality Therapy, emphasizes the need for clients to identify what they can control and what things are out of one's control. It is normal for us to blame others when a conflict takes place. It is also normal to focus on other people's behavior, such as my brother won't stop annoying me, or why does my mom insist on asking me tons of questions at the end of the day? However, when you focus on your own behavior, you are able to target things that you can change. Face it, as much as you'd like to, you cannot change other people. You can obsess about it, whine about it, cry and complain about it, but you will never change another person's behavior. Therefore, if you spend all of your energy focusing on why and how the other person should change, then you are wasting your time. However, if you focus on the behaviors you can change that might affect the situation, such as not talking to your mom unless she initiates conversation or not paying attention to your brother unless he is annoying you, you might actually see some results. In the preceding examples, if the person changed those behaviors or made other changes related to the conflicts in question, it is very likely that he or she would get different responses from her mother and brother. Similarly, if Mark decided to talk more to Liz and Christina instead of retreating to his den each day, or if Martin Jr. suddenly decided to spend more time engaging with his family instead of flying under the radar, they both would likely see different behaviors in response from Christina and Liz.

Robert Wubbolding (2000) further developed Reality Therapy by adding the WDEP model. This model enables clinicians and clients to break down their problems by having them identify what they want and what they are doing to get what they want, evaluate what they are currently doing to get what they want, and then develop a new plan for getting what they want (see Table 8.2).

Table 8.2   Wubbolding's WDEP Model

W	What do you **W**ant? This helps clients get to the heart of their issue. Oftentimes family members are so eager to find fault with other family members and have their objections heard that they forget what they are fighting about.
D	What are you **D**oing to get what you want? Sometimes family members get in their own way. For example, if a client wants her husband to spend more time at home, and she chooses to nag him about it, it usually doesn't go well.
E	**E**valuate your current actions. As mentioned above, the client's choice of action is not the best choice for getting what she wants, as it usually leads to an argument and then works against her goal of spending more time with her husband.
P	Develop a new **P**lan. Exploring more effective ways for clients to get what they want is useful as they are encouraged to examine the pros and cons of potential choices, including other family members' potential reactions to their choices.

SOURCE: Adapted from Wubbolding, R. (2000). *Reality therapy for the 21st century.* Philadelphia, PA: Taylor & Francis.

Sometimes the mere identification of what clients want can enable them to move forward easily, even without going through the other steps. Particularly in couples' counseling, clients get so mired in complaining about each other and being angry, that when they are prompted to identify what they want, they are left speechless. William Glasser (1998) has shared that he will often ask couples he is working with if they are coming to counseling for marriage counseling or if they are there for divorce counseling. Being absolutely serious, he emphasized that sometimes couples come to counseling as a last resort but have no real intentions of doing the work necessary to save their marriage. Therefore, if their answer is marriage counseling, then they will need to identify what they want to get from counseling and what they are willing to do to get it.

POSTMODERN THEORIES

Narrative Family Counseling

Narrative family counseling arose from the postmodern approach adapted in the mid-20th century by many fields of study in the humanities and social sciences. Postmodern theory holds that knowledge is socially constructed. Therefore, rather than searching for objective answers in the material world, postmodern theorists explore the experiences and social context, or environment, of individuals and groups, including families.

There are four basic premises of narrative family counseling:

1. Meaning is constructed from experience.

2. Experience is subject to multiple interpretations.

3. Language conveys a story, or narrative.

4. Narratives influence subsequent experience.

STOP AND THINK:

1. How might these premises apply to what you already know about family counseling?

2. Do these premises sound reminiscent of aspects of other family counseling theories about which you have already read?

Narrative family counselors believe that families construct meaning about their experience. Narrative family counselors therefore focus their attention on meaning, rather than on behaviors, cognitions (thoughts), or emotions. They believe the family's experience can be interpreted many ways, the family has chosen one way of interpreting their experience that then influences how they function as a family, and that the family's interpretation can be changed. They refer to interpretation of experience and its impact on functioning as the family's story, or narrative. This narrative takes on a life of its own, becoming part of the family's experience and influencing not only how they view the past but also how they view what happens in the present and future. One of the jobs of the family counselor is to suggest alternative narratives.

One way that narrative family counselors learn about the family's narrative is by attending to the language family members use to describe their experiences. The family's use of language conveys their experience to the family counselor, reflects the meaning the family ascribes to those experiences, and influences the family members as they listen to one another's description of their experiences. For example, Liz referred to her sister, Barbara, as "my sister," rather than as "Christina's aunt," when the family counselor asked who she was (Chapter 6). This choice of terms reflected her narrative of excluding her children's relationships when describing extended family relationships. Similarly, had Mark referred to Christina and Martin Jr. as being from a "broken home," the story would have been very different than when he referred to them living in a "blended family." Similarly, if Mark had referred to Liz as "my wife" the meaning would be very different than when he called her "Liz."

Social scientists sometimes use the term *dominant culture*. The dominant culture includes the ideas, values, beliefs, knowledge, norms, and customs commonly accepted as representative of the majority of a society's members. However, not everyone is part of every aspect of the dominant culture. For example, the dominant American cultural view of the family includes a legally married, heterosexual couple living together with their biological children. In reality, many families do not fit this dominant narrative about families in the United States. Some couples do not live together because of separation, divorce, or death, while others may be geographically separated for financial reasons or because of immigration status. Some people choose domestic partnerships. Still other couples either decide not to have children or want children and find themselves unable to procreate. Finally, when biological parents do not cohabit, stepparents and domestic partners may assume the role of parenting.

The Manning-Kelly and Jones families do not fit the narrative of the dominant culture in the United States. Christina's three half siblings, Emma, Matthew, and Dominique, are the only children who live with two legally married, heterosexual, biological parents. And all of the children live in either single-parent or blended families.

STOP AND THINK:

1. List all the ways a family could deviate from the dominant cultural narrative about families. Do you know at least one family who exemplifies each of the ways you identified?

2. Referring to the extended family genogram, which families within the extended Manning-Kelly and Jones extended families fit the dominant cultural narrative about family? Which do not?

3. For those who have experienced living in an alternative family form, describe its impact on how your family views itself. For those raised in a family that fits the dominant cultural narrative, speculate on what it might be like to live in a family that is different from that dominant cultural narrative about families.

The dominant cultural narrative is external to all families, whether they fit it or not. It is not only considered to be the norm but also as a preferable family form by the larger society and sometimes even by people who live in families that don't conform to the dominant cultural model of the family. When a family does not fit and yet accepts the dominant cultural form of the family as the standard by which to judge itself, the family likely will conclude that the problem resides within itself rather than the larger social context in which it functions. Narrative family counselors, however, do not accept that the dominant cultural narrative applies universally to all families. Nor do narrative family counselors accept that deviation from the dominant culture is problematic. The family counselor's view is important, because the family's belief that the family is the problem affects its narrative, its present and future experience, and its functioning. When the family counselor maintains a different viewpoint, she or he is able to better facilitate a shift in the family's viewpoint that then opens the possibility of a change in its narrative.

Narrative family counselors view the problem as residing not in the family but in its narrative about the problem. In other words, if the family accepts that it is problematic because it does not fit the dominant cultural definition of family, the narrative becomes "we are defective," which then becomes a self-fulfilling prophecy. Narrative family counselors therefore encourage the family to externalize the problem that brought the family to counseling, to remove it from prominence in the family's narrative, and to allow the family to consider an alternative story, or narrative, about itself.

To summarize, postmodern theory holds that experience is subject to multiple interpretations and is influenced by the language used to describe it. These combine to create the family's narrative, which then influences its subsequent experience and dynamics. Alternatively, narrative family counselors view problems as occurring when the family accepts the dominant cultural or constructed narratives that suggest the problem resides with them. The intervention involves externalizing the problem and constructing a different narrative about it. By separating the family from the problem, members can collaborate with each other and the counselor to create a new and more productive narrative.

The narrative family counselor facilitates family members' efforts to make sense of their experience. She or he does not evaluate or direct them. It is a collaborative approach, and so narrative family counselors disclose their own assumptions and ask families to educate them about the family's uniqueness. The family counselor does not interpret what she or he hears but rather focuses on how the family can influence the problem, externalizing the problem-saturated story, and empowering the family to reauthor its story in a way that defines the family as competent to manage its problems and accept its missteps.

The tools of narrative family counseling include the narrative metaphor, which is the story of the family; externalizing conversations; and guiding the family toward a story in which the family is competent. These tools are based on the assumptions that the family's unique narrative is a social construction, rather than a given fact, and therefore it can be changed.

Part of the Manning-Kelly and Jones families' narrative appears to be that in a blended family, parenting roles remain the same as when each family was a single-parent family between marriages. Mark does not get involved in Liz's arguments with Christina or attempt to engage Martin Jr. more in the life of the family. Additionally, he participates reluctantly in family counseling. This way of defining themselves as a blended family has an impact on them and is not the only story, or narrative, that can be attached to blended families. The Jones family that Martin has created with Daniella is also a blended family, yet the Jones family defines itself completely differently with respect to parenting the son they do not share biologically than the Manning-Kelly family does.

FC: At first, it appeared you assigned tasks based on gender, with Liz managing the children and Mark having the lead career. But as I've gotten to know you better, it seems you organize who does what based on whose biological child needs what. Is that true?

Liz: No, it's about him thinking women are supposed to do everything.

FC: And that happened in your marriage with Martin, also?

Liz: Yes.

FC: So the problem is that you've all been raised to accept that women take care of children's needs and men do not.

The narrative family counselor shifts from the problem-saturated problem that Mark and Martin expect Liz to assume the role of a full-time homemaker while maintaining a career outside the home to a new narrative suggesting the problem lies in the social context in which the adults were reared and that assumes women are responsible for children. Her statement suggests this assumption can be questioned. It also suggests that Liz's choice of husbands is not somehow flawed, nor are Mark and Martin inadequate husbands and fathers.

Liz: Yes. Well, no. I don't accept that. But how can I ask Mark to take one of my children to the doctor?

FC: Mark? How can she ask you?

This is a collaborative question. Rather than coaching Liz on how to assert herself by the presumed expert family counselor, the narrative family counselor asks Liz and Mark to work collaboratively to rewrite their family narrative.

Mark: Look, I don't have time to be running her kids around. Someone has to earn a higher income in this family than she does.

Liz: I earn a lot of money, Mark. Don't put that down.

FC: I hear a lot of distinction between "his" and "her" when discussing the children. Is the story that men's work outside the family is more important, or that you don't help one another with your children from your first marriages?

Liz: Really? It sounds like we don't want to be parents to our stepchildren? That's awful.

FC: That's one way of hearing it and what it sounded like to me. Unless you disagree, I wonder whether the problem might be this story about how your family is supposed to function.

Liz: I can't figure out a way to disagree. But I don't like that that's how we act.

FC: Let's change the story then. What else could it be?

Liz: I don't know, that men and women share responsibility? That's what I believe.

FC: OK, so how would your lives be different if the story were about shared responsibility?

Liz: Well, Christina and Martin Jr. would still be my kids.

FC: So it's also important to change the narrative about his and her children. What if the story were men and women who blend their families are equally responsible for their own and each other's children because they are now one family, and the biological relationship is therefore less important than the family relationship?

Liz: I don't know.

Mark: Not going to happen, Liz.

Christina: [To Liz] Dad treats Jamal like his own son.

Notice that Christina intervened after Mark's dismissive statement.

Liz: Christina!

C: I'm just saying it's possible.

FC: Sounds like a different story, Christina. Mark, what are you
                telling Liz about how you see your role in the family?

Apart from Christina having become part of a triangle between Mark and
Liz that effectively deflected their argument and prevented it from escalating,
the counselor also underscored the narrative family counseling premise that the
problem was external to the family, and thus the story about it can be changed.
Martin and Daniella's narrative is that they coparent all three of their children,
despite the fact that they otherwise hold very traditional roles with respect to
parenting. Mark and Liz's narrative is that they each parent their own biological children separately, despite having more egalitarian roles with respect to
work outside the home than Martin and Daniella do. Rewriting the Manning-
Kelly family narrative that a blended family is divided along biological lines
may in fact reduce some of the tension in Liz and Mark's marriage. That Mark
does not appear receptive to change is a challenge the family as a whole must
confront with the collaborative assistance of the narrative family counselor.

STOP AND THINK:

1. Identify a narrative in your own family. How does it help or hinder
    your family and its members?

2. How comfortable are you with the idea of taking a collaborative role with
    the family, rather than being the expert upon whom the family relies?

3. If you were the Manning-Kelly narrative family counselor, how might
    you approach Mark's statement that it was "not going to happen"
    that he takes responsibility for at least the logistics of coparenting
    Christina and Martin Jr.?

Narrative family counseling is uniquely suited to address cultural differences
among families. By viewing the dominant cultural narrative as only one way
of interpreting the world and listening to the family's view of its uniqueness,

a narrative family counselor is more likely to avoid imposing a single cultural view on all client families.

Additionally, any family's narrative is influenced not only by the dominant cultural narrative but also by the cultural narrative(s) of its members. For example, Diller (2007) states that tensions within biracial marriages reflect racial tensions of the larger society. He also notes that how couples resolve these tensions provides a model for dealing with society's racial tensions or the couple's biracial children. And so a narrative family counselor might explore how racial tensions between the dominant White culture and Black Americans manifested in Liz and Martin's marriage. As we turn to feminist family counseling, it is important to note that both narrative and feminist family counselors might explore the role conflict Liz experienced between the dominant male culture and negotiating a work-life balance in her heterosexual marriages.

Feminist Family Counseling

The original family counseling theories, such as the ones described in Chapters 5 through 7, were developed by men. During the 1980s, women family counselors began to examine those theories from the perspective that they were written by men and might not be applicable to families in which women were involved. Noting that experience determines one's narrative about the world, they argued that the experience of being male might lead to a different view of families than the experience of being female would. The feminist family counseling critique was not about the male perspective being wrong but rather about needing to expand the field's views about families to recognize the possibility that any one perspective might be biased. Most prominent among these feminist family counselors were four women associated with the Women's Project in Family: Peggy Papp, Olga Silverstein, Marianne Walters, and Betty Carter.

Using the tenets of postmodern and family systems theories, feminist family counselors argued that traditional approaches to family counseling neglected the role of the larger social context as part of the system in which families function. Specifically, they pointed out that the traditional models of family counseling reflected gender-based stereotypes perpetuated by the dominant society and not universally applicable.

Gender, in contrast to sex, is a social construct. Differences in biological development result in female fetuses developing female reproductive organs that subsequently allow them to bear children. Similarly, men's biological development results in complementary but different reproductive organs. By contrast, there is no biological basis, other than nursing infants, for women to raise children alone at home while men work at a distance from the home. In fact, until relatively recently in human history, all but very wealthy women did work other than caring for their homes and children, including gathering, farming, or involvement in a cottage industry based in their home. There are many other expectations for women, including their relative power in relationships to men, that are learned socially by young children with female sex characteristics and that are not biologically based. Men also learn gender-role expectations, such as not crying and being aggressively competitive with one another, and these roles are also socially rather than biologically based. The debate about whether socially learned gender related behaviors bear any relationship to biochemical differences between males and females is beyond the scope of this textbook. In either case, it is these socially learned characteristics that form a particular society's definition of gender.

Feminist family counselors questioned the assumptions promoted by several early family counseling theorists that imply that family problems result from an overinvolved mother and disengaged father. They argued that what was referred to as maternal overinvolvement and paternal disengagement derived from the fact that middle-class women of the generation from which family counseling developed were often isolated in suburban homes with young children while men traveled to work in nearby cities and therefore were outside the home many hours most days.

Feminist family counselors also criticized the implication that the only solution to family problems involved bringing the father back into the family to "fix" it. While both parents arguably need to be involved with child-rearing, it is unnecessary to assume that the children of stay-at-home mothers need to be rescued from her. Feminist family therapists argued that approaches to family counseling based on these assumptions label a woman who fulfills the role assigned to her by the dominant culture as the cause of the family's problem, while simultaneously promoting the stereotype that women and children require rescuing by more competent men. Using the same postmodern theoretical perspective taken by narrative family counselors, feminist family counselors pointed out that the traditional role, rather than the women themselves, was the problem because these roles were constructed in a way that left women more involved in the day-to-day lives of their children and men more isolated from them.

Some feminist family counselors suggested that addressing the negative impacts of gender on the family involves increasing family members' awareness of gender-based expectations and asking families to evaluate the impact of these expectations on them. The family would then be free to choose, with guidance from the family counselor, whether to change specific expectations and roles or manage their impact differently. Like all family counselors, feminist family counselors adhere to the ethical guideline that it is not the role of the family counselor to impose her or his values, in this case about gender, on the family. And feminist family counselors remain sensitive to and respectful of cultural differences in the expectations accompanying gender roles.

Differential power tends to result directly from traditional gender-based roles or expectations regarding behavior. Nichols (1984) pointed out that family counselors tend to view women as clients and men as being reluctantly dragged to counseling at the insistence of the counselor. The Manning-Kelly family provides an excellent example of how this view originated. Liz contacted the family counselor after receiving a referral from the family's physician and, in response to being asked to bring the entire family, argued that Mark was too busy at work. One of the assumptions of traditional gender roles is that the husband's work is more lucrative and therefore more important than the woman's. As a result, he has the right to decide how he and his wife use their time, including who is responsible for getting children to various appointments. We do not have specific information about whether Liz's statement reflected a traditional gender orientation in which Mark's work was more lucrative and therefore provided him with decision-making power about his involvement with the family or whether it was specifically about how they have distributed responsibility for stepchildren in their blended family.

While the writers agree that traditional gender-based roles may lead to gender-based behavior, analysis of the family counseling theories already explored suggests that the male theorists' views of both the problem and the solution might have been more complex than an analysis based solely on gender suggests. For example, Minuchin's (1974) work reflected a commitment to strengthening the marital relationship in family counseling. Specifically, Minuchin focused on the boundary between the parental subsystem and the child subsystem. He gave couples assignments that involved time alone together to strengthen their bond. He also advocated that couples collaborate about child-rearing. He specifically stated that bringing a child into the couple relationship to deflect conflict was detrimental to both the health of the child and the health of the couple. One could interpret strengthening the couple subsystem as bringing the father in to fix the mother's overinvolvement with their children. Questions remain, however, regarding whether or not that was Minuchin's intention and whether structural family counseling can be practiced from a feminist perspective. Similar arguments can be made regarding whether Bowen's (1978) and Napier and Whitaker's (1978) theories have been interpreted as more gender biased than they were intended.

Luepnitz (2002) pointed out that feminist family counseling is a perspective of the counselor's and not synonymous with promoting a feminist agenda. Nichols (1984) referred to this distinction as that between advocacy and indoctrination. Both assertions, as well as our analysis, suggest that a variety of models of family counseling could be adapted to a feminist perspective.

STOP AND THINK:

1. Did any of the three traditional family counseling theories you've studied in Chapters 5 through 7 ignore the impact of traditional gender roles on families? If so, which ones? Explain your answer.

2. Knowing what you do at this point about the Manning-Kelly family, what traditional assumptions about men's and women's roles do you think Mark and Liz hold as individuals? What do you think the impact of these assumptions has been on them as individuals and a couple, their previous marriages, and their blended family? If you do not have enough information about the family to answer these questions, what else do you need to know?

3. Do you think structural family counseling can be practiced from a feminist perspective? Why? Why not? What about multigenerational family counseling and experiential family counseling?

Irrespective of what position one takes, the concept that gender influences experience is relevant to individuals and families and therefore to family counselors. It derives from the postmodern assumption that one's approach to life is determined by one's experience, and the way society treats boys and girls, men and women, Whites and People of Color, children and the elderly, heterosexuals and LGBTQIAs, people with and without disabilities, and so on, influences individual experience, attitudes, beliefs, and behaviors. In other words, if a mother is overly involved with her children, and a father is disengaged from the family, at least one aspect of the problem may be differing role expectations for men and women, rather than a flaw within the family system. Either way, the problem may be amenable to a variety of family counseling interventions based on a variety of family counseling theories while bearing a multicultural and feminist perspective.

For the purposes of this textbook, the most important points to remember are:

1. Family counselors must avoid assumptions that individual choices and behaviors are biologically based.

2. Family counselors are advised to be mindful that each family member's experience is determined in part by his or her gender experiences, in the

same ways that he or she is affected by ethnicity, age, socioeconomic status, and so on.

3. Couples and parents may be helped by clarifying their assumptions about how each will fulfill roles, including those associated with her or his gender.

All of Christina's parents and stepparents were raised in families where roles for men and women differed along gender lines. The men worked outside the home, and the women were responsible for home and child care. We do not know exactly how and to what extent gender roles specifically affected the power distribution among Christina's grandparents and stepgrandparents. However, we do know that none of her parents or stepparents had a model for sharing role responsibilities. And Liz's role as a working mother has been one she has defined as causing problems in both her marriages.

Martin's father appears to have been far more engaged in the family's life than Mark's was, despite the traditional gender roles in both families. Notice how both Martin and Mark have repeated their own fathers' level of involvement with their own children and stepchildren. Liz's father, likely due at least in part to his substance abuse, appears to have been disengaged from his children.

STOP AND THINK:

1. How might Liz's father's disengagement from the family affect her view of herself as a mother who works outside the home and her expectations for herself and her husbands?

2. How might Liz's expectations for herself and her husbands impact Christina's views about women's roles? How might Martin's and Mark's expectations for themselves and their wives affect Christina's views about men's roles?

3. If you do not have enough information to answer these questions, what more do you need to know?

The six questions posed in the last two "Stop and Thinks" are the kinds of questions a feminist family counselor might ask the Manning-Kelly family. She or he would pose these questions with the children present, as children often have a unique and clear understanding of how their parents function and are frequently more forthcoming than their parents.

Sometimes couples argue about role sharing. Simply because a woman works outside the home does not mean she wants her partner to share cooking responsibilities, for example. Similarly, a stay-at-home mother may expect her partner to share responsibility for chores after work as she, too, has been working all day. Sometimes, each partner brings expectations to the relationship based on her or his own parents and becomes confused and upset when the other partner does not conform and has different expectations. Other times, one or both partners wants to be very different than their parents were and is either unsure how to accomplish such change or has not shared this expectation with the other partner.

Liz has indicated that she limited her career to balance her roles as professional and mother. Her daughter, Christina, said she wants a more traditional female role, as her aunt and stepmother have chosen. Liz stated that Christina's father, Martin, did not support her working outside the home.

Given the family's history, a feminist family counselor would be mindful of our society's current ambivalence about women's roles and how that ambivalence affects this family in particular. Rather than viewing Liz as overinvolved with her children while Mark remained disengaged, a feminist family counselor would examine their expectations for themselves and each other as parents and work with them to achieve a reconciliation of their differences. A feminist family counselor would also be mindful of Liz's dilemma around balancing work and mothering, as she seems to both want to prioritize mothering and resents that she has had to relinquish career advancement to achieve it. A feminist family counselor would note the discrepancy between her learned expectations for herself and the reality of her life. The feminist family counselor would also be mindful of potential anger because neither Mark nor Martin has had to make the choices she has been faced with. A feminist family counselor might wonder whether Liz's anger might be about the social environment in which they live, despite it being directed at Martin and Mark. She might also speculate about whether Martin and Mark would treat Liz differently if she had chosen a more traditional role, as their mothers, Daniella, and Shoshana did. Such speculation would be aimed at increasing awareness and choices. It is compatible with all of the schools of family counseling examined in this textbook.

INTEGRATIVE FAMILY COUNSELING

Many family counselors choose one theory and stick with it, getting more and more training in the same area throughout their careers, and so on. Others find that they feel pulled to more than one theory, rather than sticking with one approach. For example, a counselor might decide that the focus on empowerment and gender equality in feminist theory is a good fit for him or her personally, but the psychodynamic emphasis of early life experiences also rings true and warrants attention during counseling. Most theories can be integrated with others. Using an integrative approach, however, is more than being eclectic and choosing an approach out of thin air when the time comes. Just as operating from a single theoretical orientation is based on careful consideration and training, using an integrative approach is the careful selection and combination of more than one theory integrated into one's practice. The basis of theory choices should include consideration of goodness of fit with one's personality, the appropriateness for use with one's clientele, and, most importantly, the evidence of the approaches' effectiveness in counseling.

CONCLUSION

Developing a theoretical orientation is crucial for family counselors. Not only does it help counselors know how to proceed with clients, but it also ensures that they are behaving ethically by employing evidence-based practices rather than flying by the seat of their pants. Students should take their time researching the different theoretical approaches; trying them on for size; seeing how they fit with their own personalities, values, and beliefs; and seeking more training and supervision throughout their academic and professional careers.

REFERENCES

Bowen, M. (1978). *Family therapy in clinical practice.* New York, NY and London, UK: Jason Aronson.

Diller, J. V. (2007). *Cultural diversity. A primer for the human services* (3rd ed.). Belmont, CA: Brooks/Cole.

Dreikurs, R. (1947). The four goals of the maladjusted child. *Nervous Child, 6,* 321–328.

Glasser, W. (1998). *Choice theory: A new psychology of personal freedom.* New York, NY: Harper Collins.

Hutchins, D. (1979). Systematic counseling: The TFA model for counselor intervention. *Personnel and Guidance Journal, 57,* (10), 529–531.

Luepnitz, D. A. (2002). *Schopenhauer's porcupines. Intimacy and its dilemmas.* New York, NY: Basic Books.

Minuchin S. (1974). *Families and family therapy*. Cambridge, MA: Harvard University Press.

Napier, A., & Whitaker, C. (1978). *The family crucible. The intense experience of family therapy*. New York, NY: Harper & Row.

Nichols, M. (1984). *Family therapy. Concepts and methods*. New York, NY: Gardner Press.

Wubbolding, R. (2000). *Reality therapy for the 21st century*. Philadelphia, PA: Taylor & Francis.

FOR FURTHER STUDY

The Ackerman Institute: *www.ackerman.org*

Barrett, D. (2002). The 'royal road' becomes a shrewd shortcut: The use of dreams in focused treatment. *Journal of Cognitive Psychotherapy, 16*(1), 55–64. doi:10.1891/jcop.16.1.55.63701

Barry, D. (1997). Telling changes: From narrative family therapy to organizational change & development. *Journal of Organizational Change Management, 10*(1), 32–48.

Basirico, L. A., Cashion, B. G., & Eshleman, J. R. (2014). *Introduction to sociology* (6th ed.). Redding, CA: BVT.

Baucom, D. H., Epstein, N., & LaTaillade, J. J. (2002). Cognitive-behavioral couple therapy. In A. S. Gurman, & N. S. Jacobson (Eds.), *Clinical handbook of couple therapy* (3rd ed.) (pp. 26–58). New York, NY: Guilford Press.

Beck, A. T. (1979). *Cognitive therapy and the emotional disorders*. Madison, CT: International Universities Press.

Billig, J. P., Hershberger, S. L., Iacono, W. G., & McGue, M. (1996). Life events and personality in late adolescence: Genetic and environmental relations. *Behavior Genetics, 26*, 543–554.

Brodie, F., & Wright, J. (2002). Minding the gap not bridging the gap: Family therapy from a psychoanalytic perspective. *Journal of Family Therapy, 24*(2), 205–221. doi:10.1111/1467-6427.00212

Child Welfare Information Gateway. (2013). *Alternatives for families: A cognitive behavioral therapy (AF-CBT)*. Washington, DC: U.S. Department of Health and Human Services, Children's Bureau.

Christensen, T. M., & Gray, N. D. (2002). The application of reality therapy and choice theory in relationship counseling, and interview with Robert Wubbolding. *The Family Journal, 10*(2), 244–248. doi:10.1177/1066480702102020

Corcoran, J. (2002). Developmental adaptations of solution-focused family therapy. *Brief Treatment and Crisis Intervention, 2*(4), 301–313. doi:10.1093/brief-treatment/2.4.301

DeShazer, S., & Doulan, Y. (2007). *More than miracles: The state of the art of solution-focused brief therapy.* New York, NY: Routledge.

Dulwich Centre. (2015). *What Is Narrative Therapy?* Dulwich Centre Publications Pty Ltd & Dulwich Centre Foundation, Inc. Retrieved from http://www.dulwichcentre .com.au/what-is-narrative-therapy

Eckstein, D., Aycock, K. J., Sperber, M. A., McDonald, J., Van Wiesner, V. I., Watts, R. E., & Ginsburg, P. (2010). A review of 200 birth-order studies: Lifestyle characteristics. *The Journal of Individual Psychology, 66*(4), 408–434.

Ellis, A. (2005). *The war on masturbation.* Interview with Albert Ellis. Directed by J. G. M. Davi.

Gehart, D. (2010). *Mastering competencies in family therapy: A practical approach to theory and clinical case documentation.* Pacific Grove, CA: Brooks/Cole.

Gladding, S. (2011). *Family therapy: History, theory, and practice.* Upper Saddle River, NJ: Pearson Education.

The Glasser Institute. www.glasser.com

Griffin, T. L. (2002, April). The adult only child, birth order and marital satisfaction as measured by the Enrich Couple Inventory. *Dissertation Abstracts International, 62,* 4837.

Hur, Y. M., McGue, M., & Iacono, W. G. (1998). The structure of self-concept in female pre-adolescent twins: A behavioral genetic approach. *Journal of Personality and Social Psychology, 74,* 1069–1077.

Johnson, W., Krueger, R. F., Bouchard, T. J., & McGue, M. (2002). The personalities of twins: Just ordinary folks. *Twin Research, 5,* 125–131.

Milliren, A., & Barrett-Kruse, C. (2002). Four phases of Adlerian counseling: Family resilience in action. *The Journal of Individual Psychology, 58*(3), 225–234.

Napier, A. Y. (1988). *The fragile bond: In search of an equal, intimate and enduring marriage.* New York, NY: Harper Collins.

Papp, P. (1997). Listening to the system. *Family Therapy Networker, 21,* 52.

Richarz, B., & Römisch, S. (2002). Acting-out: Its functions within analytic group psychotherapy and its transformation into dreams. *International Journal of Group Psychotherapy, 52*(3), 337–353. doi:10.1521/ijgp.52.3.337.45513

Rockquemore, K. A., & Laszloffy, T. A. (2003). Multiple realities. A relationship narrative approach in therapy with black-white mixed-race clients. *Family Relations, 52*(2), 119–128.

Shalay, N., & Brownlee, K. (2007). Narrative family therapy with blended families. *Journal of Family Psychotherapy, 18*(2), 17–30.

Trauma Focused Cognitive Behavioral Therapy: https://tfcbt.org/about-tfcbt

White, M., & Epston, D. (1990). *Narrative means to therapeutic ends.* New York, NY: W. W. Norton.

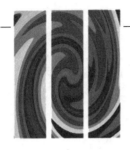

PART III

Other Aspects of
Family Counseling

CHAPTER 9

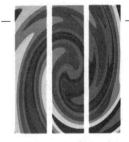

Special Topics in Family Counseling

In this chapter, we explore eight family counseling topics with which you need to be familiar because a significant number of families bring one or more of them to counseling. These are multicultural families; LGBTQIA families; single parent families; blended families; families with aging members; biomedical disease processes in families; mental health and substance abuse disorders within families; and domestic violence and child, elder, and dependent abuse. We will return to each of them again in Chapter 12, when we describe family needs for services beyond what family counselors can provide.

MULTICULTURAL FAMILIES

Basirico, Cashion, and Eshleman (2014) define culture as a "system of ideas, values, beliefs, knowledge, norms, customs, and technology shared by almost everyone" (p. 97) who shares that cultural identity. It, like race, is socially constructed (Basirico, et al., 2014, p. 99). In other words, while we associate certain physical characteristics and continents of origin with an individual's racial origin, we have agreed socially to make these connections. If you have doubts, use the following link to test your ability to identify an individual's race: www.pbs.org/race/002_SortingPeople/002_00-home.htm.

Lum (2007) offered an example of a man who was incorrectly identified upon arrival in a hospital emergency room as Latino because of the color of his skin and then assumed to be Spanish-speaking by hospital staff. As a result of the staff mislabeling his race, his inability to converse in Spanish was then misdiagnosed as a cognitive functioning delay and catatonic schizophrenia.

Culture is learned within families, transmitted between generations of the family, and reinforced by interactions within the community. As you can conclude from reading the definition above, culture is all encompassing, influencing every aspect of individuals' behavior. Clinically, both culture and race influence how both clients and counselors define the reality that influences their thoughts, feelings, behaviors, and the meaning they attach to each of these.

When family counselors work with families, the family's cultural and racial experiences are integral factors in the family's functioning as well as in its response to clinical interventions. And race is important in counseling for similar reasons.

As counselors, it is thus crucial that we examine our own views about culture and race. The term *ethnocentrism* refers to the assumption that our own cultural and racial experiences provide the standards by which to judge people. In other words, the language, values, norms, customs, and way of looking at the world learned as a child becomes the correct way of being in the world. While pride and appreciation of one's culture does not impede clinical practice, the right/wrong, good/bad dichotomy used to evaluate diverse cultures and their members is both racist and unproductive.

By contrast, cultural relativism, or a multicultural approach views each culture in its own context. Thus, whether a family is functional is determined by how consistent its norms and values are with those of the cultures with which the family identifies. Consistency with the cultures with which the family counselor identifies becomes irrelevant.

One of the social realities of People of Color in our society is the experience of being labeled as different and subsequently devalued and rendered powerless. By contrast, a social reality of being White is that one does not have to think about race as a factor in how one is treated. This aspect of the White experience is known as White privilege.

In multicultural or biracial families like the Manning-Kelly family, some members experience the prerogatives of being White whereas other family members experience the devaluation and disempowerment of being a person of color. Additionally, couples may experience negative attitudes and verbalizations about their biracial marriage from within their own extended family and social networks.

The client family and its members' experiences, as well as the family counselor's ability to maintain a multicultural perspective impact the client-therapist relationship. And the reality of a multicultural counseling relationship usually needs to be addressed for counseling to be successful. The culturally competent counselor will be mindful of and address as appropriate the multicultural nature of the therapeutic relationship between herself or himself and the family, as well as the cultural reality and ethnocentric or racist experiences of family members (Diller, 2007, Lum, 2007).

The culturally competent counselor will also recognize that the Manning-Kelly family includes several bicultural and biracial family members. Christina and Martin Jr. have a White mother and a Black father. Jason and Ashley's mother is Middle-Eastern, and their father is White.

When working with bicultural and biracial clients and families, counseling tends to be more collaborative. Christina and Martin Jr. do not share the experience of being Black with their mother, and this likely has an impact on their relationship with her. Similarly, they do not share the experience of being White with their father. And neither parent can fully understand their experience being biracial.

Additionally, within any given racial group there may be a number of different cultural influences. For example, the cultures of Japan, China, Polynesia, Guam, Saipan, Hawaii, Laos, Thailand, Korea, and Vietnam differ dramatically from one another, and yet all fall within the racial definition of Asian and Pacific Rim. Similarly, Latinos may trace their cultural origin and language to a variety of geographic locations and not all on the same continent. A final example involves the Middle East, which is a geopolitical construct from the World War II era. Even within countries, for example Iraq, there are a number of cultural groups who oppose one another in values, customs, norms, and so on.

We previously speculated that Christina and Martin Jr.'s distance from their parents and half sister might be a product of the family's life cycle stage or how it was blended. We have also considered the impact of Emma's cerebral palsy and the extra attention her mother gives her because of it on Liz's relationships with her two older children.

A culturally competent counselor would also hypothesize that Christina and Martin Jr.'s bicultural experience may play a role in their relationships with their mother, stepfather, and half sister. Tatum (1997) noted the impact of adolescence being a time of identity development and thus racial awareness. Adolescents tend to choose an identity group and then adapt their own identity to conform to it. Often, such conformity is in opposition to the dominant culture. For example, as adolescents of color become more aware of racism, they may create a group identity that rejects and opposes the cultural identity of White teenagers.

Additionally, we do not know what role racial and cultural differences played in Liz and Martin's marriage or how these differences may have contributed to the demise of their marriage. In a discussion of the socialization of biracial children, Diller (2007) noted that larger cultural tensions may manifest in the relationships of biracial couples. It is perhaps relevant that

Martin's second marriage is to a Black woman, and Liz's second marriage is to a White man.

Some research indicates that the prevalence of eating disorders is similar among White Americans and Americans of Color (Mulholland & Mintz, 2001). Other researchers have found that Blacks evidence fewer eating disorders than Whites (Abrams, LaRue, & Gray, 1993). These researchers pointed out that the prevalence of eating disorders may be associated with the degree to which Black women are assimilated into White culture, in other words, how extensively they accept and identify with the values and norms of the dominant culture. They also hypothesized a similar relationship between eating disorders and anxiety, depression, and low self-esteem. Anorexia, which entails the restriction of caloric intake and excessive exercising, has consistently been found to have low prevalence among Black women (Williams, 2011).

Christina seems to have learned her concern about weight and appearance from her mother, Liz, who evidences symptoms of restrictive eating and over-exercise. The family counselor discovered that Martin and Daniella do not share Christina's value of thinness. Yet they also appeared relatively unconcerned about Christina's weight. It may be helpful for the family counselor to learn how Christina's friends view weight and appearance and with which racial groups she identifies. It is possible that Christina isolating herself from friends is not only a result of their interest in college but also their lack of interest in maintaining the standard of thinness promoted by the dominant culture for women.

Jason and Ashley are also bicultural. Their mother is a Middle-Eastern American, and their father is White. The family structure is different from any other in the extended Manning-Kelly and Jones families, with the maternal grandparents having taken a much more active role in daily child care than Martin's, Liz's, or Mark's parents did. Similarly, there is no indication that Liz felt pushed out of her children's lives by her in-laws, Samuel and Roxanne, or that Martin felt isolated by Sally and either of her husbands during or after their marriage, an experience Mark had both during and after his marriage to Shoshana.

Middle Eastern culture is very different from Black or White American culture, and so one cannot generalize that the experiences of being bicultural or biracial are identical for these stepsiblings. Again, it is beyond the scope of this text to describe in detail culturally competent practice with each of these cultural groups. Rather, we encourage counselors to ask their clients and colleague experts about race and culture and to be mindful that they cannot make assumptions about any client family's experiences based on their own race or culture.

> ## STOP AND THINK:
>
> 1. Describe your cultural and racial experience in high school. Did you hang out primarily with adolescents of your own racial and/or cultural group? How did you view students who were members of other groups?
>
> 2. Think about someone you know whose weight or appearance seems to be a dominant focus in her or his life. What cultural values and norms underlie this focus? Does this person's family share those values and norms? Do you?

FC:	Christina, I'd like to find out a little bit more about your friends.
C:	Not my friends.
FC:	Yes, your friends. You and your mom have both said they are very focused on college. Tell me more about them.
C:	Well, they all just assume that's what's next.
FC:	Tell me other things about them.
C:	I don't know what you want to know.
FC:	Are they mostly Black, White, biracial?
C:	Black, I guess.
FC:	And what do they think about your weight loss?
C:	Not much. You know, they say it's my mom, my White side.

Notice the family counselor did not hesitate to ask about race. Culturally competent practice requires counselors to accept and value differences, rather than pretend they do not exist. Notice also that Christina's Black friends labeled her biracial and explained what might otherwise appear silly behavior to them in terms of her biracial heritage. Because conformity is so highly valued during adolescence, the family counselor speculated that the reference to her "White side" allowed her to deviate from the group's norms more than would have been tolerable had she not been biracial.

LGBTQIA FAMILIES

L (lesbian), G (gay), B (bisexual), T (transgendered), Q (questioning sexual identity), I (intersex), and A (asexual) are the terms comprising the acronym LGBTQIA. And LGBTQIA families are families with one or more members who identify their sexual identity or orientation in any of these ways. You might also hear the term LGBTQIAA, the second A denoting allies. How sexual orientation and identity affect a family depends on many factors, including the age of the LGBTQIA member, attitudes about sexual orientation and identity within the family and in its larger social context, the availability of social support, the process by which the family member came out to her or his family, and whether any family disruption resulted from the coming out process.

You may have grown up with someone who lived in a family with two moms or two dads. However, your grandparents probably did not. You also may know someone who has experienced the process of coming out to her or his family. Again, because society was very different as recently as two generations ago, your grandparents probably did not know anyone who had come out when they were young adults.

What are the similarities and differences in the experiences of children raised by heterosexual and LGBTQIA parents? Young children are wonderfully accepting of who their parents are. However, they are also sensitive to how people outside the family treat their parents and may feel protective when that treatment is discriminatory. When individuals come out to their families, they faces their parents' and extended family members' attitudes. Coming out can be further complicated by the attitudes and beliefs of the cultural identification of the individuals and their families. If the person coming out is already involved in a heterosexual relationship in which her or his sexual orientation was a secret, the partner will likely feel betrayed, angry, and confused, as will their children.

Couples in which one member is open about her or his sexual orientation and the other is not sometimes argue about the meaning of their differences. Christina's cousin Paul is gay and also out to his family. His husband, Matt, is not out to his family, despite having suffered a dishonorable discharge from the military during the don't-ask-don't-tell (DADT) years. Imagine what Paul and Matt's conversation about this discrepancy might be.

Paul: You said last Christmas that you'd be out to your family before the holidays this year. And here we are, it's November 1st, and you're not.

Matt: I know, and I've tried. But you know my dad—career military, super religious—I'm not sure he'll ever speak to me again, and that will make my mom's life miserable.

Paul: One thing I love about you is how you think about other people's feelings. But what about mine?

Matt: You know how I feel about you.

Paul: Yeah, but it feels like I'm less important to you than other people are.

Matt: That's not true. You're the most important person in my life. You and the baby we're going to adopt.

Paul: Well, it doesn't feel that way.

Imagine how much more heated this argument would be if Paul and Matt's relationship was distressed in addition to the conflict about Matt coming out to his family.

Matt was in the military for a couple of years after college, when DADT was in effect. After his commanding officer was told by someone that Matt had considered a friend that he was gay, he received a dishonorable discharge, which became part of his permanent record. Not only does he not receive veterans' benefits despite having served in Afghanistan, but also he must disclose how he left the military on job applications. This latter impacts his competitiveness for professional jobs and so both involve economic loss.

Paul and Matthew face some of the same issues of being labeled different and devalued that people of color face and that White heterosexual couples do not. Sometimes gay and lesbian partners need to keep the nature of their relationship hidden from coworkers in order to feel safe in their jobs. Other times, one or more family members may initiate a cutoff with the LGBTQIA member. And finally, one or both partners may be a member of a cultural group that holds even more negative views of sexual diversity than the mainstream. LGBTQIA clients who are not White sometimes do not identify with LGBTQIA groups that ignore the experience of also being of color.

A counselor needs to understand each family's unique experience regarding the LGBTQIA member. She or he also needs to maintain a multicultural perspective and be mindful of her or his own attitudes about those identifying as LGBTQIA.

STOP AND THINK:

1. How would or how has your family reacted to learning a member is LGBTQIA?

2. How might the family's reaction affect the LGBTQIA member and her or his spouse?

SINGLE-PARENT FAMILIES

Single-parent families happen in a variety of ways. Sometimes there was never an enduring relationship between the parents. The child may have resulted from a brief liaison or from a medical procedure such as insemination. Sometimes, the parents were never legally married but had an ongoing, committed, and loving relationship that did not achieve permanence, either through the death of one of the partners or the dissolution of their relationship. In families in which the parents were legally married, the marriage may have ended in either death or divorce.

Whether or not a legal marriage occurred has little to do with the involvement of the second parent following the termination of the relationship. A parent who never lived with the child may insist on involvement in the care of that child. Or, a parent may leave the family and fail to maintain contact with the children. When a parent has died, the death may have been sudden or the result of a protracted illness.

The impact of a parent dying is in some ways very different than the effect of a parent leaving the family while alive. Both require periods of grieving and adjustment to the change. Both involve changing roles and expectations within the family. Frequently, when there is only one parent, one of the children becomes what Minuchin (1974) termed "parental." In other words, that child may take on roles and responsibilities usually associated with adulthood. Rather than viewing the situation as an inappropriate incursion by a member of the child subsystem into the parental subsystem (see Chapter 6), in single-parent families such behavior can be viewed as necessary to maintain the family's equilibrium.

Christina's Aunt Selena, one of Martin's younger sisters, was a single parent at the time the Manning-Kelly family was seen. And Christina's maternal grandmother, Sally, was widowed, although by the time of her first husband's death their children were all adults living outside the family home. Of more immediate relevance to the family counseling, both Liz and Martin had been single parents between their separations and remarriages. Liz and Christina both described that period as difficult, although Christina described Liz's unhappiness as the greatest challenge, while Liz focused on doing the work of both parents. Shoshana, Mark's first wife, and he were single parents after their marriage ended. And finally, Christina's Uncle David, Liz's brother, is a single father who appears to have very little contact with his son, Carl. Because the Manning-Kelly family has had no contact with Christina's cousin Carl, we have no idea what the impact of a father who virtually abandoned him has had on him. Given David's polysubstance abuse, it is likely he had emotionally abandoned his ex-wife and son even before he physically left them.

Family counselors working with single-parent families also need to maintain a multicultural perspective about single-parent families. People who live in the United States tend to view two-parent families in which a legally married, heterosexual couple cohabit with their biological children as the norm, despite the fact that half of all children in this country will have lived in a single-parent family for some period of time before reaching their 18th birthdays. Family counselors therefore need to recognize that a variety of family structures are valid. For example, it is very different for a 15 year old to assume responsibility for some of the care and discipline of younger children when there is only one parent in the home than when the increased responsibility is symptomatic of a situation in which the 15 year old has been placed between her parents in a way that stops them from reconciling their conflicts.

In summary, family counselors must be mindful of the unique needs of single-parent families and avoid imposing any ideas they may have about the relative value of two-parent families upon their clients. When single parents present for family counseling with their children, it is often about child behavior problems or concerns about how their children are adjusting to the other parent's absence. You will learn more about the transition in and out of being a single-parent family in the section that follows on blended families.

STOP AND THINK:

1. Did you or someone you know live in a single-parent household for any or all of your childhood?

2. How did that household differ from households with two parents? Be as specific as you can.

3. Now ask yourself, what do I think of these differences. Do I label them as good or bad?

BLENDED FAMILIES

The term *blended family* refers to families in which at least two nuclear families have combined to create a new family. This definition implies there was a previous marriage or significant relationship that produced at least one child and then a second marriage or significant relationship that produced the new blended family.

As noted in the previous section, losing a partner or parent through death is a very different experience from losing a partner or parent through divorce. While those family members left behind may experience a feeling of abandonment in both cases, everyone with the exception of very young children knows the deceased did not really wish to leave. Additionally, the relationship between the partners was likely a primarily happy one, and so both the bereaved parent and the children can more easily reclaim happy memories of when the family was together.

Separation and divorce are very different. Parents usually continue to hold negative feelings about each other following the dissolution of their relationship. If they did not get along as partners living together, the chance that they will as coparents living apart is low. Family counselors can help separating and divorcing parents avoid fighting through their children and instead focus them on their issues with one another. For example, it is not the children's fault when one parent feels taken advantage of by the other's frequent requests to change the visitation schedule, and the children are best served by the parents refraining from discussing with or asking for help from the children in managing the visitation schedule.

Additionally, children in divorced families know their other parent is alive and so can and often do maintain the fantasy that their parents will get back together, and their family will again be whole. Even if the children are too young to remember a time when their biological parents were happy together, they may imagine what it would have been like and long for it. These wishes and fantasies may become problematic when one parent becomes involved in a serious relationship. Children often resist the new partner, and new partners often feel hurt, anxious, and enraged by stepchildren who treat them badly. Blended families may require assistance with these strong feelings and also in deciding whether the stepparent will be involved in disciplining the children, when and how the biological parent will deal with the children's negative behavior toward the stepparent, and how much time and money will be devoted to stepchildren not living in the home.

Blended families experience a number of family, as well as individual and couple issues not encountered when children's biological parents remain alive and married to one another. These include relationships among stepsiblings and half siblings, which vary depending on whether the children were raised together or in different households and how they were introduced to one another; adoption of stepchildren when the biological parent is unavailable; and coparenting, which includes managing contact between children and both biological parents and the biological parents' relationship with each other. The Manning-Kelly and Jones families do not include examples of the father having residential custody, although children do reside with their fathers and visit their mothers or spend an equal amount of time in each home.

There are four blended families in the Manning-Kelly and Jones families that affect the identified patient, Christina, and also exemplify a range of issues arising in families with remarriages. These are Sally and Jim, Liz and Mark, Martin and Daniella, and David's ex-wife, Susan, and her second husband.

Liz and Mark have created a blended family, as have Martin and Daniella. Liz and Mark are both divorced. Family counselors are not trained or licensed to provide legal counsel, and so attorneys have likely been involved in creating financial and custody agreements for Liz and Martin when they divorced and for Mark and Shoshana when they divorced a year later. Such agreements sometimes include provisions in the event either parent remarries.

The emotional sequelae of divorce and remarriage may extend beyond the legal realm. Even when custody and visitation schedules are clearly specified in divorce agreements, one parent sometimes needs to make a change in the schedule and negotiates that change with the other parent. For example, Liz wanted Christina and Martin Jr. to go to her stepdaughter's college graduation, which fell on a weekend they were scheduled to be with Martin. Sometimes former spouses can easily negotiate trade-offs. Other times, one may feel burdened and taken for granted. Martin believed that, because he was so committed to Christina and Martin Jr., Liz assumed she could change the schedule whenever she wanted and he would accommodate in order to see his children. Such a situation continuing over the 10 years they had been divorced had created a lot of ill will. It falls within the domain of the family counselor, not the attorney, to help them better manage their relationship as former spouses who need to coparent.

A similar issue arises as children move into adolescence. Christina and Martin Jr. have friends and school activities that intrude on their time with both sets of parents. However, because they live with Liz and Mark and therefore see less of Martin and Daniella, the times they have social events on weekends when they are scheduled to be at Martin's may feel like a more significant intrusion on his time with them. It is important for parents in situations like this to negotiate with each other about alternatives, rather than placing demands on their children. If Martin told Martin Jr. that it hurt his feelings when his son went to a soccer tournament on a weekend he was scheduled to be with Martin and Daniella, Martin Jr. might feel obligated to withdraw from the soccer team or resentful of Martin for pressuring him or treating him as though he were a much younger child. Similarly, if Martin asked Martin Jr. to talk to his mother about trading weekends so he would be with her during the tournament, Martin Jr. would be triangulated into his parents' ongoing distress (Chapter 6). A family counselor might coach Martin to negotiate with Liz to change the weekend Martin Jr. stays with him and Daniella, instead of asking Martin Jr. to do it for him.

Although Mark's children from his first marriage are young adults, he continued to provide financial assistance to them, in part because he believed Shoshana and her parents had disrupted the more nurturing aspects of his relationships with them. Shoshana had not remarried, and there was no way to know without talking to her whether her choice to remain single had cultural components or was a matter of personal preference. In situations where one parent has remarried and the other has not, there can be tension between the parents regarding issues of abandonment and desirability that can be played out in fights over money and children. It falls to the family counselor to determine when to suggest seeking legal counsel and when the issues being addressed by client families have more to do with emotions and coping with a reality that cannot be changed.

Both remarriages have produced half siblings for the biological children of the first marriages. Emma is Mark and Liz's daughter and the half sister of Christina, Martin Jr., and Mark's two older children. Babies, toddlers, and preschool aged children demand more time and attention than adolescents, even though adolescents need to know their parents care about and are paying attention to them. As Christina and Martin Jr. have noted, they think Emma is more important to their mother than they are. Their situation is complicated by Emma's disability. It is important for the family counselor to help Christina and Martin Jr. accept their feelings, rather than discount them out of guilt for being jealous of a disabled child. We have no idea what Mark's older children feel about Emma or even how well they know her given that they were both away at college when she was born.

Martin and Daniella have also produced half siblings for their biological children. Since Christina and Martin Jr. spend less time with these half siblings, and neither has special needs, their feelings about these children appear less fraught, although that is not the case for everyone in their situation. Some children feel replaced by a parent's new family. Christina and Martin Jr., however, think their father's younger children are cute and enjoy playing with them. They don't view them as siblings so much as a part of their father's new family, almost indistinguishable from Daniella, who they like. Daniella's older son, Jamal, lives with these half siblings and seems to accept them as part of the fabric of his everyday life. He was young when Martin entered his life, and Daniella said he was happy to have someone who treated him like a son.

Daniella was not married to Jamal's father, and he had maintained minimal contact with his son. Thus, the father's rights regarding Jamal may be unclear to the family. Since laws differ from state to state, Martin's legal role in Jamal's life is an issue only an attorney can address. However, if adoption becomes both possible and desirable, then a family counselor may be able to assist Martin and Daniella with their decision and Jamal with any emotional repercussions of it.

Finally, Carl, one of Christina's cousins, is in a blended family. His mother and Liz's brother, David, divorced when he was 2 years old, and Carl's mother remarried 2 years later. Carl now lives with his mother and stepfather. Carl's stepfather has a daughter from his first marriage who is now 20, and Carl has two younger half siblings who are now 7 and 9 years old.

Although David has been unable to contribute financially or emotionally to Carl's upbringing, and Carl's stepfather would like to adopt him, Carl's mother prefers not to trigger potential conflict. Because she and Carl's stepfather disagree, and their differing approaches to conflict may create tension in other areas of their marriage, a family counselor might be helpful to them.

Additionally, Carl has been telling himself he does not care about his biological father. Such detachment may mask a variety of complex feelings, including anger, self-doubt, and sadness. Children in Carl's position may doubt their lovability, concluding that if they were lovable, the parent who is no longer in their lives would have stayed. This is a risk in any divorce but much more so when one parent disappears from a child's life. Anger and sadness about the loss of that parent can be confusing: "I hate him for leaving" and "I wish my family were whole" is not an easy ambivalence for a young child to resolve. Thus, many children in Carl's situation say, "I'm fine. I couldn't care less about him. I really don't even remember him." Family counselors can be enormously helpful in bringing the real feelings to awareness, helping children distinguish between a parent's issues and how lovable the child is, and strategizing to find ways to manage complex and confusing feelings so they don't go underground and interfere with the child's current and future life.

As you can see, there are a variety of blended family issues, and many are evidenced in the larger Manning-Kelly family. These issues include relationships among stepsiblings and half siblings, adoption, loss, and coparenting. The Manning-Kelly family does not include examples of the father having residential custody, although that happens.

STOP AND THINK:

1. Did you or someone you know live in a blended family?

2. What were the challenges involved in relating to stepparents, step-siblings, and half siblings?

3. How did the parents handle these challenges?

FAMILIES WITH AGING MEMBERS

In Chapter 2, you read about the final stage of the family life cycle, the family in later life. You learned that as the older generation ages, there are repercussions for members of other generations in the family and most especially for their adult children. You read about the sandwich generation, people in midlife who are raising families, launching children, and simultaneously caring for elderly parents. Such care does not involve only the day-to-day tasks associated with illness and decline but also arranging for and monitoring such care, taking on decision making when elderly parents can no longer make decisions for themselves, moving them out of their homes when necessary and sometimes against their will, and other less than pleasant, often time-consuming responsibilities. Caring for aging parents also involves exchanging roles with them. This exchange, with the adult child now being the caretaker of the aging parent who cared for her or him in childhood, can be emotionally difficult for everyone. Watching beloved and formerly vibrant parents decline can also be emotionally painful. And finally, tensions among adult siblings may be manifested in conflict about the care of an aging parent and management of the parent's financial resources. How these various tasks and emotions are handled can make a huge difference in biomedical and mental health outcomes for family members.

Family counselors need to be aware of the challenges of aging parents that may be impacting the families they see. We have described Mark's responsibilities as an only child for his elderly parents, Liz's worry about her aging mother caring for an increasingly disabled husband, and Martin's parents' relative youth and independence.

In blended families, family counselors also need to be aware of tensions between each elderly parent and both his or her biological children and his or her stepchildren, as well as tension among siblings and stepsiblings. Sally and Jim married after they both were widowed, and both had grown children from their first marriages. Family counselors can recommend that all the adult children be seen together, either with or without their parents present. Helping adult stepsiblings to see one another as people who care about their parents, as well as their own interests, can help open lines of communication so that they can more effectively deal with issues surrounding aging, death, and disbursement of any remaining resources and assets. We will address this possibility in more detail in Chapter 12.

As the U.S. population ages, there is an increasing need for family counselors and other human service practitioners with training and experience in gerontology to deliver counseling and other services to the elderly and their families. Family counselors can be helpful with many aging issues, including managing the impact of the aging members' coping on their families when they face physical and mental decline, loss of independence, and impending mortality; strategizing about how adult siblings distribute care-taking responsibilities and helping them support one another; and helping aging spouses find a way to balance one's need for care with the toll giving the care takes on the other's health and well-being. Family counselors can also provide grief groups for widows and widowers, support groups for caretakers, and reminiscence groups for some dementia patients.

Liz's stepfather, Jim, has recently been diagnosed with Alzheimer's disease. Although he is still living at home, his decline is clear to his children and stepchildren. They report that he wanders out of the house, leaves the kitchen after turning on the stove, and easily becomes enraged at Sally. They say he is often withdrawn from interactions among family members. Jim and Sally contend that the children are exaggerating his symptoms and argue that he and Sally are more than capable of managing him at home. Family counselors are often asked to see the aging couple and some or all of their adult children and are expected to help the adult children convince the parents that the patient requires a higher level of care. While making the kinds of life-changing decisions Sally and Jim face is not part of a family counselor's role, family counselors can help family members clarify their thoughts and more effectively communicate with each other so that everyone's perspective is heard and considered as decisions are made. At the same time, family counselors need to be careful to avoid taking sides, irrespective of what they think the merits of a particular family member's arguments are.

As aging family members lose independence and function, their reactions may create additional difficulties for the rest of the family. For example, when patients with dementia or circulatory disease are no longer able to drive, they may rage and attempt to manipulate family members to give them their car keys.

These relatives may find it difficult to say no, even when they know that driving would be unsafe. Family counselors can be helpful to these family members in learning to assert themselves despite their complex feelings about the parent's deterioration and the parent's reaction to losing independence. Family counselors can also encourage family members to seek further information from the medical team when questions arise that are beyond the family counselor's knowledge or scope of practice.

Mark's parents, Emily and Bryan, present a different set of challenges. They both have age-related health problems, though neither suffers from dementia or a life-threatening disease. They are less able to care for their home than they were and yet do not wish to move to an apartment or retirement community where they would have less responsibilities. Mark is concerned about their nutrition because Emily, who had been a traditional housewife, no longer likes to cook or go to the grocery store. Because Mark is an only child, he does not have the power that a sibling group might have in approaching his parents with his concerns. Additionally, he does not have siblings to share the burden of their care. He also does not need to cope with the dynamics of a sibling group in which their disagreements and old battles might be fought over current issues with aging parents.

Sandwich Generation. Family counselors can help members of the sandwich generation manage the challenges of both caring for children or launching adult children and caring for aging family members. The demands of both may be enormous, and members of the sandwich generation must find ways to prioritize, create a balance between their families of procreation and their aging parents, and take care of themselves.

Both Mark and Liz are members of the sandwich generation. Barbara, Liz's older sister, is not because her children are in their mid-20s, both married with their own families. Her children, however, have been in the position of being in a sandwich generation when they were helping their father and Barbara during Barbara's cancer treatment while maintaining independent lives and families of their own.

Panini Press Generation. You will not find the term *Panini press generation* in the family studies or family counseling literature. It is a term coined by someone one of the authors knows. It refers to an adult balancing care of a sick or aging spouse with care of an elderly parent. Barbara's husband, Peter, was in the Panini press generation when Barbara's cancer overlapped with his father's final illness. The need for support, balance, and managing family relationships is similar to that of the sandwich generation.

STOP AND THINK:

1. Are your parents or the parents of someone you know experiencing the challenges of the sandwich or Panini press generations?

2. How are they coping?

3. What else could they be doing?

FAMILIES WITH BIOMEDICAL CONDITIONS

While biomedical diseases require diagnosis, intervention, and ongoing care by physicians and allied health professionals, family counselors can help patients, caretakers, and the entire family adapt to the changes, emotional challenges, and demands brought about by ongoing, or chronic, diseases. Family counselors may be called upon to help the family understand the full meaning of the diagnosis and prognosis, find ways to cope with the patient and her or his disease, and make decisions when the patient requires more care than the family can provide at home. The biopsychosocial model provides a template of how attention to the mental health aspects of care intersects with biomedical care. It holds that the biological, psychological, and social aspects of the individual patient must be addressed for effective treatment of any one aspect. Physicians who subscribe to the biopsychosocial model attend to the psychological and social health of their patients, including their families, as part of any treatment. Family counselors have an important role to play in psychosocial care.

A family's genogram (Chapter 3) sometimes provides information about biomedical diseases that appear in multiple generations of a family. There are at least six examples of chronic biomedical conditions in the Manning-Kelly family: Jim's Alzheimer's disease, Emma's cerebral palsy, Barbara's breast cancer, potential health sequelae of Christina's eating disorders, David's metabolic syndrome, Martin's mother's chronic heart condition, and Sally's elevated blood pressure. None of these specific conditions appears in more than one family member.

Jim's dementia was discussed earlier in this section. At the other end of the life cycle, 4-year-old Emma experienced brain trauma during delivery and has been diagnosed with cerebral palsy. While cerebral palsy is not a progressive disease, it cannot be cured, and so the patient and her family need to accommodate to her special needs and both the impact of these needs and the meaning of the diagnosis on the family.

All parents have expectations for their children. Some parents are very specific about these expectations, as some readers well know. But even parents who are not insistent about their child majoring in business or premed or going to a university at which they are a triple or quadruple legacy assume that their children will be as smart and accomplished as they are. And no parent wants to see his or her child suffer, for example, when teased about the way he or she walks. The family counselor can normalize these feelings, help the parents grieve the loss of their hopes and dreams for their child, and refocus on the child's strengths and abilities.

Rereading the description from the first session with the Manning-Kelly family, one hears both verbal and nonverbal messages that suggest Liz may be overly involved with Emma. While this dynamic may have arisen because Emma is so much younger than Christina and Martin Jr., there may also be an unspoken assumption within the family that Emma is more helpless because of her cerebral palsy. A family counselor could help Liz redirect some of her attention to the developmental needs of her older children, which include their need for a mother to whom they feel important.

Finally, when a child is born with special needs or becomes chronically ill, her or his parents may each cope differently. The family counselor can assess the adaptability of the marital relationship, to facilitate prevention or treatment of marital deterioration secondary to discrepancies in how the parents cope. Liz chose to sit with Emma and apart from Mark in the first session, and Emma spoke only to Liz. A family counselor would wonder whether Mark has been excluded or removed himself from Liz and Emma's relationship and, as a result, whether intervention can restore whatever previous closeness may have existed between Liz and Mark.

Barbara's breast cancer is in remission, which means there is no evidence of cancer cells. However, until a patient has been cancer free for an extended period of time, usually 5 years, she is not considered cured. The risk that the cancer will recur decreases over time and eventually returns to the level of the general population in the absence of a recurrence, or relapse. In the interim, patients and their families experience a great deal of uncertainty about the future. To fully assess the impact of this uncertainty on the family, it is important to ask what the initial diagnosis and treatment were, how long the patient has been in remission, and whether she has relapsed. If, for example, Liz said her sister was diagnosed with stage 3 cancer (metastatic), underwent a mastectomy followed by chemotherapy and radiation, and had been cancer free for 2 months and also claimed she was not worried about her sister's health, the discrepancy between the facts and her stated reaction would be worth pursuing. If, on the other hand, Liz said her sister was diagnosed with stage 1 cancer, underwent a lumpectomy, did not require further treatment, and had been cancer free for 3 1/2 years, her lack of worry would be consistent with the facts and not require further exploration by the family counselor.

During treatment, immediate family members often turn to friends and extended family members for assistance. Barbara and Pete's adult children were not available to help on a regular basis. Paul lived too far away to visit frequently, even though he took time off work to be with his parents during Barbara's hospitalizations. Patricia was pregnant and had a very young child and said she could not be with her mother during every chemotherapy and radiation treatment. Sally, Barbara's mother, was in her 70s and attempting to care for her husband, Jim, at home because they do not think his Alzheimer's requires assisted living yet. And David, her brother, could not be counted upon. Pete worked full time, had already taken family medical leave during Barbara's hospitalizations, and so had turned to Liz for help.

Given that Liz had a full-time job and 3 children for whom she assumed primary responsibility, additional time demands to help with Barbara's care may have placed increased stress on her and her family. It cannot be overemphasized that while family counselors cannot treat biomedical diseases, they can be enormously helpful with how the family copes and the mental health outcomes for family members. Imagine a situation in which Liz tried to balance her career with the needs of her husband and children and then added 5 or 6 hours a week rotating with Pete driving Barbara to treatments and helping them at home. Add conflict about Mark's belief that Barbara's adult children needed to find a way to help out more. Finally, consider that Liz might have wished to protect her aging mother, who was coping with her stepfather's deterioration, from worry about her older daughter. This was a cauldron of stress over which Liz had little control and that may have produced both emotional and physical symptoms and exacerbated Christina and Martin Jr.'s negative behaviors in response to even less attention from their mother. Notice also that Sally has been excluded from requests for help without anyone asking her what she preferred.

STOP AND THINK:

1. Have you, a close friend, or a family member experienced a significant biomedical condition? If yes, how has that affected the patient and her or his family?

2. Have you known anyone your age who has lost a parent? How have her or his friends reacted? How have you reacted?

3. Some people, especially when they are young, do not want others to know they are suffering from a biomedical condition. How would you react if a friend told you she or he had been diagnosed with a chronic biomedical condition such as multiple sclerosis, chronic fatigue syndrome, diabetes, or cancer?

FAMILIES COPING WITH MENTAL
AND SUBSTANCE ABUSE DISORDERS

Mental disorders and substance abuse have been combined in this section. Most diagnostic systems and insurance policies combine mental health and substance abuse under the same umbrella. Both bridge the biomedical and psychosocial aspects of the biopsychosocial model. It has been estimated that as many as 90% of psychotherapy and counseling clients have been affected by substance abuse in some way. Estimates of mental illness also suggest a significant part of the population has experienced a family member's struggle with mental illness, if not their own.

Mental Disorders. Whenever an individual or family presents for counseling, there is an assumption that some mental disorder exists. In the present mental health funding climate, a mental disorder must be diagnosed in order for clients to qualify for financial reimbursement from their health insurance plan. It is beyond the scope of this textbook to cover the process and criteria for diagnosing a mental disorder. Instead, its impact on families will be the focus of this section.

Like aging and biomedical diseases, the presence of a mental disorder in one member of a family affects other members of that family. Sometimes, as when a member is depressed, she or he withdraws from the family, resulting in hurt and anger in the spouse and a feeling of abandonment and unlovability for the children. At other times, the disorder's symptoms can be frightening, as when a thought-disordered family member makes statements that appear detached from the rest of the family's reality or a substance abuser becomes angry or violent. The family may organize around denying or preventing these outbursts, creating anxiety and a sense that emotional closeness is not safe.

An examination of the Manning-Kelly family genogram reveals a multigenerational history of eating disorders. Sally was described as concerned about her daughters' appearance and attractiveness, and both Barbara and Liz have restricted intake. Christina described Liz as exercising more than any of her friends' mothers, suggesting that Liz may overexercise. Eating disorders are associated with a number of biomedical problems and can be life threatening. Family counselors often work with physicians and nutritionists when treating clients with eating disorders.

There is some indication that David suffers from a mental disorder beyond polysubstance abuse. However, mental health issues cannot be diagnosed when an abuser or addict is using. Whether his behavior has been influenced by both a mental disorder and polysubstance abuse or only one of these, it has resulted in a cutoff (Chapter 8) with his son, Carl. How his father's behavior has affected Carl is unknown because he is also cut off from his father's extended family.

STOP AND THINK:

Mental illness is often stigmatized in our culture.

1. What is your family's attitude toward mental illness and mental health counseling?

2. How might your family's attitude affect you when a client exhibits symptoms of mental illness or reports a previous diagnosis?

3. How might your family's attitude affect you if a client says she or he should not be in counseling because it is only for weak people who cannot fix their own problems?

Substance Abuse. Substance abuse is a mental health issue. There are also physiological components of addiction. Substance abuse refers to the use of alcohol, prescription medication, or illegal drugs in such a way that the client's health, occupational/educational, psychological, or social functioning is compromised. For example, a physician might tell her or his patient that the amount of alcohol she or he consumes may be associated with decreased liver functioning and continuing to drink may be life threatening. If the patient continues to drink, she or he is abusing alcohol. Another patient may go to multiple physicians and pharmacies complaining of the same symptom in order to obtain multiple prescriptions for the same medication to which she or he is addicted. Abusing various substances not only might undermine relationships with friends and family members but also may cause legal problems, such as drinking while driving citations, underage drinking, and possession of illegal substances or prescription medications without a prescription.

A family counselor looking at the Manning-Kelly family genogram would notice that substance abuse appears in at least two generations in Liz's family of origin and that her second husband, Mark, also appears to be abusing alcohol. Bill, Liz's father, died of cardiovascular disease associated with his drinking, and there is a history of alcohol abuse among her mother, Sally's, siblings and parents. The genogram tells us nothing about the use of drugs and alcohol by any of the teenaged and young adult children in Christina's generation. It also reveals nothing about substance use in Martin's or Mark's families. Because family counselors use genograms to assess the presence of multigenerational issues, it would be helpful to ask about prescription medication use and abuse and experimentation or use of nonprescription drugs, as well as alcohol use, throughout the family. Because of their history of restricting food intake, both Liz and Christina also may be at risk of abusing appetite suppressors in all forms.

STOP AND THINK:

Substance abuse may be even more stigmatized than mental illness.

1. What are your views about substance abuse and the people who abuse substances?

2. How might those views affect you as a counselor when a client tells you she or he or a family member is a substance abuser?

DOMESTIC VIOLENCE AND CHILD ABUSE

Bent-Goodley (2001) defined domestic violence as repetitive assault and/or coercion. Domestic violence can be physical, sexual, or emotional. When coercive, it can include threats, stalking, and withholding of money, love, food, and other necessities of life. Power and intentionality can be assumed, although neither may be conscious on the part of the perpetrator.

Domestic violence usually refers to an abusive relationship between domestic partners. Although victims may experience their situation as precluding escape and may, in fact, be threatened with violence if they leave, the presumption is that they are physically, if not emotionally, capable of escaping the violence. By contrast, child, elder, and dependent abuse is perpetrated against someone who is unable to physically leave the situation. While the legal status of dependents, including minor children and the elderly, differs from that of domestic partners, the family counselor has a clinical role in both situations.

Family counselors are responsible for assessing the possible, or suspected, presence of domestic violence and child, elder, and dependent abuse. Because of their prevalence, it is important to attend to the possibility of physical, emotional, or sexual abuse in any client family. Family counselors are also responsible for providing a partner who is the victim of domestic violence with information about safety, as well as her or his counseling options. Finally, family counselors are among the professionals who are bound by reporting laws to inform the appropriate authorities when they suspect a minor child, elder, or disabled person is being, has been, and in some cases, is at risk of being abused or neglected.

The presence, history, or risk of domestic violence or child, elder, and dependent abuse is more likely to emerge during family counseling sessions than during an initial assessment of the family. Family counselors who routinely work with families in which domestic violence or child, elder, and dependent abuse has occurred may see families for which the violence or abuse is the presenting problem. All family counselors must be sensitive to risk factors and willing to ask about domestic violence and abuse because of its prevalence, as well as because of their obligation to protect clients.

What follows is an excerpt from a session with the Manning-Kelly family demonstrating how family counselors might learn about domestic violence when it is not the presenting problem. Prior to this session, the family counselor did not suspect the presence of any kind of domestic violence or child, elder, or dependent abuse.

FC:	Last week was a powerful session, and I'm wondering how this week has been.
Liz:	Good. Christina and I had a wonderful talk after last week's session, and she's agreed to explore options for a gap year after high school.
FC:	That's great.
C:	[Glares at her mother]
FC:	What's up, Christina?
C:	Nothing.
FC:	Liz?
Liz:	Sometimes she's still so angry at me. And I never know what I've done.
FC:	Christina?
C:	[To her mother] Nothing. [To FC] I don't know what she's talking about.
Liz:	I wasn't even home most of last week. What could I have done? [To FC] I rarely have to travel for work. I don't like to, and no one is used to it. If that's the problem, I don't know what more I can do about it.

FC: Sounds like it's difficult for everyone.

Liz: Yes. Emma went to my sister, Barbara's, and as you know, she doesn't like to be away from me. But Barbara is wonderful, and I left dinners in the freezer that Mark or Christina could fix. [Pause. To Christina] It was only 4 days.

Martin Jr., who is usually very still, began fidgeting, and Mark repeatedly tapped his right toe. Emma stopped coloring and attempted to get her mother's attention. Christina looked away.

FC: I must be missing something. The tension in the room suddenly became enormous.

C: You think?

Liz: [Simultaneously] I'm not sure what you mean.

FC: [Pause] I'm also curious as to why Emma didn't stay at home while you were away.

C: [Sarcastically] She's safer with Aunt Barbara.

Liz: Christina!

FC: Safer?

C: He [Indicating Mark with a head gesture] can't take care of anything. Not even himself. [Her face contorts with rage and disgust.]

Liz: Christina! He's your father.

C: No! He is not my father! He's your husband. I guess.

Liz: I don't like your tone.

C: Have you ever wondered why Ashley doesn't speak to him . . .

Liz: That's complicated, Christina. You don't understand it.

C: . . . and Emma is afraid to be anywhere you're not when he's home?

Liz: I don't know where you're going with this, Christina, but I don't like it.

Mark: [To Liz] You know she lies. She's told you she's stopped cutting, but I caught her while you were away.

C:	Tell her how you did that, Mark.
FC:	Tell me how he did that, Christina.
C:	[Beginning to cry] He came into my room. [Angrily to Liz] He does that, you know, sometimes even when you're home.
FC:	He came into your room?
Liz:	Christina, this is completely out of line.
FC:	Mark?
Mark:	Who knows. Something she made up in her head.
C:	[Expletive] you, Mark.
Liz:	Christina!
FC:	I'm confused. Did you "catch" her cutting when you went into her room or somewhere else?
C:	[To FC] He knows exactly what I'm talking about. And she [Indicating her mother with a head gesture] does, too. Or she's more out of it than I think she is.
Liz:	[Softly] What . . . ?
C:	Yeah, Mom.
Mark:	Liz!
FC:	Christina, could you fill me in about what you and your mom are talking about?
Mark:	[To FC] I can't believe you're listening to this lying brat.
Liz:	[To Mark] Watch how you talk about her.

Mark gets up and begins to walk toward the door.

FC:	Mark, I need you to stay.
Mark:	And I need to sue your incompetent [Expletive].
FC:	For now, we need to finish this conversation, and it would be better with you in the room. [To Christina] I need you to tell me what happened when he caught you cutting.

C:	[Crying, head bent forward] He, he locked the door, like he always does. And he hit me and called me a little slut, like he always does. And then . . . No . . .
FC:	I know it's hard. But we need to protect you, and we can't if you won't tell us what you need protecting from.
C:	[Looking at FC] Don't you know?
FC:	I think I do, and I don't want to make an assumption. It's too important.
C:	He told me to shut up, and then he pushed me. And then he held me down and . . . and . . .
FC:	[Gently] And what?
C:	[Looking down again and crying harder] And then, you know, he touched me and things, made me do things. [To FC] Please don't make me say more.

Liz has also started to cry as she stares at Christina. Mark's face is very red. Emma is trying to get her mother's attention by patting her, hard and repeatedly, and Liz is ignoring her. Martin Jr. is shaking his head and mumbling, "Oh no, oh no, oh no."

FC:	No. That's fine, Christina. I know that was very, very difficult. For you, for all of you.
Mark:	[To Liz] You believe her? And this [Expletive] counselor? Your darling Christina who every boy in school has had it off with, and you believe her?
Martin Jr.:	Hey!
Mark:	[To Martin Jr.]: You stay out of this if you know what's good for you.
Liz:	[Simultaneously] Shut up, Mark. [To Martin Jr.] It's ok, MJ.
FC:	I cannot even imagine the pain you're all in at this moment. The only good thing is that now that it's out in the open, your mom can protect you all, and you can begin to repair your relationships. But first, Mark and Liz, as I mentioned in my intake materials, this is the sort of thing I'm required to report.

Liz:	No. You can't. He's an attorney. This will ruin him.
C:	You didn't say that.
Liz:	I'm sorry. I'm so sorry, Christina. [To FC] Go on.
FC:	There are several ways to handle this. I can make the call, with or without you here, or you can make the call, though I'll need to be in the room with you. The choice is yours.
Mark:	[To Liz] I cannot believe you. Your precious daughter is lying, you're siding with her and this incompetent [Expletive] of a therapist who's done her best to undermine our family and is going to lose her license and everything else that matters to her before I'm finished, and if you don't get off it you're going to lose me, you'll have another failed marriage to explain to the next poor jerk who gets mixed up with you.
Liz:	What marriage, Mark?
Mark:	Good question. But I suppose if you'd taken the time to be a wife after you got Emma from me . . . [Gets up again. To FC] You'll regret this until the day you die.
Liz:	[Screaming as he leaves] Don't blame me for this, or her. [Gets up and walks to put her arms around Christina, Emma remaining at the chair her mother has just vacated] Honey, my sweet daughter, why didn't you tell me?
C:	[Sobbing] I thought you knew.

STOP AND THINK:

1. What are your reactions to this transcript of the family counseling session?
2. What is your reaction to Mark? To Christina? To Liz?

The family counselor must now not only report the sexual abuse but also help the family heal from it. Once reported, a legal process will begin over which the family counselor has no control. However, she may be called upon to release her case notes about the family and to testify if the case goes to trial. At the same time, the family may ask for her professional services as they go through the process, including helping them make decisions and heal the relationship wounds brought about by multiple violations of trust. Christina may also need individual counseling for symptoms of trauma and to ensure her self-esteem and long-term relationships are not adversely affected by the experience of being abused.

Many family counselors believe that the nonabusive parent always knows about the abuse, and, as a result, the victim's anger at the nonabusive parent for allowing the abuse to occur and repeat must be addressed as part of the family's healing. Liz reacted to her daughter's revelation by believing, comforting, and apologizing to Christina. Not all nonabusing parents do what Liz did. Rather, some refuse to believe the victim or blame her or him for encouraging the abuser. The mental health consequences for both the victim and the family are deeper and more prolonged when the nonabusing parent denies the reality of the abuse.

CONCLUSION

You have read about eight issues, or special topics families bring to counseling. All family counselors need some competence in each of these issues, because they will see families struggling with them over the course of their careers. However, these issues are often accompanied by needs for service beyond what a family counselor is trained or licensed to do. In Part IV, you will learn about situations in which families require family services other than family counseling and what other services are available to families. First, however, we will address the experience of the family counselor and the ethics involved in the practice of family counseling.

REFERENCES

Abrams, K. K., LaRue, A., & Gray, J. J. (1993). Disordered eating attitudes and behaviors, psychological adjustment, and ethnic identity: A comparison of black and white female college students. *International Journal of Eating Disorders, 14*(1), 49–57.

Basirico, L. A., Cashion, B. G., & Eshleman, J. R. (2014). *Introduction to sociology* (6th ed.). Redding, CA: BVT.

Bent-Goodley, T. B. (2001). Eradicating domestic violence in the African American community. *Trauma Violence Abuse, 2*(4), 316–330.

Diller, J. V. (2007). *Cultural diversity: A primer for the human services* (3rd ed.). Belmont, CA: Brooks/Cole.

Lum, D. (2007). *Culturally competent practice. A framework for understanding diverse groups and justice issues* (3rd ed.). Belmont, CA: Brooks/Cole.

Minuchin, S. (1974). *Families & family therapy.* Cambridge, MA: Harvard University Press.

Mulholland, A. M., & Mintz, L. B. (2001). Prevalence of eating disorders among African American women. *Journal of Counseling Psychology, 48*(1), 111–116.

Tatum, B. D. (1997). *"Why are all the black kids sitting together in the cafeteria?" and other conversations about race.* New York, NY: Basic Books.

Williams, M. T. (2011). Guess who's coming to dinner? *Psychology Today, 12/29/2011.*

FOR FURTHER STUDY

Atwood, J. (1992). A systemic-behavioral approach to counseling the single-parent family. In J. Atwood (Ed.), *Family therapy: A systemic behavioral approach* (pp. 191–206). Chicago, IL: Nelson-Hall.

Braithwaite, D., Olson, L., Golish, T., Soukup, C., & Turman, P. (2001). Becoming a family. Developmental process represented in blended family discourse. *Journal of Applied Communication Research, 29*(3), 221–247.

Carlson, J., & Sperry, L. (2005). Tailoring treatment: The impact of culture. In *Family therapy techniques: Integrating and tailoring treatment* (pp. 121–139). New York, NY: Routledge.

Carlson, J., & Sperry, L. (2005). Tailoring treatment: Families under stress. In *Family therapy techniques: Integrating and tailoring treatment* (pp. 143–164). New York, NY: Routledge.

Corey, M. (2007). Knowing your values. In *Becoming a Helper* (6th ed., pp. 39–63). Belmont, CA: Brooks/Cole.

Doherty, W. J., & Baird, M. A. (1984). *Family therapy and family medicine.* New York, NY: Guilford Press.

Gonzales, J. (2009). Prefamily counseling. Working with blended families. *Journal of Divorce and Remarriage, 50,* 148–157.

Howell, L. C., Weers, R., & Kleist, D. M. (1998). Counseling blended families. *The Family Journal, 6*(1), 42–45.

Koch, A. Y. (1983). Family adaptation to medical stressors. *Family Systems Medicine, 1*(4), 78–87.

Koch-Hattem, A. (1987). Families and chronic illness. In D. Rosenthal (Ed.). *Family stress* (pp. 33–50). Rockville, MD: Aspen.

Liepman, M. R., Silvia, L. Y., & Nirenberg, T. D. (1989). The use of family behavior loop map ping for substance abuse. *National Council on Family Relations, 38*(3), 282–287.

Meyer, G. (1992). Family therapy with divorcing and remarried families. In J. Atwood (Ed.), *Family therapy: A systemic behavioral approach* (pp. 159–173). Chicago, IL: Nelson-Hall.

Morgan, O. J., & Lizke, C. H. (2012). *Family interventions in substance abuse. Current best practices.* New York, NY: Routledge.

Patterson, J., Williams, L., Edwards, T., Chamow, L., & Grauf-Grounds, C. (2009). When a family member has a mental illness. In *Essential skills in family therapy: From the first interview to termination* (2nd ed.). New York, NY: Guilford Press.

Rockquemore, K. A., & Laszloffy, T. A. (2003). Multiple realities. A relationship narrative approach in therapy with black-white mixed-race clients. *Family Relations, 52*(2), 119–128.

Shalay, N., & Brownlee, K. (2007). Narrative family therapy with blended families. *Journal of Family Psychotherapy, 18*(2), 17–30.

Smith, A., & Cok-Cottone, C. (2011). A review of family therapy as an effective intervention for anorexia nervosa in adolescents. *Journal of Clinical Psychology in Medical Settings, 18*, 323–334.

CHAPTER 10

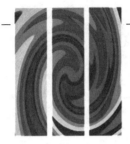

The Counselor's Experience Working With Families

The majority of this family counseling textbook has focused on the clients who seek family counseling. But what about the family counselors who work with them? Family counselors are also people who participate in relationships with their clients. Family counselors have feelings about their clients, themselves in relationship to their clients, what is happening in their personal and professional lives in addition to counseling a particular family, and the work of family counseling. Family counselors work with multiple clients, have lives and demands made upon them outside of work, and need to find balance between their professional and personal selves as well as practice the self-care necessary to function in multiple settings and avoid unethical behaviors associated with burnout.

In this chapter, we examine what it is like to work with families and what family counselors need to do for themselves in order to work effectively and professionally. This chapter is in no way exhaustive of the topic. Like the rest of this book, it is intended to provide you with an introduction to the concepts, practices, and experiences of family counselors.

THE POWER OF FAMILY SYSTEMS

Just as the family as a system is more powerful than its individual members, so the family system is more powerful than the family counselor as an individual. Some family counselors approach families from a theoretical perspective that views the family counselor as expert authority (Haley, 1963). The family counselor as expert helps level the playing field when working with a family. Other family counselors embrace a one-down position, using their position to build a healing relationship with the client family and empower its members to participate in their own growth and change (Napier & Whitaker, 1978). Still others view the relationship collaboratively, despite the power of the family system over any one individual including the counselor (Dulwich Centre, 2015).

Whatever theoretical model informs your work as a family counselor, it remains important to be respectful of the power of the family system. As an entity that is greater than the sum of its parts, the family system can be conceptualized as existing somewhat independently of its individual members. Thus, the family counselor's relationships with individual members are insufficient to address the family counselor's relationship with the family as a whole.

Additionally, as we have seen in Chapter 4, family systems strive to maintain equilibrium. So, as unhappy as members may be, change risks destabilizing that equilibrium and members also tend to fear the consequences. Sometimes, in fact, the consequences are devastating. Often, however, they are not, and the fear of change is far worse than the consequences of the change. Working with individuals, a counselor can explain this phenomenon and examine the client's specific fears about changing. The dynamics of the family are usually outside family members' awareness and therefore more difficult to address with them. Yet, as with individuals, nothing will be revealed that wasn't there already. It is simply a matter of making the covert overt (Sager, 1981) and dealing with it so that it stops interfering with both individual and family functioning.

Since this is an abstract way of viewing the family, let us examine a specific example from the Manning-Kelly and Jones families. In Chapter 6, you read transcripts from their first two family counseling sessions. You read about the repetitive arguments between Christina and her mother, Liz, in the first session and saw a glimpse of the repetitive argument between her mother and father, Martin, in the transcript of the second session. These two arguments, being repetitive, are part of the family dynamics, locking members into particular roles. As suggested in Chapter 1, Christina may not be able to decide what she wants to do after high school until she no longer has to defend what may have started as one of several possibilities and then congealed through her response to her mother's response into her position. Similarly, these repetitive fights isolate Liz, because while Christina is supported by her father, stepmother, and to some extent her brother Martin Jr., Liz has no one. Her husband, Mark, is emotionally distant from the family and acknowledges he does not become involved in the specifics of parenting Liz's children. It was not until the family counselor was willing to challenge the effect of the family dynamics that isolate Liz that these two arguments could begin to change.

When the family counselor pointed out Liz's isolation, she was bringing the family dynamics from a covert, unacknowledged position to an overt one that could no longer be ignored (Sager, 1981).

The Manning-Kelly family also illustrates how a family life cycle event can threaten a family system's equilibrium. Christina is preparing to be launched into adulthood, and that change alone will alter the family system. In this case, the repetitive argument between Liz and Christina, like Liz's overinvolvement with Emma's disability, keeps Liz focused away from her husband's drinking and distance. Perhaps the family system is subtly encouraging Christina not to leave, because leaving would result in Emma's development being even more impeded by the family system's need to keep children dependent on Liz so Liz will not confront Mark about his drinking and disengagement from her and the family. In a family in which the marital subsystem is strong, young adult children leaving home may be sad and yet is not threatening to the family system. It is only when children distract their parents from problems within their couple subsystem that family life cycle changes are threatening.

It is not uncommon for repetitive arguments such as those in the Manning-Kelly and Jones families to continue despite the family counselor's intervention. The family system requires members to function in a way that maintains its equilibrium. Additionally, the family is, by definition, stronger than the individual members or the family counselor. Thus, the logic that no one likes the argument is insufficient to stop it. So is suggesting various alternatives to arguing. In sum, it is incredibly difficult for families to change their dynamics, because the system will strive to maintain equilibrium and is also greater than the individuals who comprise it and wish to change it. Family counselors must be able to tolerate frustration and uncertainty about when and under what circumstances the family will be willing to risk disequilibrium in order to attain a new way of interacting. This tolerance for frustration and uncertainty rarely is natural and must be cultivated by the family counselor.

HOW FAMILIES INDUCE FAMILY COUNSELORS INTO THE FAMILY SYSTEM

Because family members usually become used to their distress and on some level accept it as the price they pay for the security of the family system's equilibrium, they not only may be reluctant to change but also feel threatened by the family counselor's attempts to help them change. In other words, the family system may be highly motivated to induce the family counselor into itself so that she or he will refrain from efforts to place it in disequilibrium. There is usually pressure, often subtle, on the family counselor to accept the status quo even as the family asks the counselor for help changing.

The Manning-Kelly and Jones families provide an excellent example of this phenomenon. Liz was convinced of two things: (1) Christina's eating and cutting behaviors were not as severe as the primary care physician believed them to be, and (2) it was crucial for Christina's future that she first visit and then apply to college for the fall following high school graduation. Christina and the rest of the family agreed with Liz's first belief. However, Christina was as convinced that she needed to experience life, work, and prepare for her role as a stay-at-home mother instead of going directly to college as Liz was that such a course of action would ruin her life. While the family counselor viewed the family's dynamics as the focus for change, the family members would have preferred that she accepted their view that Christina was fine and take sides in the conflict between Liz and Christina about Christina's immediate future. The pull on the family counselor was powerful, and yet succumbing to it would have undermined family counseling by taking the counselor's focus off of changing the family dynamics.

One of the challenges family counselors face is how to decline pressure to be induced into the family system without denying the family's members' reality. If the family counselor ignores the experiences of the individual family members, she or he risks leaving them feeling unheard and, as a result, mistrustful of the family counselor. Unfortunately, there is no simple solution to recommend. At best, family counselors must be alert to both the family system dynamics and the need to empathize with each family member. Unfortunately, the pressure to maintain the family system's equilibrium sometimes undermines family counseling. Inducing the family counselor into the family system is an effective mechanism to protect the system from the disequilibrium that accompanies change while also undermining the desire for change that brought the family to counseling.

An example of induction into the family system involves pressure on the family counselor to agree that the presenting problem resides in the identified patient rather than the family system. Had the family counselor agreed that Christina's eating and cutting disorders or her refusal to explore college as an option for the fall following high school graduation was the problem, there would have been no threat to the equilibrium of the family system. However, by hypothesizing that the family dynamics aimed at avoiding the distress in Liz and Mark's marriage were the true problem, the family counselor threatened the family's equilibrium by engaging in techniques aimed at redefining and addressing the family dynamics. Transcripts in Part II of this book illustrate this point, as do arguments between Liz and the family counselor later in this chapter.

STOP AND THINK:

1. Find specific examples of how the Manning-Kelly and Jones families attempted to engage the family counselor in their view that Christina, the identified patient, was the problem.

2. How, specifically, did the family attempt to induce the family counselor to accept their view?

3. How might you handle the temptation to take sides in the family's situation?

MANAGING MULTIPLE RELATIONSHIPS

When doing individual counseling, there is one relationship to attend to during sessions, the one between the client and the counselor. When doing family counseling, there are multiple relationships to attend to and manage. These include the relationship between the family counselor and each family member, the relationships among the family members with each other, the relationships both within and among various groups (spousal, sibling, parent-child) within the family and between each of these groups and the family counselor, and the relationship between the family as a whole and the family counselor. We have already discussed the power of the family system. In this section, you will become acquainted with the multiple relationships a family counselor must also manage.

Sometimes, these relationships conflict with one another. For example, as already described, the family system maintains its equilibrium by avoiding change, and so, while family members may be unhappy and turn to the counselor for help, the family as a whole may resist the family counselor's efforts to disrupt its equilibrium. Additionally, what is good for one family member may not be good for another member or for the family as a whole. In the Manning-Kelly family, for example, Christina's symptoms and Emma's dependency may both have masked the marital conflict between Liz and Mark and thus served a positive function of maintaining the family's equilibrium. However, anorexia, cutting, and age-inappropriate dependency are not beneficial to Christina and Emma as individuals.

How does a family counselor manage the multiple relationships, their complexity, and the conflicts among them? We have previously discussed this challenge in terms of the family counselor needing to avoid being induced into the family and taking sides regarding the labeling of the identified patient. It is also important that the family counselor facilitate the family's ability to balance individual and group needs in a way that works best for the family and its members. This not only empowers the family but also allows for cultural and value differences between the family counselor and any particular family.

Even when knowledge of child abuse emerged, the family counselor did not decide what the family needed to do. She did, however, comply with the laws of the state in which she practiced, as specified in her intake forms and took the required step of reporting the abuse. Note that in carrying out her legal obligation, she offered the family options for how she would report the abuse, specifically whether she would report with or without the family present or they would report with her present. It was then up to state officials to decide what happened next.

Being human, family counselors are drawn to some people more than others. So of course we find ourselves sometimes drawn more to some members of a client family than to others. For example, the family counselor found Mark's distance from his family and irritability with her off-putting even before she learned he had been abusing Christina. She also liked Liz and empathized with the many ways she seemed stuck in her position and isolated from her family.

STOP AND THINK:

1. Have you ever read a book or seen a movie that, while well written, was full of characters you disliked? Did you finish reading the book or watching the movie? If you did, how did you cope with your dislike of the characters, and were you tempted to stop reading or watching at any point?

2. Which family member in the Manning-Kelly and Jones families do you feel most drawn to, and why?

3. To whom do you react the most negatively, and why?

4. What can a family counselor do when she or he likes and sympathizes with one family member more than others?

5. What can she or he do when she or he experiences a strong dislike of one of the family members?

Clients may find it difficult to trust someone who does not like them. Similarly, family counselors may find it difficult to do their best for people they dislike. It therefore becomes essential for family counselors to examine their feelings, both positive and negative, about the members of client families. This involves the family counselor

1. being honest with herself or himself about what she or he likes and dislikes about each family member,

2. examining what those preferences say about her or him, and

3. asking herself or himself what she or he may be overlooking about each family member.

It may be helpful to remember that people tend to do the best they can, given who they are and their circumstances, so that you view characteristics or behaviors you dislike as genuine though ineffective attempts on the part of family members to be likable people.

Family counselors must also manage family members' behaviors toward one another. Some members talk for one another, others interrupt, and some are hostile and challenging to other family members and/or the family counselor.

STOP AND THINK:

1. How might a family counselor set limits on one family member's behavior without intimidating other family members who are behaving respectfully?

2. How might she or he avoid conveying judgment that a family member is rude or mean? In a role-play, practice setting these limits with another classmate.

Family counselors need to be self-aware in order to effectively manage the multiple relationships that the practice of family counseling involves. They need to recognize when they are feeling annoyed or judgmental and quickly soothe themselves. They need to remember that the family requires firm and respectfully conveyed limits from a caring family counselor, and that they are capable of providing that. They need to remind themselves that they can deal with their hurt or outrage or disgust or whatever other negative feelings may arise, though not during the session. This is very similar to what family counselors need to do when clients raise their personal issues:

1. Note it.

2. Avoid allowing it to leak into the work with the client family.

3. Deal with it outside of the time the counselor is working with the family.

As described in the section about avoiding induction into the family system, family counselors also need to avoid accepting the family's views about its members and instead form their own clinical impressions. It is tempting to see Christina's eating and cutting disorders or Liz's repetitious revisiting of the college discussion as the problems. However, viewing Christina as a self-harming and obstinate mess and her mother as a badgering nag would not have been conducive to effectively helping the family. Additionally, neither view was the entire story. What was relevant to the family counselor was that both Christina's and Liz's behaviors were ways of dealing with a family system dynamic that was not working for them as individuals or for the family as a whole, and that neither would be able to change her behavior until that dynamic was addressed. It was the family counselor's job to remind herself that the family had the potential to change in a way that would leave its members more likable.

Finally, one or more family members may remind the family counselor of someone she or he holds negative feelings about. Once again, self-awareness is key. The counselor can use her or his self-awareness to remind herself or himself that the client and the other person are not the same. The family counselor may need to remind herself or himself of this fact repeatedly during sessions.

COMFORT WITH DIVERSITY

STOP AND THINK:

1. What has your experience of diversity been?

2. Were you raised in a multicultural or homogenous community?

3. Were you raised in a multicultural family?

4. What were your parents' and grandparents' attitudes toward people who looked or behaved differently than they did?

5. If you are *not* a White, middle- or upper-class, Christian, straight male, how have you been treated by the dominant society with respect to your "deviant" characteristics (non-White, working poor or impoverished, non-Christian, female or transgendered, gay or lesbian or bisexual), and what are your feelings about that treatment?

6. If you *are* a White, middle- or upper-class Christian, straight male, how has your privileged position in the dominant culture affected how people treat you, and what are your feelings about that treatment?

7. How might your personal and family histories impact your experience working with families who do not share your demographic or cultural background?

Multicultural issues and the need for family counselors to be culturally competent were discussed in Chapter 9, and references were provided for students who wish to learn more about culturally competent counseling than is possible to address in an introductory textbook. This section of this chapter turns the focus to the person of the family counselor experiencing the practice of her or his profession.

Two situations come to mind. In the first, the family counselor is a member of the dominant culture. He has had no personal experience of being discriminated against and is aware that his situation reflects White privilege or freedom from being treated as less-than because of race, ethnicity, socioeconomic status, gender, religion, age, sexual preference, or other characteristics. White women share many of the privileges associated with being White, although there is variation based on other personal and familial characteristics, and both need to assume a non-White family has had a very different and less generally positive experience.

The second situation involves a family counselor of color working with families who are either White or of a different race or ethnicity than the counselor. Differences may include biracial or bicultural families, even though one of the races or cultures is the same as the counselor's.

Diller (2007) and Lum (2007) summarize various approaches to cultural competence, including the contributions of various mental health professions. Although there are many ways to conceptualize and label the essential skill set for culturally competent counseling practice, for purposes of introducing you to the topic, Diller's (2007, p.18) five cultural competent skill areas are included here. These are awareness and acceptance; self-awareness; dynamics of difference; knowledge of client's culture; and adaptation of skills. Awareness and acceptance involve being aware of, valuing, and creatively using cultural differences in one's counseling practice. Self-awareness requires counselors to recognize the potential impact of their own ethnicity and attitudes on their clients and actively working to mitigate it. Dynamics of difference involves the family counselor being alert to potential miscommunication and misunderstanding because of the cultural differences between counselors and clients and using their clinical skills to resolve them as they arise. Knowledge of client's culture is self-evident. Culturally competent counselors seek information from experts, members of the particular culture, and clients themselves in order to more fully understand the client within her or his cultural context. Finally, adaptation of skills involves adapting counseling theory, assessment, and intervention to account for cultural differences and to more fully serve clients.

Clients differ dramatically in their level of acculturation to the dominant culture, as well as in the ways their own culture and interactions with members of the dominant culture have affected them. Thus, it is as culturally incompetent to apply a one-size-fits-all model to every member of any one cultural or racial group as it is to ignore the impact of culture on the client family. To practice ethically, family counselors need to recognize and respect the uniqueness of each client family and its members while remaining accepting of and adaptable to cultural differences.

Family counselors who are not part of the dominant, White culture are usually far more accustomed to adapting themselves to culturally different individuals, groups, and institutions than White family counselors are. The concept of White privilege specifically refers to the reality that Whites rarely think about racial issues, whereas non-Whites are confronted not only by racism but also by the need to adapt to the dominant culture in order to succeed in it. Thus, the challenges of practicing culturally competent counseling may differ for counselors of different races and ethnicities. Whatever an individual family counselor's challenges are, it remains imperative for her or him to learn to practice in a culturally competent manner.

Culturally competent family counselors also need to recognize the unique needs of bicultural, biracial, multicultural, and multiracial families. As noted in the previous chapter, Diller (2007) also pointed out that racial and ethnic tensions in the larger society are often played out within the family context, and children in biracial families such as the Manning-Kelly family face challenges that children in either Black or White families do not.

An example unrelated to the Manning-Kelly family involves one of the writers' experiences as a preschool teacher in a predominantly Native American prekindergarten setting. A member of the community told her that asking a direct question is indistinguishable from giving an order. Now, when working with Native American clients in her clinical practice, she is careful to word questions in a speculative and indirect manner.

EXPERIENCING THE FAMILY

We all grew up in families. Over the years, we have asked family counseling students to create a genogram (Chapter 3) for their own family. We have also asked family counseling students to apply some of the family concepts we discussed in lecture and this textbook, such as triangles and secrets, to their families. As family counselors learn during training and their work with families, every family has idiosyncrasies. Sometimes, families also exhibit serious dysfunction. It is important for family counselors to learn to distinguish between idiosyncrasy and dysfunction, both in the families with whom they work and in their own families.

Imagine for a moment that you have experienced conflict with your parents about your college major. They think you should choose a major that will prepare you for a high earning profession. You are taking a family counseling class, so unless you intend to use it in a medical school or legal practice, you are likely not headed for a large income. Because this hypothetical version of you has never felt that your family accepted or valued your career choice, you can easily empathize with Christina as her mother insists she choose the path that she, Liz, thinks is best for her, rather than the one she has chosen for herself. As the Manning-Kelly and Jones families' counselor, you would need to bear in mind that Liz is both isolated and defensive about her position that Christina should be preparing to apply to college in a few months, because as a young adult child who has felt the need to defend your right to choose a major and not empathize with your parents' fears for you it would be easy to overlook Liz's perspective. While avoiding empathizing with your own parents may be a coping tool in your interactions with them, avoiding empathizing with Liz would render you ineffective as a family counselor.

Bearing this distinction between your own family and your client families in mind requires you or anyone intending to practice family counseling to establish clear boundaries between your personal and professional lives. Further coursework and structured, frequent supervision during the early years of your work with families will facilitate the creation and maintenance of your boundaries. Additionally, you may decide to work with a counselor to be certain your own personal history does not interfere with your work as a counselor. When and how to decide whether any student of family counseling would benefit from seeking her or his own counseling is beyond the scope of this textbook. Your supervisor will be able to help you draw the line between supervision and your own counseling, and if your issues frequently cross it, that is an indication that going to counseling may be appropriate for you.

Returning to the Manning-Kelly and Jones families, think about what your own reactions might be if you were the family counselor in the following excerpt.

FC: So, Christina, it sounds as though it's important to you to take time after high school before going to college.

Liz: Are you telling her she doesn't need to go to college in the fall? Because it is way over the line for you to intrude in our lives in that way. I'm her mother, and I know what's best for her.

STOP AND THINK:

1.   Was it predictable that Liz might view empathy for Christina as undermining her authority as Christina's mother? Explain your answer.

2.   If Liz were to confront you and accuse you of undermining her mothering, how might you react? And how might you handle your reaction?

At this point, the family counselor could do one of several things: apologize to Liz, attempt to appease Liz, become defensive, address Liz's anger at her, or address the family dynamics evident in the exchange. We will continue this piece of the family counseling session in all five ways.

Scenario 1: Apologize to Liz

FC: Liz, I'm so sorry. I simply wanted to clarify that I'd heard what Christina said. The last thing in the world I want to do is undermine you.

Liz: Well, I want you to be clear with Christina that you don't support her.

Notice that the family counselor is now trapped. Telling Christina she does not support her is tantamount to saying she does not empathize with her. It will likely undermine any trust Christina has developed for the family counselor and thus the potential for effective intervention with Christina and her family in the future. Additionally, Liz now has the power to undermine the family counselor's interventions whenever she or the family system becomes uncomfortable.

Scenario 2: Appease Liz

FC: I was only clarifying and empathizing. That's my job, and I'm so sorry it upset you.

Liz: Well, I don't think Christina needs your empathy. What she needs is to listen.

Once again, the family counselor has trapped herself. For all practical purposes, she has agreed not to use empathy in her interactions with Christina. And without empathy, it may be difficult if not impossible for Christina to trust the family counselor. Additionally, the family counselor has aligned herself exclusively with Liz.

Scenario 3: Become defensive

FC: No, no. I'm not taking sides in this.

Liz: Really? Because it sounds as though you're telling her she doesn't have to go to college, and I don't appreciate that.

The family counselor has trapped herself for a third time. She now needs to convince Liz that her intention was not to disrupt the mother-daughter relationship, which would have been unethical, rather than continue her efforts to facilitate effective change in the relationship between Liz and Christina and in the family.

Scenario 4: Address Liz's anger at her

FC: You sound really angry at me, Liz, and I think it would be helpful for us to talk about it.

Remember, this is a family that avoids allowing conflict to continue until it resolves. One of the family counselor's goals is to demonstrate continuing conflict long enough to resolve it.

Liz: I'm not angry at you. I do think you should be more careful about your role here, though.

FC: Let's talk about that. When you say careful about my role here, I'm not sure exactly what you would like to be different. Please tell me what you'd like me to do differently.

Liz: I expect you to support my parenting, not undermine it. If you can't do that, then we can't keep seeing you.

FC: I wouldn't want it to come to you stopping counseling. My goal is to support everyone in the family. I'd like to let Christina know I've heard what she's saying while supporting you as her parent. Any suggestions about how I might do that?

| Liz: | You're the counselor. You tell me. |
| FC: | Let's both think about it. |

By avoiding arguing about whether Liz was angry and yet continuing to acknowledge there remained a problem to resolve, the family counselor was able to encourage Liz to engage with her in the process of resolving it. She also avoided becoming defensive in the face of Liz repeatedly challenging her. While they did not resolve their conflict, the family counselor communicated that she believed empathizing with Christina was not mutually exclusive with supporting Liz and modeled both empathetic listening and ways to proceed in the face of conflict. Both are positive; however, neither addresses family dynamics.

Scenario 5: Address the family dynamics

| FC: | Right now I'm feeling like I need to defend myself. And I'm curious whether that's how you all feel when the arguments about college begin. Martin Jr.? |
| MJ: | Yeah, I guess. |

Notice the difference in Scenario 5. In the first four scenarios, the family counselor was induced into the conflict between Liz and Christina. In the fifth, however, she used her experience of the family's attempt to induce her to address a dynamic she had not previously noticed. Liz did not interrupt, and the argument was deflected into the more productive focus on the family dynamic. We will return to how family counselors can use their experience of being induced into the family dynamic to change it later in this chapter.

If the family counselor had been re-experiencing her own conflict with her parents, she might have identified with Christina to the extent that she over-looked the possibility of Scenario 5. And this is the primary reason that, when families raise the family counselor's own issues, the family counselor needs to seek supervision or her own counseling so that her family issues do not inter-fere with her effectiveness while working with the family.

You may be thinking, most people would not be as hostile to an authority figure or someone from whom they have sought help, like a counselor, as Liz was in these scenarios. While many individuals may be hesitant to confront a counselor, some are quick to react, even if they feel anxiety or remorse about it later, and others do not hesitate to confront a counselor. Additionally, the family system frequently protects its equilibrium (Chapter 4) by covertly appointing one of the members to defend it. Whether that defense is Christina refusing to go to college or Liz confronting the family counselor is irrelevant from the perspective of the family's dynamics. In the scenarios, Liz was acting as the spokesperson for the Manning-Kelly family and thus protecting the family system as well as herself.

Many family counselors begin their careers feeling intimidated or put off by aggressive adult clients. New family counselors are often younger than the adult members of the families with whom they work and are also not yet secure in their ability to manage a group of people. To further complicate the situation, some family counselors were raised in families in which one or both parents were aggressive, either verbally or physically. And those who are attracted to family counseling as a profession may have been the placaters (Satir, Stachowiak, & Taschman, 1975; Chapter 7), or peace makers in their families, rather than the ones who pushed family members to change. Recognizing one's desire to placate is the first step toward learning to override the temptation when the family needs the family counselor to gently and continuously confront them.

STOP AND THINK:

1. How did you learn to treat authority figures?

2. What was your role in the family in which you were raised?

3. What experience have you had with aggressive adults?

4. How did you react reading the five scenarios of how the family counselor might have approached Liz's anger?

5. How might your family experience affect how you reacted?

As you read this section about experiencing families and responded to the Stop and Think questions, you may have noticed that the work of a family counselor can be emotionally difficult. Two recommendations have been mentioned: supervision and counseling. After describing these, we will turn to a third: self-care.

Supervision can take many forms. All graduate programs require some form of practicum or internship in which students work with clients under the clinical supervision of a licensed professional. State licensing laws include a mandatory minimum number of practice and supervision hours, and graduate training programs are designed to help students meet predegree licensing requirements in the state in which the graduate program exists. Supervision itself usually occurs at least once a week, although sometimes only once every 2 weeks, and includes one-to-one interactions between the student counselor and her or his supervisor. Some training programs also offer supervision groups of two or more students meeting with the supervisor. Additionally, licensing laws require postdegree experience, again under the supervision of a licensed professional. Clients are told they will be working with a student counselor when they enter counseling and sign a form that allows the student counselor to consult with her or his supervisor. Ultimately, the supervisor is responsible for the clients' welfare and the quality of the student counselor's work.

After becoming fully licensed, counselors often join peer supervision groups. These are groups of professionals who meet regularly to learn about new research and treatment modalities or to provide feedback to one another about their counseling work. Cases are presented, and client confidentiality is carefully protected in peer supervision groups. Although not required, peer supervision helps family counselors with accountability, avoiding isolation, and staying connected with a professional network.

The decision to engage in individual counseling is ultimately a personal one. The writers believe that a willingness to examine one's own issues is crucial to the ethical practice of counseling. Additionally, the experience of being a client gives a counselor tremendous insight into the vulnerability that being a counseling client entails. It is humbling and may circumvent a tendency on the part of some counselors to view themselves as in some way superior to their clients. Such an attitude risks treating clients in a condescending manner. And respect for the client and the client's autonomy is crucial to the ethical practice of counseling.

Self-care is a third component of practicing any form of counseling. You have begun to see how personally challenging family counseling can be. Even when families are not recreating a counselor's issues, revelations and dynamics can be exhausting and lead to burnout. A specific plan for self-care is essential.

Self-care can include anything that restores the well-being of the family counselor. There are daily practices, such as meditation, exercise, and taking a few minutes for oneself in or out of the office before resuming the nonprofessional aspects of one's life. There are also practices that family counselors engage in less frequently, such as attending professional conferences and workshops and going on vacation. As you progress through your training, you can observe yourself, your peers, more seasoned professionals, and eventually your colleagues to learn what might work best for you.

Before we leave the topic of the family counselor's experience working with families, it is important to note that none of us progresses through life without stress. Sometimes stress is positive, such as weddings and births. Sometimes it is not, for example, when aging parents require additional care and die. And sometimes it occurs when one of our own children or our significant relationship is in distress. At these times it is especially important for the family counselor to both engage in self-care and seek whatever assistance, through supervision or counseling, that facilitates her or his emotional health and personal and professional functioning.

EXPERIENCING THE MANNING-KELLY AND JONES FAMILIES

Bear in mind that the family counselor is, like the Manning-Kelly family, a fictional character loosely based on the writers' experiences working with families and supervising students learning to practice family counseling. Given that both she and the Manning-Kelly family are composites of real people, her experience working with the Manning-Kelly family is hypothetical, as is the family itself.

The family counselor disliked Mark's aloofness from the beginning. She felt he was disengaged, and, as a professional working outside the home and a mother raising children in a two-parent family, she was put off that he seemed to leave parenting entirely to Liz. She was aware that her values about parenting did not need to match her clients' and worked to avoid judging him. The family counselor was also puzzled that he had known his stepchildren as long as he had and yet did not appear to be interested in them or their well-being. He also seemed to avoid interacting with his biological daughter, Emma.

Similarly, the family counselor disliked and was put off by Mark's blaming stance toward his first wife. According to him, he was the passive victim of her and her parents, pushed out of the family and alienated from his children. However, he seemed to overlook his own role, which may have been as simple as acquiescing. However, the family counselor hypothesized that she was seeing something similar in his second marriage and current family. Perhaps his disengagement had led to his first wife, Shoshana, and her parents taking over his role rather than victimizing him. On the other hand, if they had in fact colluded against him then perhaps his current disengagement reflected a reluctance to be rejected again. Clinically, these hypotheses could be helpful to the family.

However, the family counselor had to remain alert to her negative feelings about Mark and attentive to managing them in a way that allowed her to genuinely convey empathy, support, and openness to her second hypothesis, rather than dislike and blame. She also wondered whether both Shoshana and Liz had felt the same critical dislike of his disengagement, passivity, victim stance, and aloofness she was feeling.

The family counselor also identified with Christina's feelings about being controlled by her mother. The family counselor had grown up in a family in which her mother appeared to dominate the family while her father appeared passive while goading her mother's controlling behavior. The family counselor had recognized this dynamic between her parents as an adult in her own individual counseling. As a child, she had viewed her mother in much the same way Christina viewed hers and her father as a helpless victim of her mother, just as she was. She had since learned no adult really has to be passive, and thus believed both her father and Mark's passivity was by choice. However, she needed to be cautious about conflating Mark with her father. Mark did not appear to goad Liz, though he clearly chose to be a passive, disengaged parent.

As a family counselor, such personal experience with family dynamics underlying unlikeable behavior can be helpful. However, because the family counselor needed to be alert to her reactions to Liz and Mark to avoid treating them as though they were her own parents, she talked about her feelings in her peer supervision group, being careful to protect the privacy of the Manning-Kelly family and maintain the focus on keeping her own issues out of her work. She sought guidance about how to approach Mark from professionals she trusted who were not emotionally involved in the way she was.

The family counselor's inclination was to protect Christina, to step in and mother her the way Liz seemed unable to do. She also recognized that she did not wish to undermine but rather wanted to strengthen the mother-daughter relationship, guiding them toward a way to communicate that allowed Christina the autonomy appropriate to her stage of development and facilitated resolution of their disagreements.

The family counselor felt much the same way about Emma that she did about Christina. She wanted to lure her away from her mother and demonstrate Emma's ability to be a more autonomous four-year-old. Once again, however, this intervention would have been detrimental to the family and so she talked about and sought suggestions from her peer supervision group.

As you have probably noticed, there were a number of times when Liz was confrontational and even hostile toward the family counselor. And, in Chapter 9, Mark verbally threatened her while standing up, towering over her to further convey power.

The family counselor noticed she felt defensive when Liz confronted her and scared when Mark threatened her. In both situations, she knew she needed to remain calm and soothed herself, both during and after the session, that she would be all right. As a new counselor, she had been intimidated by strong, successful women like Liz. Fortunately, that was no longer the case. However, she continued to experience a desire to defend herself and needed to be aware when that desire arose so she could continue to support Liz while firmly setting boundaries with her.

Her fear of Mark was more difficult to manage. While she knew she needed to maintain her focus on helping the family cope with both the crisis and the need to report his abuse, she was intimidated by the fact that he was an attorney and knew how to cause her a lot of trouble, both in the courts and with her licensing board. While she was confident she was behaving legally and ethically, ethical behavior does not preclude time-consuming and expensive efforts to defend oneself from accusations. She also worried about her reputation if he made his accusations public. Even if he was ultimately convicted of child abuse, the damage to her reputation of any publicity associated with his claims against her, however unfounded, would be difficult to overcome. So she was frightened for her counseling business. Self-awareness of these feelings and self-soothing that she would survive whatever happened allowed her to remain sufficiently focused on the needs of the Manning-Kelly family to complete the session in an ethical manner and as effectively as she did.

Finally, the family counselor was repulsed by Mark's abuse of Christina. She had heard similar stories and was impressed that Liz virtually avoided the temptation to blame the victim in order to hold her marriage together. But no amount of experience with abusive families numbs the horror and disgust one feels when confronted with a situation in which a child who is a dependent and cannot yet leave the family is repeatedly traumatized by helplessness and violation by an abusive adult. The family counselor needed to accept her own feelings and also put them on hold to be dealt with outside of the session, for example, by talking about them in peer supervision where colleagues would validate her reactions and share their own. A family counselor who is numb to the pain and horror that are natural aspects of learning about abuse would need to take action to restore her or his empathy.

SELF-AWARENESS, SELF-CARE, AND ETHICAL PRACTICE

Earlier chapters and sections of this chapter have alluded to the importance of the family counselor's self-awareness in working with the Manning-Kelly family. Had she not been aware of her reaction to Liz, she would have likely followed one of the first four scenarios and been entrapped by the family dynamics, induced into their system, and unable to maintain her counseling role to help them change their dynamics. She may have sided with Christina against Liz, alienated Mark early in counseling, or overlooked the differences between her own ethnic and racial background and those of the biracial family and the impact of these differences on her counseling work.

Self-awareness involves checking in with oneself on a regular and frequent basis. You can begin your practice of self-awareness by noticing what is happening around you at any particular moment and noticing yourself within your context, also at any particular moment. Practice observing, without evaluation or analysis. What does the ice cream in your mouth taste like right now? And then what does it feel like as the cold moves down your throat? Avoid thinking about whether you "should" be eating ice cream or what it might be doing to your weight or cholesterol. Similarly, as you walk across campus, notice the feel of the air on your skin and the smell of the plants around you. Avoid thinking about the work you have to do, the meeting you need to get to quickly after class, or whether you'll have time for lunch. If you are hungry, notice the feeling of hunger in your stomach and then the taste of your lunch and the increasing feeling of fullness as you eat.

Once you begin to notice these daily occurrences, begin noticing your body's reaction to the people in your life. Do you lean toward one friend when she or he is telling you a secret and start thinking about what else you'd like to be doing when another complains about the same thing for the umpteenth time? Do you find it more difficult to concentrate in some classes than in others? Now observe what is happening—the temperature in the room, what students sitting near you are doing, and the tone of the professor's voice—when you notice your concentration has wandered. Finally, ask yourself about the level of your well-being. Again, simply notice, without evaluating or judging.

When one practices self-awareness, one is more likely to recognize both physical and emotional responses that alert one to trouble. The family counselor working with the Manning-Kelly family may have recognized tightness in her shoulders when Liz verbally challenged her and then flagged her body's response as an indication she was feeling the need to protect herself despite the absence of a clear threat. She would thus have been alerted to the need to pay careful attention to her response in order to avoid reacting to Liz in a way that would convey hostility or defensiveness. Remember that Liz's family members respond to her with hostility and defensiveness, and it would have been tempting for the counselor to have been induced into the family system and responded in similar ways. Without the awareness of what was happening in her body and what it meant, the family counselor would not have been able to successfully avoid a similar reaction.

This level of self-awareness requires careful attention to oneself, how one responds, and where one carries messages from one's mind in one's body when one does not recognize them as thoughts. And the reflection necessary to attain and use this level of self-awareness is simply a matter of practice. Sometimes it also requires input from someone other than the counselor, for example a supervisor, members of a peer supervision group, or the counselor's own counselor.

Self-care is closely associated with self-awareness. Because both self-awareness and the experience of counseling families require concentration, emotional openness to pain, and quickly processing lots of information from lots of people, the work can be exhausting. Many counselors practice self-care to manage all these aspects of their job, as well as demands from their own families and friends. Self-care can include exercise, meditation, rituals like lighting a candle or drinking herbal tea before leaving the office, peer supervision groups, friends and family with whom to unwind, mental health days, and vacations.

Many family counselors rush from their last client of the day to care for their children and, when in the sandwich generation (Chapter 2), their aging parents as well. Sometimes, the people for whom family counselors are responsible in their personal lives seem to appreciate them even less than their clients do. For example, adolescent children may be uncooperative and treat their family counselor parent as though they think she or he is an idiot. Her or his aging parents may resist changing their lives to accommodate the changes in their functioning and blame their adult child family counselor for a situation that is beyond everyone's control. Or, the family counselor may be going through a particularly difficult period with her or his intimate partner. Counselors in private practice may further be tempted to accommodate a client's need to change times at the expense of other important aspects of the counselor's life, such as time with family and friends and self-care, in order to maintain her or his income stream. All of these occurrences require and simultaneously conspire against the family counselor's routine practice of self-care.

Why is self-care important? For the same reason self-awareness is. If a counselor does not practice self-care, she or he is more likely to experience burnout: distraction, lack of empathy, and lack of genuineness that is conveyed when verbal messages conflict with nonverbal messages. When counselors experience burnout their nonverbal messages scream, "I need to get out of here!"

even though the counselor would never dream of uttering those words. When counselors fail to balance their professional and personal lives, they risk their personal issues leaking into and contaminating their professional relationships with their clients.

The Manning-Kelly family was scheduled at the end of one of the family counselor's work days. The family counselor often left sessions with the Manning-Kelly family feeling good about the work she had done and yet sad or anxious. She thought about whether these feelings were reflections of the family's sadness and anxiety, feelings she had had as a child in her own family, or exhaustion from the experience of being with so many distressed families during the day or with this family in particular. She lit a candle, did some deep breathing and muscle relaxation, and then drank a cup of herbal tea while writing case notes for the day. After that, she closed the office, went home, and enjoyed the evening with her family and sometimes also with friends.

You will read about ethics in the next chapter. Some of the most common ethical errors made by family counselors who are not practicing self-awareness and self-care include violating client boundaries by behaving like a friend or family member instead of a counselor and self-revelation that fulfills no clinical purpose. In addition to the ethical violation, such behavior may also leave the already stressed family counselor feeling badly about her or his lack of professional behavior. And a negative spiral can easily follow.

In sum, the practice of family counseling requires that counselors learn and practice self-awareness and self-care in order to avoid burnout and to practice ethically and effectively. The writers advise anyone hoping to become a family counselor to begin a practice of self-awareness and self-care now, so that both are more likely to be habits by the time the student reaches the point in graduate training when she or he will begin to counsel families.

THE SCHOOL COUNSELOR'S EXPERIENCE WITH FAMILIES

In school settings, the counselor serves many roles in addition to counselor. These roles may include consultant, testing coordinator, special program coordinator, student organization advisor, registrar, testing proctor, substitute teacher, witness for disciplinary referrals (these last two are unfortunate and not appropriate for school counselors, but they do happen), and trip chaperone or even talent show judge. Serving in all of these roles can make maintaining boundaries tricky. The counselor-client relationship for school counselors is not confined to the counseling office. School counselors see their clients every time they walk down the hall, into a classroom, or attend a school event. Many students view their school counselors the same way they view their teachers, in that the ones they really connect with they treat like friends or even extended family. It is not unusual for school counselors to receive gifts, birthday party invitations, and return visits from their former clients after they have graduated from school. While these practices would be strongly discouraged in the mental health agency or private practice setting, they are commonplace in the school counseling world. Managing these boundaries requires careful consideration of what is in the best interest of the client and what is appropriate or inappropriate for the school counselor's role. Therefore, it is important for the school counselor to be familiar with the appropriate code of ethics (see Chapter 11) and to stay abreast of the latest developments in his or her profession. In addition, school counselors should seek supervision when faced with a difficult boundary issue.

School counselors work frequently with their students' families. Oftentimes, the student of concern is in trouble, academically, emotionally, socially, or a combination thereof. For school counselors, having empathy for the students is easy. They chose this profession because they like and understand children and adolescents. Empathizing with the children's parents is not always as easy. When the school counselor meets with the parent or parents, it is important to maintain empathy for them, imagining, or perhaps remembering, what it feels like to be summoned to the school because you or your child is in trouble. Upon entering the school building, many parents are transported through time back to their own childhoods, feeling as though they are being called to the principal's office because they did something wrong. In addition, when parents and teachers have a conflict, territoriality can rear its ugly head. Parents feel as though the quality of their parenting is being questioned, while teachers feel as though their quality of teaching is being questioned. Here again, it is important for the school counselor to remain empathic, validating each person's perspective and expertise related to the child of focus. School counselors are just as susceptible to family induction as counselors in any other setting. The same temptations to side with certain family members (often the child client) can pull at the counselor, just as the same negative feelings toward certain family members may surface. Furthermore, the same self-care practices apply. Finding a supervisor for school counselors maybe a challenge, since there is often only one school counselor in a given school, and sometimes one school counselor serves more than one school. Still, it is important for school counselors to seek supervision with peers in order to protect themselves from burnout. School counselors may connect with counselors from other schools, for individual or group supervision.

CONCLUSION

Family counselors, also being human beings, react to the individuals and family systems with whom they work. The family counselor's awareness of her or his own reactions and how she or he manages them so that they do not disrupt counseling or interfere with what client families need are crucial to the ethical practice of family counseling. Clearly, these counseling tasks must occur simultaneously with assessing the family system and the impact of interventions informed by the family counselor's theoretical approach. Learning to balance all these factors takes time and requires the supervision by an experienced clinician that is part of all graduate programs and required for all licenses.

We will now turn to the ethics of family counseling. Bear in mind that the ethical family counselor is a person like you. In other words, she or he never has all the answers.

Extend Your Learning:

1. What self-care practices are you using now to cope with the stress of being a student?

2. What parts of your self-care routine have you neglected lately? How might you attend to those areas?

3. Most colleges and universities have free counseling services offered for their students. There is no better time than when counseling is free to give counseling for yourself a try. Even if you don't think you have any issues to work through, sitting in the client's seat can be a very helpful experience for counselors-in-training. Honestly, at what other time in your life will there be a person who will give you 50 minutes of uninterrupted attention, to talk about whatever you want to talk about, and for free? As you make plans to see a counselor for the first time, ask yourself and respond in your journal:

    (a.) Why haven't I done this before?

    (b.) How do I feel about making the appointment?

    (c.) Am I nervous? If so, what about?

    (d.) Am I excited? If so, what about?

    (e.) After the first session, take note: What surprised you? What did you like about how the counselor worked with you? What did you not like? How did being in the client's seat affect your view of yourself as a future counselor?

REFERENCES

Diller, J. V. (2007). *Cultural diversity. A primer for human services* (3rd ed.). Belmont, CA: Brooks/Cole.

Dulwich Centre. (2015). *What is narrative therapy?* The Dulwich Centre. Retrieved from http://dulwichcentre.com.au/what-is-narrative-therapy

Haley, J. (1963). *Strategies of psychotherapy.* New York, NY: Grune & Stratton.

Lum, D. (2007). *Culturally competent practice. A framework for understanding diverse groups and justice issues* (3rd ed.). Belmont, CA: Brooks/Cole.

Napier, A. Y., & Whitaker C. A. (1978). *The family crucible.* New York, NY: Harper and Row.

Sager, C. J. (1981). Couple therapy and marriage contracts. In A. S. Gurman & D. P. Kniskern (Eds.), *Handbook of family therapy.* New York, NY: Bruner/Mazel.

Satir, V., Stachowiak, J., & Taschman, H. A. (1975). *Helping families to change.* New York, NY: Jason Aronson

FOR FURTHER STUDY

Backer, A., Goodnough, G., Levitt, D. H., & Moorhead, H. H. (2013). Boundary issues. In D. H. Levitt, & H. H. Moorhead (Eds.), *Values and ethics in counseling: Real-life ethical decision making* (pp. 43–48). New York, NY: Routledge/Taylor & Francis Group.

Bradley, N., Whisenhunt, J., Adamson, N., & Kress, V. E. (2013). Creative approaches for promoting counselor self-care. *Journal of Creativity in Mental Health, 8*(4), 456–469.

Gushue, G. V., Constantine, M. G., & Sciarra, D. T. (2008). The influence of culture, self-reported multicultural counseling competence, and shifting standards of judgment on perceptions of family functioning of white family counselors. *Journal of Counseling & Development, 86*(1), 85–94.

Herlihy, B., & Corey, G. (2015). *Boundary issues in counseling: Multiple roles and responsibilities* (3rd ed.). Alexandria, VA: American Counseling Association.

Hung, L. (2011). Experiences of school counselors in ethical decision making. *The Archive of Guidance & Counseling, 33*(2), 87–107.

Klein, R. (2015). The nuances of difference in the therapeutic relationship. In L. French, & R. Klein (Eds.), *Therapeutic practice in schools, Volume two: The contemporary adolescent: A clinical workbook for counsellors, psychotherapists and arts therapists* (pp. 129–134). New York, NY: Routledge/Taylor & Francis Group.

Lenz, A. S., & Sangganjanavanich, V. F. (2015). Wellness and self-care for professional counselors. In, *Introduction to professional counseling* (pp. 221–244). Thousand Oaks, CA: Sage.

Pieterse, A. L., Lee, M., Ritmeester, A., & Collins, N. M. (2013). Towards a model of self-awareness development for counseling and psychotherapy training. *Counseling Psychology Quarterly, 26*(2), 190–207.

Pope, M., Pangelinan, J. S., & Coker, A. D. (2011). *Experiential activities for teaching multicultural competence in counseling.* Alexandria, VA: American Counseling Association.

Simpson, L. R., & Falkner, J. (2013). Self-care and self-growth: A professional responsibility. In D. Capuzzi, & D. R. Gross (Eds.), *Introduction to the counseling profession* (6th ed.) (pp. 123–150). New York, NY: Routledge/Taylor & Francis Group.

Tse, P. C. (2014). Connecting self and relationship through ego state analysis and the action method for performing group counseling supervision: The IF model. *Asia Pacific Journal of Counseling and Psychotherapy, 5*(1), 45–61.

Yokoyama, K., Magraw, S., Miller, J., & Hecht, L. (2011). Cultural genograms. In M. Pope, J. S. Pangelinan, & A. D. Coker (Eds.), *Experiential activities for teaching multicultural competence in counseling* (pp. 269–270). Alexandria, VA: American Counseling Association.

CHAPTER 11

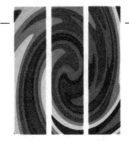

Ethics of Family Counseling

Why do we have ethical codes? Once you have completed your training and pursued and received licensure (if applicable), you will have multiple practice settings to consider as you plan your career. Agencies, schools, hospitals, and private practice are just a few of these options. Because there is such a wide variety of settings and practitioners in the helping professions, and because helping professionals work in a variety of roles with their clients, it is important to have some standards in place in order to ensure that people are receiving the best possible care. Ethical standards are in place to serve as a guide for our behaviors and choices as we work with clients. Simply put, ethical standards are in place to keep us from doing harm. In medicine, the Hippocratic Oath "First Do No Harm" is used frequently in reference to patient welfare. Just as physicians must keep in mind the best interests of their patients, family counselors must be mindful of the best interests of their clients. Ethical standards are also in place because we cannot possibly know all of the potential outcomes of our actions. The ethical codes have resulted from years and years of professional practice and prompt practitioners to consider the implications of their choices when working with clients.

The counseling professions have several ethical codes, depending on what type of training and licensure a professional has. The American Counseling Association (ACA) is for licensed professional counselors, the American Association for Marriage and Family Therapists (AAMFT) is for licensed marriage and family therapists, and the National Organization for Human Services (NOHS) is for professionals who have either an undergraduate or graduate degree in a human services field, and therefore serves a broader population of helping professionals. While there are many more professional organizations that serve the helping professions, for the purposes of this book, we focus on the three aforementioned organizations.

It is the responsibility of every helping professional to read and be familiar with his or her profession's ethical standards. Students usually read their ethical codes during undergraduate or graduate school, and supervisors typically require their supervisees to read the standards again at the beginning of their supervisory relationship.

PROTECTING CLIENTS

Legal statutes as well as professional ethical codes governing the practice of family counseling have been designed to protect clients. In so far as possible, licensing laws, all of which specify minimum levels of training and postdegree clinical supervision, protect the public from inadequately trained and unscrupulous family counseling practitioners.

Each state has its own licensing requirements and legislated ethical codes governing the practice of family counseling. These include penalties for practicing without a license, misrepresenting one's credentials, working outside what is called one's scope of practice, engaging in any relationship with a client other than counseling during and for some period following the counseling, and reporting suspected abuse or neglect of minor children, the elderly, and the disabled. Scope of practice may be an unfamiliar concept. It simply means that family counselors must be trained and supervised to practice in the areas for which they advertise. So, for example, family counselors cannot give medical advice beyond recommending that a client consult with an appropriate physician. Similarly, a family counselor cannot present as competent to work with domestic violence unless she or he has had specific training and clinical supervision working with families in which domestic violence is an issue.

A third topic that deserves mention involves the differential power of the family counselor and the clients with whom she or he works. Family counselors must recognize that, even if their world view and theoretical orientation involve a collaborative relationship with their clients, they remain the authority on whom the clients depend for mental health care. Family counselors are therefore ethically bound to practice the profession of family counseling in a manner that does no harm, including the harm of abusing the power inherent in being a practitioner of mental health care or ignoring its reality.

Recognition of the potential power of being in the role of family counselor may help you think about some of the other topics addressed in this chapter. For example, if the family counselor is more powerful, then bartering for services, while potentially of financial benefit to both the counselor and the client, would be biased in favor of the one with more power.

STOP AND THINK:

1. If a client offered to paint your house in exchange for an agreed-upon number of counseling sessions and discovered the house was in such bad condition that painting took two or three times longer than she or he had anticipated, do you think she or he would be reluctant to suggest you renegotiate the arrangement? Why, or why not? And how might her or his trust in you be affected?

2. If you were unsatisfied with the client's painting job, how might that affect your feelings about and work with the client?

Client Rights and Family Counselor Responsibilities

Family counseling clients have rights, and family counselors have certain responsibilities, including protecting those rights. These are specified by both state and federal legal codes. It is beyond the scope of this textbook to detail them all. Following a summary of client rights and family counselor responsibilities, two questions unique to family counseling will be addressed: who is the client? And, what are the boundaries unique to family counseling?

Clients have the right to privacy, and family counselors are responsible for protecting that right in all their dealings with client families. This sometimes raises the question of who is the client, for example, when one family member calls to tell the family counselor something she or he does not want the rest of the family to know. We address this situation further in the next subsection.

Clients also own their medical records. This means that, although it is incumbent on family counselors to maintain detailed records of their contact with client families, the family counselor can be asked to give the family a copy of those records. Again, there are various ways to handle this imperative, including advising the family to read the records in the presence of the family counselor so that she or he can soften the impact of technical jargon and diagnoses.

Finally, family counselors have the responsibility to keep those family members who are dependent on other family members for care safe in so far as possible and to keep the public safe from a family member who the family counselor suspects may harm one or more people outside the family. State statutes and legal precedents such as the *Tarasoff v. Regents* (1976) case specify when and how a family counselor must report abuse or neglect and when family counselors must turn over medical records to the court or its agent and/ or testify. While there are some options, such as the ones the family counselor provided the Manning-Kelly family (Chapter 9), failure to report can leave the family counselor criminally and civilly liable for any harm that is done, and failure to comply with court orders can lead to the charge of contempt of court.

The authors recommend seeking legal counsel when any of these issues arise. If a family counselor's employer does not have an attorney on staff, then the liability insurer that covers the practice will.

Who Is the Client?

When family counselors see more than one family member, the question arises regarding who the client is. Specifically, is the family or one of the individuals in it the client? The answer to this question is especially important with respect to the issue of confidentiality. It also may direct the family counselor to focus on particular assessments and interventions rather than others. Finally, there may be a conflict of interest between the family and one of its members. Deciding who the client is helps the family counselor decide how to resolve such a dilemma.

Consider the initial sessions with the Manning-Kelly family. The family counselor might have concluded that Christina's interests would be best served by helping her identify and resolve her anger at her mother's choices and their impact on her. Such work in counseling might allow her to make decisions about her own future independently of her reactions to Liz. Such an approach would involve individual, rather than family counseling, and the client would be an individual, in this case Christina.

Alternatively, the family counselor might have concluded that the family would best be served by addressing the way Liz and Mark handled the tension between them, as well as any remaining tension between Liz and Martin, and seeking alternatives that did not involve their children. The family counselor who chose this approach would theorize that removing Christina from her position within the marital subsystem would free her to make decisions about her own future independently of her family's needs. And in this case, the family system would be the client.

Deciding whether Christina or the family is the client would help the family counselor to conceptualize the problem, develop a working hypothesis, and choose a theoretical approach to intervention. Either choice would presumably result in greater age-appropriate autonomy for Christina and a resulting reduction in her symptomatology. Because this is a textbook about family counseling, the second approach has informed the examples throughout the book. However, for the purpose of this discussion about the ethics of family counseling, the critical point is that the answer to the question of who is the client is very different in the two approaches.

None of the ethical codes reviewed for this book address the issue of identifying the client, in other words, whether the client is an individual or the entire family, when counseling client families. Thus, answering the question about who the client is involves ethical decision making. Models of ethical decision making are addressed later in this chapter.

Most ethical codes specify confidentiality requirements when parents ask a family counselor for information about her or his work alone with a minor child. As you continue your training, you will learn to think in an ethical way about what to do if a family member calls between sessions to speak privately with you or when you do sessions with subgroups or individuals within the family in addition to sessions with the entire family. Some family counselors are firm about not seeing individual family members when also seeing their families and instead refer these individual family members to other counselors for individual counseling work. Others believe that individual sessions are sometimes indicated and should not be considered mutually exclusive of working with the family in its entirety. For example, because Christina was 17 years old, and the Manning-Kelly family was about to enter the launching stage of family development, a family counselor might decide to recommend individual sessions with Christina while also seeing the family intermittently. And while a child counselor might also work with a much younger child and only see the parents intermittently, a family counselor would look to the family system as the key to change rather than to the child.

STOP AND THINK:

1. Based on what you have learned, how do you think the outcomes might differ if Christina were seen in individual counseling by a child counselor rather than with her family by a family counselor?

2. If the identified patient was a younger child, what would your answer to question 1 be?

3. Based on what you have learned, do you think one approach might be more effective than the other? Why?

The question of multiple relationships with clients, also referred to as dual relationships in some ethical codes, thus arises when family counselors see entire families and any member or subgroup of the family separately. Dual relationships involve having more than one relationship with a client. Family counselors are prohibited from engaging in dual relationships outside of counseling with clients. This is why family counselors do not barter for services with their clients or engage in social, romantic, or business relationships with clients. Because of the power differential, clients are unable to engage in any of these kinds of relationships as an equal participant with their family counselor.

Are situations in which a family counselor has two counseling relationships with a client dual relationships in the sense of a power differential? Or, because both relationships happen in the context of counseling, are they ethical? If nothing else, this question provides an excellent example of using ethical decision making.

STOP AND THINK:

1. Would seeing Christina both individually and with her family have the potential to harm her? If so, how? If not, what led you to that conclusion?

2. Referring to the section of this chapter about ethical decision making, follow the steps and discuss your conclusions.

Now consider the potential situation in which Mark has been ordered by a court to obtain treatment for his sexual abuse of Christina. The Manning-Kelly family may ask the family counselor to work with Mark individually to fulfill this condition of his obligation to the court. There are many reasons why the family counselor would say no, including that treating sexual abuse is beyond her scope of practice. Another would be the dual relationship she would then have with Mark and the rest of the family. Imagine that she said yes, and then a month later, Liz called to ask how Mark was doing with his individual counseling. Had the family counselor referred Mark to another counselor for treatment, the new counselor could easily explain to Liz that her or his work with Mark was confidential, and she or he was therefore unable to discuss it with Liz. The family counselor, however, already has a counseling relationship with Liz that she is ethically bound to protect. So, while she would have to decline to discuss Mark's individual work with Liz, her choice might be disruptive of her clinical relationship with Liz and thus of her work with the family.

Issues around dual relationships and conflicts of interest extend far beyond what has been covered in this section. If you pursue a graduate degree and licensure in family counseling, you will learn more about these and other specific issues, as well as how to approach them ethically, in your coursework, internship training, and postdegree clinical supervision.

Boundaries and Ethical Behavior

Power was addressed earlier in this section as a way of conceptualizing the client-counselor relationship in an ethical way. Another way to think about these issues involves respecting client boundaries. As defined in Chapter 4, boundaries are physical and emotional spaces that individuals, families, and subsystems within families create around themselves.

Respecting a client family's boundaries involves attention to every level of the family system. Individual boundaries may differ, as may the boundaries among subsystems and between the family as a whole and those external to the family. In the previous chapter, you read about the need for family counselors to avoid being induced into the family system in order to maintain their ability to work on behalf of the family and all its members. Conversely, rigid family boundaries may challenge the family counselor to negotiate sufficient engagement in the family system to form a counseling alliance.

The Manning-Kelly family presents a clear example of respecting boundaries. As an abused member, Christina had received unwanted touching from her stepfather. A family counselor who approached the family from the beginning with respect for boundaries would not have initiated any physical touch with its members. Had the family counselor touched Christina in some way, even if she had intended to convey support, she could have inadvertently traumatized Christina with yet more unwanted touch from an adult. Additionally, and as an aside, touch can easily be misinterpreted by clients, and so the authors do not recommend touching clients. While there may occasionally be exceptions, though never initiated by the counselor, the detailed considerations are beyond the scope of this textbook.

REPORTING LAWS

Client Safety. Every state has laws protecting dependent people from physical and sexual abuse and from neglect by those who are responsible for their care and safety. The protected people include children, the elderly, and people with disabilities. These laws also require certain professionals, including family counselors, to report suspected abuse or neglect. If you become a licensed or provisionally licensed member of one of the professions required to report abuse, you will need to become familiar with the statutes in the state in which you are licensed in order to learn what the reporting procedures and time frames are for that state. These professions include all mental health practitioners, educators, and physicians.

What does all this mean? First and most importantly, it means family counselors have a legal obligation to use their knowledge, experience, and skills to assess the probable risk or presence of abuse or neglect. Neglect is difficult to define. Physical and sexual abuse are less difficult to define, though the specifics of how to define and assess for them are beyond the scope of this textbook. With respect to sexual abuse, it is important to remember that when someone has power over another, the person of lesser status cannot consent to sex because the option of saying no is unavailable. In other words, if a person does not have the option to say no, then they do not fully have the option to say yes. This is one of several reasons why family counselors and other mental health practitioners, educators, and physicians are prohibited from engaging in romantic or sexual relationships with their clients.

You may have noticed that the criterion for reporting is suspicion of abuse or neglect. It also applies only to dependents, including minor children, the elderly, and the disabled. While a family counselor who engages in a romantic relationship with a client who does not meet these criteria is still in violation of the law, it is assumed that an adult who of reasonable intelligence and physical capacity can refuse to consent or remove herself or himself from contact with the abuser. While in reality this is not always possible—for example, adults can be coerced to remain in abusive relationships—to our knowledge, family counselors do not need to report this kind of domestic violence.

Family counselors reporting abuse of a member of a group legally defined as requiring reporting do not need to be investigators. They do not need to present proof beyond whatever led them to reasonably suspect abuse or neglect, such as what happened during the session discussed in Chapter 9. In other words, counselors need to fully document what has led them to suspect abuse or neglect.

When reporting laws first appeared, many mental health professionals were concerned because reporting was a violation of the client's confidentiality, one that could easily lead to mistrust and the end of the counseling relationship. Some argued that it would be more beneficial to the perpetrator to continue treatment than to become the subject of an investigation. Today, decades after reporting laws became codified in all 50 states, students ask what reporting does to the counseling relationship.

Concerns about trust and future counseling, either with the counselor who reported the abuse or someone else, are reasonable. However, the subject is not available for argument. Rather, the law is very clear that family counselors must report or face charges of being complicit in the abuse. The court considers a mental health professional who fails to report to be behaving like a parent who stands by doing nothing or ignores a child being abused by the other parent, a close friend, neighbor, or relative.

Students also ask about the issue of compliance with reporting laws being a violation of client confidentiality. Family counselors are legally and ethically required to maintain the privacy of what their clients say to them, as well as of the existence of the counseling relationship. This is true whether the client is an individual, a couple, or a family. However, the law also states that a family counselor's suspicion of abuse or neglect overrides legal and ethical prohibitions about revealing client information and requires that the family counselor report to the appropriate agency. The law does not, however, give the family counselor the right to reveal confidential information elsewhere. If a client subsequently sues the family counselor for violating her or his confidentiality, the law protects the counselor from being found guilty so long as the counselor can document reasonable suspicion. Again, maintaining complete records, which all family counselors must do anyway, provides sufficient documentation of reasonable suspicion. The example from the Manning-Kelly family speaks to this point. If, at some point subsequent to the session during which Christina revealed she had been abused by Mark, she said she was lying, the family counselor would still be protected because, based on the information she had at the time and documented in her records, she had reason to suspect. It is, of course, possible that Christina was lying, but the family counselor does not need to serve as investigator and decipher that. There are also reasons other than lying that someone would retract an accusation, for example, fear of what was subsequently happening to the family.

In addition to abuse and neglect of dependents, family counselors also need to protect clients who appear to be a danger to themselves or someone else or who appear unable to accomplish the tasks of daily living. In other words, if a client indicates that she or he intends to kill herself or himself or someone else and has a specific plan to carry out that intention, the family counselor must report it. As with abuse and neglect, the laws of each state specify to whom the report is made. And, although the family counselor needs to be in the room when the report is made, she or he can offer the client the option of making the call herself or himself. We address a family counselor's duty to warn the intended victim in the next section.

Most counselors recommend empowering individuals and families as much as possible under the circumstances when abuse or harm must be reported.

This involves allowing them to choose whether to make the reporting call from the counselor's office, be in the room while the counselor makes the call, or of being absent when the family counselor reports. The Manning-Kelly's family counselor gave them these options in Chapter 9. Once the abuse has been reported, responsibility for what to do with the information rests with the agency to which the report was made.

In cases of intended suicide or homicide, the reporting call must be made promptly. The authors recommend that the family counselor only make the call in the presence of the client or offer the client the option of making it if she or he feels safe revealing to the client that the call must be made.

All mental health professionals include a reference to the circumstances under which they must report suspected abuse or neglect, as well as danger to self or others, in the privacy policy clients sign when they begin counseling. However, clients often skim the materials or forget the content. Part of the family counselor's responsibility is to verify that clients who are old enough to sign consent for treatment are capable of understanding the privacy policy and have the opportunity to ask questions about it.

Some families become enraged by the counselor's decision to report, irrespective of how thorough and careful the family counselor was in explaining the limits of privacy. Mark was angry and threatened the family counselor verbally. Other families appear to have considered the possibility of a report and accept its inevitability. Additionally, some families are able to continue counseling after a counselor has filed a report, while others are not. Reporting suspicion of abuse, neglect, suicide, and so on is very difficult for both clients and family counselors. Situations like these are some of the many reasons supervision needs to be a lifelong process.

Duty to Warn. The California Supreme Court set a precedent almost 50 years ago that has since been upheld. In the *Tarasoff v. Regents* (1976) case, the court held that mental health professionals are responsible for not only reporting homicidal intent to the appropriate authorities but also warning the intended victim of life-threatening harm.

The *Tarasoff v. Regents* (1976) case is complicated and interesting. However, the critical point for family counselors is that if a client threatens to kill someone, the family counselor must not only report this threat to the appropriate law enforcement agency but must also report it to the victim. As such, this is another level of client privacy. Family counselors can be reasonably sure of what may happen when they call the police or sheriff. However, the intended victim can tell anyone she or he wants to that not only is the client threatening her or him but also that the client is working with a family counselor. Again, the criterion for family counselors involves documenting reasonable suspicion. In the case of a family counselor's duty to warn, it is important to be familiar with the laws of the state in which one practices, as the *Tarasoff v. Regents* (1976) precedent is not federal and thus may not be the standard in all states.

LAW AND ETHICS

What is the difference between law and ethics? Laws are statutes passed by an elected legislative body that govern, among other things, licensure and practice of various professions including family counseling. These laws are reasonably specific, and violation of them results in reasonably predictable consequences.

Ethics are codes of appropriate professional behavior codified in licensing laws and also in professional organizations' codes of ethics. Violations of ethical codes can result in suspension or revocation of one's license to practice counseling. Links to the Codes of Ethics for the American Counseling Association, the American Association for Marriage and Family Therapy, the National Association of Social Workers and the National Organization for Human Services are included at the end of this chapter. When a family counselor applies for licensure in a particular state, she or he is also required to pass an exam that includes statutes governing the practice of marriage and family counseling in that state, including ethics.

A related issue involves the federal government's Health Insurance Portability and Accountability Act (HIPAA) provisions regarding ownership and protection of client information (U.S. Department of Health and Human Services, n.d.). The law was first passed in 1996 and was also known as the Kennedy-Kassenbaum law. Because technology, the storage of medical records, and forms of communication have changed in ways that could not have been anticipated in the 1990s, the law has been and will continue to be updated, as are state laws regarding legal and ethical practice. All family counselors must be in compliance with the HIPAA provisions, which include monitoring changes and adapting one's policies to fit them.

Technology and social networking also have ethical implications for family counselors. For example, neither Facebook nor Skype are HIPAA compliant as of this writing. However, a family counselor can set up a professional page on Facebook, and clients can like it, even though family counselors cannot friend their clients or former clients on Facebook. Additionally, there exist alternatives to Skype that were developed specifically for physicians, are used by clients, and are HIPAA compliant. HIPAA has also been updated to include specifics regarding record keeping and protection and transmission of electronic records.

Texts and e-mails are now dealt with in ethical codes and statutes to an extent they were not as recently as 10 years before the first edition of this textbook. Family counselors need to inform their clients about the limits of their ability to protect confidential information transmitted through either and are encouraged to ask clients to use them only for business purposes such as scheduling appointments.

Finally, family counselors who agree to accept payments from insurance companies and those who work for agencies or hospitals that accept insurance payments for their family counseling services must be in compliance with laws regulating practitioners doing business with the insurance industry. These also change from time to time, and family counselors who elect to engage in a business relationship with insurance companies must remain familiar with them.

Professional codes of ethics are constantly being revised to keep up with changes and new challenges associated with clinical practice. In the past 2 decades, e-mail, texting, tele-therapy, and social media have arisen. There was no mention of any of these in professional ethical codes in 1990. Yet all of these developments involve issues around protecting the confidentiality of client information and counselor-client interactions. And due to rapid changes in technology, it is impossible for ethical codes to address new issues the moment they arise.

Reading about legal statutes and ethical codes can be intimidating. Additionally, new family counselors often have no idea what to do when faced with a situation with no guidance from a specific clause in her or his professional organization's or licensing law's code of ethics. Gray areas will always exist, and that is one of the many reasons family counselors need to learn ethical decision making as part of their training, carry professional liability insurance, and maintain lifelong supervisory relationships.

REFERRALS

In Chapter 12, we address when and to whom family counselors may need to refer families for additional services. Family counselors may also need to refer individual family members to another counselor for individual counseling. In this section, we address how to make referrals as well as the risks of violating ethical and legal prohibitions against abandonment of clients.

There are many reasons clients are reluctant to accept referrals. Some people do not like to ask for help. Others worry about the expense. Still other people find it difficult to establish trust when meeting a new professional. As a result, family counselors may be asked by clients to provide services that are outside their scope of practice or involve dual relationships. How the family counselor handles such a request, as well as the entire referral process, is important not only in terms of the outcome of the referral (that it is accepted and needed services are obtained) but also in how it influences the family counselor's continuing professional relationship with the family.

When making a referral, it is important to clarify for the family the reasons why the referral is necessary—for example, the family counselor cannot provide neuropsychological or legal advice for an aging parent—as well as the family counselor's confidence in the people or agencies to whom she or he is referring. The family counselor must do everything possible to inspire confidence within the family about accepting the referral and the importance of acting upon it. Family counselors often follow up during subsequent sessions to learn whether the family has contacted the referrals provided and, if not, what has prevented them from doing so and when they might agree to do it. If the family has not elected to accept the referral, the family counselor may be able to help them address and alter their reluctance or give them an alternative referral.

Sometimes a family needs to address something that is outside the counselor's scope of practice. For example, a family counselor may not have special training and supervision in treating substance abuse or eating disorders. If this is the case, the family counselor is ethically bound to make a referral, explaining to the family that they need someone who knows more about how to help them than she or he does. Again, families may be reluctant to accept a referral. The family counselor can offer to see the family at a future date, after the specialized work is completed, or refer a member for individual counseling while the family counselor continues to work with them on family issues. Alternatively, the family counselor could, if interested, pursue training and supervision in the specialized topic and continue working with the family as part of her or his training if they are amenable.

At other times, family counselors find they do not want to work with a particular family. They may be overwhelmed with difficult cases and started seeing the family thinking it would be less challenging. Or, an issue could arise during family counseling that raises the family counselor's own issues at a time when she or he would prefer not to address them. Sometimes, family counselors simply don't like a family that wants to work with them. Unfortunately, these situations all risk abandonment of the client.

Family counselors are enjoined not to abandon clients. And while referring a family because the family counselor does not possess the training or licensure to help them in a particular way is behaving ethically, referring the family because the family counselor does not want to work with the family constitutes abandonment. It could be argued that a family counselor who does not want to work with a particular family may not be an appropriate counselor for that family and the family might be better served by working with someone else. And from that perspective, a referral to another family counselor would be ethical. However, ethical codes embedded in statutes would overlook that argument and hold that if the family counselor engaged in a counseling relationship with a client and the services needed by the family remain within her or his scope of practice, referring the family can be construed as abandonment.

Abandonment is different from a situation in which a family counselor is unable to continue seeing the family. Family counselors get sick, change jobs, move, and retire. They may also take a family medical leave to care for a newborn child, an elderly parent, or an ill spouse or life partner. These do not constitute abandonment. However, whenever possible, family counselors need to take time to prepare clients for the transition to a new mental health practitioner. Again, we recommend using ethical decision making or contacting the attorney at your liability insurer if you feel you are in a gray area regarding abandonment.

SELF-CARE

Years ago, one of the authors, who is in private practice, received a call from a physician the week before she was scheduled to go on vacation asking that she see one of the physician's patients. The psychotherapist was exhausted and knew she needed a vacation and told the physician so. The physician responded that this middle-aged patient's father had died recently, and she thought the patient needed someone to talk to about a straight-forward issue of grief. So the therapist agreed to see the patient before she left for vacation. About halfway through that session, the patient said, "There's something else you probably don't want to hear," and the psychotherapist, who very much needed her upcoming vacation, thought, you're right, I don't want to hear it. Because she routinely practiced self-awareness, she noticed the thought, knew it would be unethical to say it aloud, knew also that it was a sign of how burned out she was, and reminded herself of her usual empathy, looked attentive, and said, "Tell me about it." While it would be a violation of the client's confidentiality to repeat what the client then said, it was one of the more painfully awful stories the psychotherapist, who had been in practice for about 15 years at the time, had ever heard. The point, however, is that she was self-aware and practicing self-care sufficiently well to behave ethically with the client in the situation in which they found themselves.

> ## STOP AND THINK:
>
> 1. Imagine you have experienced a very painful event and have worked up the courage to seek professional help. Because you know the story may be burdensome to others, you preface it by saying the psychotherapist or counselor probably doesn't want to hear it. How would you feel if she said, "You're right, I don't really want to listen to you talk about something painful today"?
>
> 2. Now imagine you are the counselor. You feel as though you will explode or break down and cry if you have to empathize with one more client's pain before you have had time away from your practice, and someone tells you she's about to reveal something awful. How would you feel? Would you want to run from the room, tell her to be quiet, or something else?

Self-awareness and the practice of self-care are both critical to the mental health of family counselors and therefore to their ability to practice ethically. If the psychotherapist had not already known she needed a vacation, one would hope she would have been self-aware enough to recognize that thinking she did not want to hear what a client so obviously needed to say was a clear warning sign that she needed to take better care of herself.

Self-awareness is a lifelong practice required of all mental health professionals. It involves noticing what is happening with oneself. Such noticing includes tension in one's body, thoughts, and feelings. During sessions with clients, mental health professionals use this awareness to inform them of the impact the client and her or his issues are having on both the practitioner and the client. For example, in the scenario above, the psychotherapist noticed her thoughts were unusual for her and not conducive to effective work with the client. She was thus able to shift her focus back to the session, reserving her awareness of how badly she needed a vacation until after the work was finished. And, luckily, she had a vacation scheduled beginning at the end of the following work day.

Other times, mental health practitioners notice they are feeling incompetent or very tense in a certain part of their bodies. Perhaps the client is feeling powerless and saying things that are intentionally designed to disempower the practitioner. When Liz told the family counselor that family counseling was not working for them and making the situation worse, the family counselor began to wonder what she had overlooked and what she could have done differently. She noticed those thoughts, told herself she would address them later, and refocused on addressing Liz's obvious frustration and being certain she heard what Liz wanted. Without that self-awareness, she might have become defensive, which would likely have worsened Liz's frustration and might have led to the family choosing to stop family counseling.

Self-care is similarly a lifelong practice required of all mental health practitioners. Empathizing with individuals and families who are distressed and in pain, remaining present with them and avoiding defensiveness when they say hurtful things, tolerating the frustration when clients cannot change quickly, and shifting from one client to another throughout the day are emotionally and intellectually exhausting components of the work. Most family counselors also go home to their own families, where they need to be available for their children's and partner's needs, as well as the needs of aging parents, friends, and colleagues. A family counselor whose relationship is going through a difficult time may feel like even more of a failure if her clients' relationships are not solid and thus overlook issues that need addressing to ensure those same relationships continue if possible. Most family counselors discover they become anxious from time to time, feeling that they are seeing the same problems in their own families that their clients have brought to counseling.

Family counselors engage in a number of ways of caring for themselves, and you will need to discover those that work best for you. Possibilities include lighting a candle or incense at the end of the day to cleanse the office, stopping somewhere for a cup of tea before re-engaging in one's personal life, exercise, meditation, creative pursuits, hobbies, lifelong supervision with peers or privately with another professional, a strong social support network, regular vacations, and going to counseling or psychotherapy to address the family counselor's own issues that are raised by clients. Counselors and psychotherapists use specific activities such as gardening, working on cars or motorcycles, chopping wood, taking classes unrelated to their work, bubble baths, massages, and pedicures for self-care. We recommend to students that they ask themselves what they enjoy doing, what helps them relax, and what is reasonable to do on a regular basis given the time and other resource constraints of their lives.

Hopefully, it is obvious why family counselors and other mental health professionals need to practice self-care. Self-care is a way of keeping ourselves from burning out, making careless mistakes, and avoiding the ethical violations inherent in careless mistakes. A family counselor whose relationship with her or his spouse or children is going through a difficult time may turn to her or his clients for comfort, becoming overly involved, subtly and inadvertently asking them to take care of the counselor. Self-awareness allows the family counselor to recognize when these and related problems arise. However, only self-care actually prevents or resolves them.

SCOPE OF PRACTICE

Scope of practice refers to those areas and types of clients that any particular mental health practitioner is competent to see in her or his practice. The most critical question is, what is the scope of the practitioner's license? Each family counselor must be familiar with what her or his license allows her or him to do in the state in which it was issued. For example, family counselors who have not completed medical education and training in psychiatry or psychiatric nursing cannot prescribe medication, even when they think a family member might benefit from it. They must, instead, refer to someone who is licensed to prescribe. In a very small number of states, licensed psychologists who have completed a rigorous training program may become licensed to prescribe psychotropic medication. Violating laws associated with practicing outside one's scope of practice may result in civil and sometimes criminal penalties.

For what a particular family counselor's license allows her or him to practice, she or he must also be able to demonstrate appropriate training, involving both education and clinical supervision. Practicing outside areas of training can lead to sanctions by one's licensing board and professional organization. It can also, as when a counselor presents with competence to give legal or medical advice yet has not been to law or medical school, lead to civil and even criminal punishment. If you practiced law or medicine and then received a family counseling degree and license, you could, in fact, give legal or medical advice as long as you have remained current with legal statutes or remained board certified in medicine. If you have not done all of these things, you can only tell clients that in your professional opinion they might benefit from a legal or medical consultation. You can also provide them with a list of names, usually three, of professionals you have worked with and trust and who are licensed to provide the services the client needs.

The Manning-Kelly family provides an excellent example, as you will see in Chapter 12. If Christina and her family had not been referred by a physician, the family counselor, noting Christina's weight, would have been ethically bound to ask when she had last had a routine medical examination by a primary care physician. She would also have been ethically bound to suggest that Christina see a physician as soon as possible if she were not under the care of one already. Finally, in cases where there are medical issues beyond the family counselor's scope of practice and especially those that can be life-threatening, the family counselor can insist that the client also be in treatment with an appropriate physician as a prerequisite for seeing the client herself or himself. Such insistence actually protects the family counselor from charges that she or he has attempted to treat the medical aspects of anorexia nervosa, for example, behavior that would be outside her or his scope of practice both legally and ethically. With respect to Christina in particular, the family counselor could, with permission, contact the primary care physician to discuss the possibility that she would benefit from psychotropic medication and whether the primary care physician would prefer the family counselor refer Christina back to her for medication assessment or to a psychiatrist.

SUPERVISION AS A LIFELONG PROCESS

It is a counselor's ethical responsibility to obtain supervision throughout his or her practice with clients. Of course, clinical supervision is required for anyone who is seeking licensure. The number of hours varies from license to license and sometimes from state to state for the same license. Additionally, if a counselor, already licensed in one state moves to a new state, she or he may be required to obtain additional supervision hours prior to being granted licensure.

It should emphasized, however, that supervision should continue even after licensure has been obtained. Although many professionals in the field do not seek supervision unless there is a problem, we recommend supervision as a lifelong activity. Many practitioners within agencies and hospitals participate in teams that meet regularly to discuss clients and can use those meetings to ask for help with their own reactions to a particular client. Family counselors in private practice usually join a peer supervision group. As long as no identifying information about clients is revealed, peer supervision is entirely ethical. Most peer supervision groups focus on a particular topic or on the counselor's response to clients (see Chapter 10).

As mental health professionals, we run the risk of becoming islands unto ourselves. Seeking supervision throughout the time we practice not only helps us break out of our isolation but also protects us and our clients from the narrowness of any one person's perspective.

ETHICAL DECISION-MAKING MODEL

Laws and ethical codes do not keep up with changes in practice. For example, when Facebook and Skype were introduced, there were no laws or ethical codes covering their use in practice. Now, we know that neither is compliant with federal codes governing the protection of patient information. However, most, if not all, codes of ethics do not specifically address the types of social media that can and cannot be used in practice. It is up to the family counselor to use what she or he knows along with ethical decision making to determine how to act when, for example, a client "friends" her or him on Facebook or asks for a Skype session while out of town for an extended period of time for work or to care for a family member.

Additionally, ethical decisions are not always clear. Sometimes trying to do the right thing for a client is in direct conflict with what's best for a counselor's agency or a third party, such as the client's spouse. In cases like these, where choices are not clear, it is helpful to have a model in place for making decisions. The following step-by-step ethical decision-making model comes from the work of Corey, Corey, and Callanan (1998):

Step 1: Identify the problem.

Step 2: Identify the potential issues involved.

Step 3: Review relevant ethical guidelines.

Step 4: Know relevant laws and regulations.

Step 5: Obtain consultation.

Step 6: Consider possible and probable courses of action.

Step 7: List the consequences of the probable courses of action.

Step 8: Decide on what appears to be the best course of action.

Pay special attention to Step 5. It is important to consult with your supervisor throughout the process.

CONCLUSION

With appropriate coursework and supervision in the principles and practice of family counseling, professionals holding a variety of licenses may practice family counseling. These include psychiatry, psychology, social work, counseling, marriage and family therapy, pastoral counseling, and human services. We have included the ethical codes from the professional organizations responsible for the practices of social workers, counselors, marriage and family therapists, and human services professionals. We recommend that if you pursue one of these professions you also familiarize yourself with the ethical codes codified in the laws of the state in which you practice.

Extend Your Learning:

1. Apply the eight-stage Ethical Decision-Making Model to any ethical questions you may have had about working with the Manning-Kelly family. What is the problem? Which ethical guidelines applied? Which laws applied? What were the possible consequences? What course of action did you decide upon and what are your conclusions after working through the eight steps?

2. Locate other ethical dilemmas or cases online or in other resources, and repeat the activity above with the cases you find.

ETHICAL CODES

American Counseling Association Code of Ethics http://www.counseling.org/resources/aca-code-of-ethics.pdf

National Association of Social Workers Code of Ethics http://www.socialworkers.org/pubs/code/default.asp

American Association for Marriage and Family Therapy Code of Ethics https://www.aamft.org/iMIS15/AAMFT/Content/Legal_Ethics/code_of_ethics.aspx

National Organization for Human Services Code of Ethics http://www.nationalhuman services.org/ethical-standards-for-hs-professionals

REFERENCES

Corey, G., Corey, M., & Callanan, P. (1998). *Issues and ethics in the helping professions* (5th ed.). Pacific Grove, CA: Brooks/Cole.

Tarasoff v. Regents of the University of California, 17 Cal. 3d 425, 551 P.2d 334, 131 Cal. Rptr. 14 (Cal. 1976).

U.S. Department of Health and Human Services. (n.d.). *Understanding health information privacy*. Retrieved from http://www.hhs.gov/ocr/privacy/hipaa/understanding/index.html

FOR FURTHER STUDY

Chamow, L., Patterson, J., Williams, L., Andrews, T., & Grauf-Grounds, C. (2009). Getting unstuck in therapy. In *Essential skills in family therapy: From the first interview to termination.* (2nd ed.) (pp. 223–225). New York, NY: Guilford.

Corey, M., & Corey, G. (2011). Stress, burnout, and self-care. In *Becoming a helper* (6th ed.) (pp. 304–331). Pacific Grove, CA: Brooks/Cole.

Corey, M., & Corey, G. (2011). Ethical and legal issues facing helpers. In *Becoming a helper* (6th ed.) (pp. 217–254). Pacific Grove, CA: Brooks/Cole.

Cottone, R. R., & Claus, R. E. (2000). Ethical decision models. A review of the literature. *Journal of Counseling & Development, 78*(3), 275–283.

Kiser, P. M. (2008). *The Human services internship: Getting the most from your experience* (2nd ed.). Belmont CA: Brooks/Cole.

Pope, K. S. (2010). *Ethics in psychotherapy and counseling: A practical guide* (4th ed.). New York, NY: Wiley.

Roth, H., & Meisel, A. (1997, May). Dangerousness, confidentiality, and the duty to warn. *The American Journal of Psychiatry, 134*(5), 508–511.

Wilcoxon, A., Remley, Jr., T., & Gladding, S. (2013). Legal issues in marriage and family therapy. In *Ethical, legal, and professional issues in the practice of marriage and family therapy* (5th ed.). New York, NY: Pearson.

Zur, O. (2007). *Boundaries in psychotherapy: Ethical and clinical explorations.* Washington, DC: American Psychological Association.

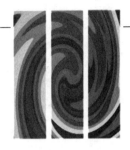

PART IV

Current Trends in Family Counseling

CHAPTER 12

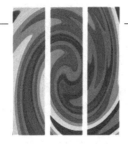

Issues Requiring Services Beyond the Counselor's Scope of Practice

The Manning-Kelly family is replete with issues that require services that family counselors are not trained to provide. Emma, for example, may require both speech and occupational therapy. And family counselors may facilitate support groups for breast cancer patients, like Barbara, and their families; grief groups for family members following a death; or caretaker support groups for women, like Sally, who are caring for an ailing spouse. However, only a professional with medical training and licensing can diagnose a biomedical problem, prescribe and administer medication, or perform surgery.

Licensing laws and codes of ethics for all counselors and psychotherapists mandate working only within the licensee's scope of practice. This means that unless the counselor or psychotherapist is trained, experienced, and holds a license to practice a particular service, she or he must refer to someone who has these qualifications. Sometimes, even when the need is within the family counselor's scope of practice, she or he must refer to another professional in order to avoid a dual relationship. For example, it might be appropriate to refer Christina to a physician who is licensed to prescribe medication for assessment regarding its potential usefulness. Unless the family therapist also holds a license to prescribe medication (e.g., if she were a licensed psychiatrist who completed family counseling training), she must make this referral because medication assessment and management is outside her scope of practice. Alternatively, following revelation of the abuse, Christina might benefit from individual counseling to deal with its impact on her sexuality, something she might not want to talk about in front of her mother, brother, and half sister. Even if working with abuse survivors is within the family counselor's scope of practice, she would need to refer Christina because her relationship with the family precludes a second, or dual, relationship with Christina.

Knowing when to refer, to whom to refer, and how to make referrals to maximize the possibility of a good outcome are critical skills for all counselors and psychotherapists. Ethically, family counselors are required to provide a list of at least three professionals when they make a referral, so that the client can choose, in other words, to maximize the client's autonomy. In order to generate these lists, family counselors must get to know other professionals and organizations in their communities and maintain working relationships with the professionals to whom they refer.

In this chapter, we will revisit the eight family issues discussed in Chapter 9 and describe more specific situations in which family counselors may need to refer families for other services. To review, these eight issues are multicultural families, LGBTQIA families, single parent families, blended families, families with aging members, biomedical disease processes in families, mental and substance abuse disorders within families, and domestic violence.

CULTURAL COMPETENCE IN MULTICULTURAL FAMILY COUNSELING

Cultural competence was described in Chapter 9, and the authors recommend you read Diller's (2007) and Lum's (2007) books for more details. Additionally, Ann Fadiman's (1997) book is an excellent case study about the pitfalls of not practicing in a culturally competent way.

Family counselors need not be experts about every culture. It is appropriate to ask clients for information the family counselor does not know about the family's culture. First, even if the family counselor is knowledgeable about the particular culture, she or he has no way of knowing unless she or he asks how enculturated the family is into the dominant culture. And second, there exists tremendous variation among individuals and families within cultures, and thus assuming all families of a particular culture are alike is a form of stereotyping that devalues them.

STOP AND THINK:

1. Do you have parents or grandparents who were born in another country? If not, do you know someone who does?

2. Notice whether and how identification with the traditions of that country's culture have changed or not over the three generations of your family.

When working with bicultural and biracial clients and families, family counselors tend to practice more collaboratively. Clients can easily recognize differences between their own and the family counselor's experiences. These differences are also a factor within biracial and bicultural families. Christina and Martin Jr. did not share the experience of being Black with their mother, which may have impacted their relationship with her. Similarly, they did not share the experience of being White with their father. And neither parent could fully understand their experience of being biracial, because neither parent was.

The writers have speculated that Christina and Martin Jr.'s distance from their parents and half sister could have been a product of the family life cycle stage; how Emma's cerebral palsy had been handled within the family, particularly the extra and possibly unnecessary attention their mother gave her because of it; unresolved tension between their biological parents; or the family's dynamics. A culturally competent counselor would also wonder whether Christina and Martin Jr.'s biracial experience played a role in their relationships with their parents and siblings. Finally, we do not know what their father's, stepmother's, and grandparents' experiences of being Black were, given that they grew up prior to the civil rights movement, when public facilities, including schools, were often segregated and their own parents could not vote.

The family counselor also would not know unless she asked about the impact of cultural differences on Liz and Martin's marriage and how those impacts were managed. She did not know how their extended families reacted to their marriage and how the community in which they lived reacted to them and their biracial children. It is interesting, though perhaps coincidental, that Martin's second marriage was to a Black woman, and Liz's second marriage was to a White man, and it would be appropriate for a family counselor to ask whether their choices were intentional.

The prevalence of eating disorders among White and Black women was addressed briefly in Chapter 9. Irrespective of culture, Christina seems to have learned her concern about weight and appearance from her mother and grandmother, the "White side," as she put it, of her family. It would have been important for the family counselor to ask more about how Martin, Daniella, and their extended families viewed and related to Christina's behavior and attitudes about food and weight.

Jason and Ashley were also bicultural. They were first generation Americans on their mother's side, as she was a Middle Eastern immigrant, and their father and his family are of western European descent. Their family structure was also different than the one in which Christina and Martin Jr. were raised. Their maternal grandparents took a much more active role in daily child care than it appears either Liz's or Martin's parents did. Thus, Jason and Ashley were regularly exposed to their grandparents' cultural attitudes, behaviors, dress, and other traditions and may have been challenged by their grandparents when they behaved like other children in the dominant culture.

Middle Eastern culture is very different from Black culture, and immigrant parents whose children are born and raised here may be very different from families of the same ethnic or racial origin who have lived here longer. The difference is enculturation, that process by which individuals and families take on aspects of the dominant culture in which they live. Families vary tremendously in terms of how enculturated they become over time. The only way to determine how enculturated or conflicted Jason and Ashley were would have been to ask.

A family counselor cannot generalize that the experiences of being bicultural are identical for these pairs of stepsiblings. And, again, it is beyond the scope of this text to describe in detail culturally competent practice with each of these cultural groups. Rather, the authors encourage counselors to learn from reading, continuing education, supervision, and colleagues; asking their clients questions; and remaining mindful that they cannot make assumptions about any client family's experiences based on either their own or generalized information about another culture.

Since not all members of the same cultural or racial group share identical experiences or values, it is not necessary to refer clients to members of their own racial or ethnic group. What is necessary is to practice in a culturally competent way, respecting the uniqueness of the client family and its members' experiences.

Although it is easier for clients when the family counselor speaks their first language, it is often difficult to find a family counselor who speaks a particular family's first language, when it is not English. Unless a client family is unable to communicate in a language the family counselor speaks, there exists no ethical reason to refer.

LGBTQIA CLIENTS

Christina's cousin, Paul, is gay, and he and his life partner Matthew were in the process of adopting a child. They lived in a state that did not recognize same-sex marriages or domestic partnerships even when the partners are heterosexual. Thus, there were complex legal issues in the adoption process and in protecting the child once adopted that would not have arisen for a couple that was able to marry. Their adoption may have therefore required more involvement by professionals other than family counselors and incurred more expense than it would have if Paul and Matthew's commitment to one another were legally recognized.

Even if they had not been in the process of adopting a child, Paul and Matthew would have faced some of the same issues of being labeled different and devalued that people of color face and that White heterosexual couples do not. Sometimes gay and lesbian partners, as well as transgendered individuals, need to keep the nature of themselves and their relationship hidden from coworkers in order to feel safe in their jobs. Other times, one or more family members may initiate a cutoff with the LGBTQIA family member. And finally, one or both partners may be a member of a cultural group that holds even more negative views of homosexuality than the dominant White community does. LGBTQIA clients who are not White sometimes cannot identify with LGBTQIA groups that ignore the experience of also being an American of color.

Helping Matthew and Paul manage these challenges so that they do not undermine their relationship is within the scope of practice of a family counselor who is culturally competent to work with LGBTQIA couples and families. A family counselor needs to understand Paul and Matthew's unique experiences within their families, professions, cultures, and the larger society in order to be most effective.

There are a variety of issues that also arise in any adoption. These include whether the adoption is of an infant or older child, identified special needs child, domestic or international, or bicultural. Adoption often involves an agency, and the family counselor working with clients who are adopting may be asked for an assessment of the prospective parents' mental health and family stability. The agency wants to ensure that the adopted child will be safe and well cared for, which no family counselor can guarantee. Sometimes prospective parents experience the seemingly endless process of interviews and paperwork as obstructive and become defensive and guarded, and family counselors can support the couple through these hurdles. And finally, adoption always involves an attorney, who may also want information from the counselor and who may become a source of stress for the prospective parents.

SINGLE-PARENT FAMILIES

Family counselors may refer the members of single-parent families to grief or divorce groups in order to adapt to the loss that resulted in becoming a single-parent family. Additionally, a number of legal and financial issues may arise following a divorce or the death of a spouse or parent, requiring the family to seek financial, legal, or court-appointed services.

This is further complicated when a domestic partnership was not legally recognized by the state in which the family resides. If the remaining parent is not biologically related to the children or a parent of record in the adoption, she or he may not have parenting rights, and the deceased or estranged partner or her or his family may attempt to gain custody. She or he also would have no financial rights nor the ability to make decisions for a dying partner.

Sometimes parenting issues also become part of legal proceedings, particularly when there are custody disputes or mutual accusations of incompetence. The family counselor may need to work collaboratively with other professionals, with appropriate consent from the client. Most importantly, the family counselor cannot provide legal or financial advice unless trained and licensed to do so. However, the family counselor can advise clients to seek legal or financial counsel elsewhere and provide a list of professionals.

The majority of single-parent families include a mother and her children. And data indicate that female-headed families are more likely to live in poverty than male-headed families. When family counselors work with families living in poverty, they may need to refer them for support services such as food stamps, subsidized housing, and Medicaid health insurance coverage.

BLENDED FAMILIES

The term *blended family* refers to families in which at least two nuclear families have combined to create a third family. Blended families involve at least one of the spouses having been in a previous relationship that produced at least one child. There are always issues of loss when a family dissolves and, when grief remains unresolved, emotional issues may affect subsequent relationships. Additionally, there are legal issues that may continue into a new relationship, for example managing shared custody or visitation by the noncustodial parent and child support when a relationship has dissolved or inheritance when a parent and partner has died. The family counselor needs to be prepared to refer when emotional issues are beyond his or her scope of practice and when legal issues need to be addressed by an attorney.

There are three blended families in the Manning-Kelly and Jones families that exemplify a range of issues that may require a referral from the family counselor. These were described in detail in Chapter 9 and will be briefly reviewed here.

Sally and Jim's situation is not uncommon. They were both widowed and remarried and had assets from their previous marriages, as well as objects of sentimental value to their adult children. Couples who find themselves in Sally and Jim's situation may need to be referred for financial and legal consultation in order to protect one another and their own and each other's adult children.

Family counselors need to be aware of tension between the aging parents' biological and stepchildren, as well as tension within each sibling subsystem. As Jim's dementia progresses, his ability to function independently and Sally's ability to care for him will deteriorate, thus incurring decisions about his care and related expenses. Health insurance supplements to Medicare, long-term care insurance, and Medicaid may alleviate some of the financial burden. However, Sally and Jim's adult children may express anger regarding whose money is being spent on whom and who will support Sally living independently after Jim has entered assisted living or depleted their joint resources.

While family counselors cannot advise clients about creating wills and prenuptial agreements, they can recommend that remarrying couples consult with an attorney to create both, as well as health care directives. They can ask remarrying couples how they want to handle their money in the event one of them becomes sick or dies and then recommend that the spouses discuss what they want with an attorney who will use her or his knowledge of the law to create legally binding documents.

A family counselor can recommend counseling with all the adult children together, either with or without their parents present. Helping adult siblings and stepsiblings to see one another as people who care about both parents as well as their own interests can open lines of communication so that the adult children can more effectively deal with issues surrounding their parents' aging, death, and the use and disbursement of resources and assets.

Liz and Mark have also created a blended family, although most of their children live at home, as have Martin and Daniella. While Mark and Liz already had a divorce settlement and child support and custody in place, any conflict around either necessitates a consultation with their attorneys, even though the family counselor can address emotional and family systems aspects of the conflict. It is important for parents to negotiate with each other about alternatives when there is conflict, rather than triangling their children into their conflict. If they cannot, it remains preferable for them to communicate through their attorneys or a mediator. If the family counselor cannot facilitate their communication or they decline his or her help, the family counselor should recommend they seek legal assistance and provide referrals if needed.

Although Mark's children from his first marriage were young adults, he continued to provide financial assistance to them, in part because he believed Shoshana and her parents had disrupted the more nurturing aspects of his relationships with his young adult children. Mark and Liz have argued about his continued support of Jason and Ashley, as described in previous chapters, and addressing the conflict was within the family counselor's scope of practice. Because Ashley and Jason are no longer legal dependents, there are no legal issues requiring referral to an attorney.

Although Daniella and Martin had created a blended family, she was never married to Jamal's father. From a legal perspective, this means that Martin may have been able to adopt Jamal without Jamal's father's legal relinquishment of parental rights. Laws vary from state to state, and adoption is an issue only an attorney can address. It is not the family counselor's role to suggest adoption but rather to respond if the family brings it up by suggesting and providing a referral. Additionally, if Jamal's father were to become a problem for Daniella and Martin, which appeared unlikely given that he had remained in contact with Jamal, the family counselor could suggest they consult with an attorney if the situation warrants.

As with all families, understanding the issues, dynamics, and pitfalls of blended families and knowing how to intervene effectively does not preclude the need for professionals other than the family counselor to become involved. As part of training and licensing, family counselors learn about their own scope of practice, what additional services to recommend under what circumstances, and how to present referrals to maximize the likelihood the family will follow through with them.

FAMILIES WITH AGING MEMBERS

As the U.S. population ages, there is an increasing need for family counselors with gerontology experience to deliver counseling and other services to the elderly and their families. In Chapter 9, the authors described issues relating to aging family members that counselors can manage. To review, these include clients facing physical and mental decline, loss of independence, and impending mortality; adult siblings disagreeing about how to distribute caretaking responsibilities; and aging spouses balancing one's need for care with the toll giving the care is taking on the other's biomedical and mental health. Although family counselors can provide services such as grief and caretaker support groups, there remain other services family counselors must refer to other professionals.

Family counselors may need to be part of a team of in- and out-patient medical staff, extended care facility staff, hospice staff, and physical, occupational, and speech therapists. Coordinating legal services for health care power of attorney, living wills, and do not resuscitate documents may also be a part of the job, although family counselors cannot provide the actual legal services.

Finally, in some settings, family counselors may be called upon to coordinate in-home services, such as home health care, transportation to and from medical and senior citizens' facilities, and meals on wheels delivery. The cost of care may also be an issue, and family counselors can help connect family members to the various financial services available in their community.

Both Liz and Mark were facing issues around their parents' aging process that may have required services beyond the family counselor's scope of practice. Liz's stepfather's decline was clear to his children and stepchildren. Additionally, its toll on Sally's health concerned them.

Family counselors are often asked to see aging couples who are in situations similar to Sally and Jim's and are expected to help the adult children convince the parents that the patient requires a higher level of care or help the parents convince the children more care is unnecessary, depending on who arranged the appointment. While making the kinds of life-changing decisions Sally and Jim faced was not part of a family counselor's role, family counselors can help family members clarify their thoughts and more effectively communicate with each other so that everyone's perspective is heard and considered. Family counselors can also provide referrals to support services within the community, such as senior centers, adult day care, home health services, and experts at county departments of aging.

As noted in previous chapters, all states have reporting laws which include a family counselor's duty to report a reasonable suspicion that someone is a danger to self, others, or unable to care for himself or herself. If, in the family counselor's professional opinion, Jim's rage and forgetfulness posed a danger to Sally or his wandering put him at risk, he or she would have to report the concerns to the appropriate legal or social service agency. You will need to be familiar with the laws of the state in which you practice to know to whom to report concerns. You can also make an anonymous call to ask whether the situation requires reporting, if you are uncertain.

If Jim and Sally decided to pursue an assisted living facility for him, the adult children could help them research and visit facilities that might be a good fit for him. The diagnosing physician would also need to be involved in the referral process. Additionally, there may be legal and financial decisions, including whether Jim was mentally competent, whether the cost of maintaining a home for Sally while Jim was in assisted living was feasible, and the impact of maintaining separate domiciles on Sally's financial security. While family counselors cannot provide any of these related services, we can explain the process as well as make referrals, when necessary. For example, because Jim's dementia could be at least in part a result of the traumatic brain injury (TBI) he sustained in combat during the Korean War, he may have been eligible for Veteran's benefits that would have deferred some or all of the additional expenses for his care. Alerting the family to this possibility and either suggesting they contact the local Veterans' Affairs office or providing them with a phone number and perhaps a contact person are within the family counselor's scope of practice.

Because Jim and Sally have created a blended family, the legal and financial considerations might be complicated by disagreements among the stepchildren. Sally's children were protective of both her health and her financial security, whereas Jim's children contended that since Jim was better off financially when they married, much of the money was not Sally's to use. The legal aspects of this conflict would have been much simpler if Jim and Sally had specified how their assets would be used during their lifetimes and distributed after their deaths in a prenuptial agreement prior to their marriage. While a family counselor cannot write such a prenuptial document, she or he can suggest a remarrying couple do so with an attorney.

Helping adult children cope with the emotional repercussions of being told by an attorney that what one thought was one's mother's money was not her own falls within the scope of practice of a family counselor. These emotions may include anger, anxiety, hopelessness, and incredulity, which is more often referred to as denial. In Sally and Jim's situation, they were legitimate feelings, and family members needed to acknowledge them, accept them, and do what needed to be done to protect Sally while getting both her and Jim the services they needed.

Mark's parents, Emily and Bryan, presented a different set of challenges, as noted in Chapter 9. Aging family members like Emily and Bryan do not have a compelling need for the types of services Jim did. So a family counselor's approach to Mark's concerns about their health and well-being and to their upset that their son was pushing them to move would not be considered issues of safety. The family counselor could focus exclusively on the dynamics of the parent-son relationship, the family's realistic assessment of the pros and cons of Emily and Bryan remaining in their home, and then guide the family through the decision-making process. A family counselor's familiarity with services available in Emily and Bryan's community and the mechanism for determining whether they qualified for any would be helpful. However, because this family counselor was not in the state where Mark's parents lived, she might not have been familiar with services and qualification requirements in their state and could have instead suggested they or Mark call their state or county department of aging for suggestions.

Emily and Bryan needed to consider the relative costs of staying in their home or moving, as well as their ability to maintain their home. Pragmatics and emotions can be difficult to balance, especially when aging family members equate moving from their home with losing their independence. If they decided to move, they would also need to decide whether to remain in the city where they currently lived and presumably had a social support network or move closer to Mark so he could be more involved with obtaining and monitoring care and other services as they continued to age. These were difficult decisions, with multiple factors in favor of each option. A family counselor can help with some but not all of them; for example, she or he cannot advise the family about the financial consequences of their decisions.

Martin's parents were both in their mid-60s and were the center of Martin's extended family, which included his siblings and their children. Martin's father's health was excellent, but his mother had suffered mild cardiac (heart related) problems for a number of years. She became very ill about the time her youngest child left for college, which may have affected her daughter's adjustment to living away from home. Since then, her condition had been well managed, and she was active and independent. At the time the family was in family counseling, she only needed routine medical care to monitor her health. The family counselor would have no role in referring her for services unless she needed to find a new cardiologist or primary care physician.

FAMILIES WITH BIOMEDICAL CONDITION

While biomedical diseases require diagnosis, intervention, and ongoing care by physicians and allied health personnel, family counselors can help patients, caretakers, and the entire family adapt to the changes, emotions, and demands brought about by ongoing, or chronic, diseases. We discussed the biomedical diagnoses present in the Manning-Kelly and Jones families in Chapter 9 and those related to aging in a previous section. In this section, we review the need to refer for medical and allied health services.

We have already discussed some of the issues associated with Jim's Alzheimer's. Additionally, the medical team that treats an Alzheimer's patient will explain to the family the associated health consequences, which include infections associated with decreased functioning as the brain deteriorates. The family counselor may benefit from conversations with the medical team, so that she or he can determine, for example, whether a family's anxiety is medically warranted.

Family counselors may be called upon to help the family understand the full meaning of a diagnosis and prognosis, find ways to cope with the patient and her or his disease, and make decisions about when the patient requires more care than the family can provide at home, as recommended by the medical team.

As patients lose independence and function, their reactions may add another level of difficulty for the rest of the family. For example, when patients with dementia or circulatory disease are no longer able to drive, they may rage and manipulate family members, and these relatives may find it difficult to say no even when they know that the patient's driving is unsafe. Physicians can be helpful in deciding when it is no longer safe for the patient to drive, and family counselors can be helpful to family members in learning to assert themselves despite their complex feelings about the patient's deterioration and the patient's reaction to losing independence. Family counselors can also encourage family members to seek further information from the medical team when questions arise that are beyond the counselor's knowledge or scope of practice.

At the other end of the life cycle, 4-year-old Emma experienced brain trauma during delivery and had been diagnosed with cerebral palsy. While cerebral palsy is not a progressive disease, it cannot be cured, and so the patient and her family need to adapt to her special needs and the impact of these needs and the diagnosis itself on the patient and family. Depending on the severity of diagnosis, Emma may be unable to reach her full intellectual or physical potential. That she walked and communicated verbally with Liz and attended preschool suggested that she will become fully independent as an adult.

As mentioned in Chapter 9, one hears both verbal and nonverbal messages that suggest Liz may be overly involved with Emma in transcripts of family counseling sessions. A family counselor could, with permission, communicate with the medical team and then, if appropriate, help redirect Liz's attention to include the developmental needs of her older children, who needed a mother to whom they felt important. However, only the medical team could advise the family about what the family could expect for Emma and how much parental attention her disabilities required. Similarly, if she were to need care after Liz and Mark died, an attorney would need to help them make arrangements for her.

As discussed in Chapter 9, when a child is born with special needs or becomes chronically ill, each of her or his parents may cope differently. The family counselor can assess the adaptability of the marital relationship and facilitate prevention or treatment of marital deterioration secondary to how the parents cope. However, if the marriage does not survive the stress of a special needs child, the family counselor can refer both partners to attorneys.

When Emma was diagnosed with cerebral palsy, Liz was distraught. Mark understood that the doctor did not yet know how severe her disability would be and decided to defer being upset until they knew with what they were coping. He also thought Liz was overly emotional and that it might have helped her if he remained calm. So he showed virtually no emotion following the diagnosis. Liz interpreted his behavior as lack of empathy or attachment to her or their daughter. Mark was confused and hurt by her lack of appreciation for his strong demeanor. Perhaps these discrepant ways of coping and related misunderstanding were the origin of Liz's overinvolvement with Emma. And perhaps they were also the beginning of the deterioration of Liz and Mark's marriage.

Barbara's breast cancer was in remission and also a factor in the lives of the Manning-Kelly family members. Unless there was a compelling reason for the family counselor to include Barbara in family counseling, there would be no need for her to speak to Barbara's medical team. However, if a member of the immediate family had cancer, even if it were in remission, the family counselor would be well advised to consult with someone from the medical team. Family challenges with which the family counselor can be helpful were described in Chapter 9.

Returning to the identified patient, Christina, it was also important for the family counselor to know whether there were biomedical consequences of her eating disorder. These may include cessation of menstruation, damage to bones, and consequences for heart, kidney, liver, and immune system functioning. When weight loss is extreme, death may occur, and anorexic patients are usually admitted to hospitals when their weight drops below a certain percent of their ideal body weight. When self-induced vomiting occurs with bulimia, glandular, dental, and esophageal damage may occur. Although the literature does not mention damage to the pancreas, anecdotal observation suggests that family counselors need to assess whether there is a history of an eating disorder when clients in their 20s present with diabetes and no other health or family risk factors, as eating disorders can disrupt treatment for diabetes.

Family counselors need to be sure that clients presenting with either anorexia or bulimia are also under the care of a physician. Monitoring weight is beyond the scope of a family counselor's practice. In addition, it may place her or him in the role of a controlling parent, and anorexia is sometimes a way of telling an overcontrolling parent that the patient cannot be fully controlled. Replicating that dynamic in the client-counselor relationship could undermine the healing potential of the counseling relationship. Minuchin, whose theory of structural family therapy was described in Chapter 6, would tell the mothers of hospitalized anorexic patients to force them to eat. This intervention was aimed at highlighting the battle for control over the client's body.

Increasingly, eating disorders are being treated with psychotropic medication, particularly antidepressants. While there is some indication that seizures can be triggered when patients with a history of bulimia take certain antidepressants, there is also evidence that some antidepressants stimulate appetite in anorexic patients. If you are counseling a client with an eating disorder, it is important to ask whether she or he has been assessed for medication and request permission to exchange information with the prescribing practitioner if she or he is taking medication.

Clients are best served when family counselors work with their physicians, irrespective of the biomedical or mental health diagnosis. You must obtain written permission to exchange information with the specific physicians and allied health professionals involved in the patient's care prior to sharing information about the client, even if the information might be helpful to the physician with her or him. If a client declines permission, it may be helpful to explore her or his concerns.

There are a number of in-patient treatment programs for patients with eating disorders throughout the United States. Best practices include a family counseling component. Because of the way medical costs are reimbursed, eating disordered patients may need to leave treatment before they are stabilized. For example, a client with whom one of the authors recently worked learned how to eat to gain a normal weight, but then funding for her care ran out before she achieved her target weight and learned how to maintain it. Family counselors can suggest clients in similar situations ask their physicians about the availability of nutrition counseling and obtain permission to communicate with both the physician and nutritionist in order to best coordinate care.

Christina's uncle, David, suffered from metabolic syndrome. This diagnosis refers to a combination of type II diabetes, high blood pressure, and high cholesterol. Prolonged substance abuse can compromise a variety of organ systems, and metabolic disease is also related to obesity. If David were a part of the family system in your office, it would be helpful for you to obtain permission to talk to his physician. Depending on the specifics of David's health and history, the physician would be able to provide information about prioritizing weight loss and treatment for substance abuse. Because David had been abusing substances for an extended period of time, his treatment would most likely begin in an in-patient program and your work would involve assessing for relapses, monitoring his compliance with out-patient treatment recommendations, and working with the family to change the family dynamics that may have contributed to his tendency to abuse substances. For weight loss, you would likely also want a specialist in diet and exercise for people with compromised cardiovascular functioning involved in his care.

It is not unusual for caretakers to exhaust themselves and become ill caring for a patient to the exclusion of themselves. Sally's blood pressure and sleeplessness, while possibly secondary to the stress of caring for Jim, required medical assessment. Family counselors who work with physicians can help clients manage stress while the physicians monitor the health consequences and biomedical symptoms.

FAMILIES COPING WITH MENTAL
ILLNESS AND SUBSTANCE ABUSE DISORDERS

Mental Illness. As family counselors, our job is to diagnose and treat mental illness from the perspective of the family's impact. So you may wonder why you are reading a section about mental illness. There are two reasons. First, diagnosis and treatment of the mental disorder itself may not be within the scope of practice for all family counselors. Some states preclude family counselors who are not also psychologists or psychiatrists from doing some kinds of diagnostic work, such as psychological testing. And all states preclude family counselors from engaging in medication management, brain scanning, and interpretation of the results of biomedical tests. Additionally, your training may not include work with certain patient populations, such as substance abusers or psychotic patients, and so you cannot engage in work with them without more specific training and supervision.

The second reason to include a section on mental illness is that some patients require services that your agency or practice may not be able to provide. These include, but are not limited to, substance abuse programs, in-patient treatment, day treatment, sheltered living situations, and assessment of cognitive impairment. However, if you continue your training in family counseling, you may be able to provide support services for the families of these patients and referrals for the patients themselves.

The Manning-Kelly family contained at least four members with diagnosable mental disorders and a fifth who potentially did: Liz and Christina both evidenced eating disorders; David had a history of bipolar disorder complicated by his polysubstance abuse; and Jim suffered from dementia, which is an organic mental disorder. It is also possible that Emma had developmental delays associated with her cerebral palsy. Each of these would have been addressed, as well as the client and family's need for services beyond family counseling.

Eating disorders are, in part, a disturbed relationship with food. As such, they often reflect or serve as metaphors for disturbed relationships in other parts of the client's life. For example, induced vomiting has been viewed as a metaphor for spewing anger and overeating for stuffing down unwanted emotions. In either case, anger and other feelings that might be productively dealt with within the client or her or his relationships are avoided and thus remain unresolved.

In many cases, eating disorders can be treated with out-patient psychotherapy. Family counselors may require additional training and supervision, depending on what the program from which they graduated and their postdegree supervision provided. Eating disorders are complex, usually involving internalized cultural beliefs about attractiveness and health, individual and family histories, family dynamics that subtly support the eating disorder or prevent change, trauma, and entrenched beliefs about perfection, control, goodness, comfort, and food. Clients who present with eating disorders may also engage in other dissociative self-harm, such as cutting. A family counselor working effectively with eating disordered clients must be able to diagnose and treat trauma, psychodynamic processes, and family systems processes, as well as the behaviors apparent in the disorder's symptom picture. For all of these reasons, family counselors must know when to refer a client with a diagnosed eating disorder to another mental health professional, as well as to a physician.

Eating disorders can be life-threatening. Anorexia, which involves restricting caloric intake and overexercising, can cause bone, cardiovascular, reproductive, and brain damage. Bulimia adds the potential of esophageal, glandular, and dental damage to the mix. As when treating any mental disorder, family counselors must prioritize addressing life-threatening and other self-destructive behaviors and use whatever supports are available, including assessment for in-patient admission and referral to a psychiatrist for medication assessment and management, when necessary. For most patients with bulimic symptoms, interventions that facilitate binging without purging reduce the immediate risks.

Some clients with eating disorders have been hospitalized at least once for the disorder. Some have been in residential treatment programs, either in or out of a hospital facility. Any client with an eating disorder is best served when under the simultaneous care of a physician with whom the mental health professional has a good working relationship. The physician can monitor weight and health sequelae, or consequences, as well as assess and prescribe psychotropic medication. And, although nutritionists cannot change disordered eating, working with a nutritionist can help clients identify what they need to eat to regain and then maintain a healthy weight.

Because Christina was referred by her primary care physician, the family counselor could assume her weight did not suggest a need for immediate medical intervention. However, it would have been helpful for the family counselor to obtain consent to exchange information with that physician so that the two could work together to be sure Christina got the care she needed. Given Christina's age, a family counselor who works with eating disorders might either schedule an individual session to more fully assess Christina's disorder and then make recommendations for treatment or refer her to someone who was not concurrently seeing the family. The family counselor might also discuss the value of a referral for nutritional counseling with the physician, if she or he had not, either now or at some point in the future when Christina was more willing to change her eating behavior. It is beyond the scope of this text to describe how the family counselor might facilitate Christina's progress to that point. As with many clients, Christina was in a situation in which other people thought her eating was problematic, and she had not yet endorsed it as an issue for her. This stance complicated and extended treatment.

Given what you have learned about family systems, it may not surprise you that Liz had also struggled with an eating disorder, as has her sister Barbara. A family counselor would ask Liz about the history of her eating disorder, when it began, what she thought triggered it, and how she managed it. The family counselor, whether seeing Christina individually or within the context of her family, would focus on the family dynamics and intergenerational messages that support eating disorders and prevent change. Some clients model their parents' relationship with food. Others find that their problem serves a function in maintaining family system homeostasis (see Chapter 4). For example, Christina's symptoms may have distracted her parents from emotional pain and conflict, and so she may have experienced subtle pressure to continue. Unfortunately, family dynamics usually reside below the level of family members' awareness, and family members do not comprehend an intellectual description of the pressures the client experiences to remain the same.

Imagine saying to Liz and Martin or to Liz and Mark, "I think Christina can't stop starving herself because she's afraid you'll fight more." Some family counselors would say exactly that (see Chapter 7). However they would say it to "gently perturb the system" and not because they expected the family to intellectually grasp the concept. Had the counselor said that in the first or second session, Liz and both Mark and Martin would likely have become so defensive that they would have left counseling. So family counselors work to change the dynamics, based on the assumption that changing the dynamics will remove impediments to client change.

If you are interested in working with families in which a member has an eating disorder or individually with eating disordered clients, who are often affected by the dynamics of the families in which they grew up or with whom they live, then you need specific training and supervision in diagnosing and treating eating disorders on both individual and family system levels. You also need to form and maintain both referral and working relationships with physicians, psychiatrists when medication is needed or the client arrives from the hospital already taking medication, and nutritionists.

Liz's brother, David, exhibited symptoms of bipolar disorder, although it was complicated by his polysubstance abuse. His substance abuse will be addressed in the next section of this chapter.

Bipolar disorder usually involves at least one hospitalization, depending on the age of the patient, and on-going care by a psychiatrist to manage the regular use of psychotropic medication. However, manic episodes are often ego-syntonic, meaning the patient views them as pleasurable while they are happening. Therefore, many bipolar patients do not take prescribed medication regularly.

Based on the information we have about David's history, he may have needed a number of services, including individual psychotherapy, medication management, medication oversight, substance abuse treatment in- and/or out-patient, sheltered living, and perhaps legal services for questions of child support and competence. We do not know much about his divorce, alienation from his son, or his inability to support himself. We also do not know whether he has had legal issues resulting from his polysubstance abuse. All may be related to one of his two mental disorders, bipolar disorder and polysubstance abuse.

Family counseling for David, his son, and his extended family may have been helpful, not in changing David but in changing the family dynamics that may have supported his symptoms. Just as eating disorders can serve as the mechanism that keeps the family system in equilibrium, David's inability to achieve financial and behavioral independence and fulfill his role as a father may serve a function in the family dynamics.

Jim's dementia was yet another example of a mental disorder requiring services beyond family counseling. Dementia is an example of an organic mental disorder, meaning it is a biomedical brain process. Because of the biomedical aspects of the disease, all dementia patients require medical care from both a specialist and their primary care physician. They may benefit from medication, again necessitating a physician to prescribe and manage. Early in the dementia process, Jim may have benefited from counseling, either individual or family, to cope with the enormity of the diagnosis and make some anticipatory decisions while he remained competent.

Decision making for Jim may have included what is termed a *living will* and a DNR, or do not resuscitate directive. While no one can fully anticipate the disease process, Jim could let his family know his wishes and codify them legally.

Sally, her children, and Jim's children may have benefited from family counseling around managing the emotions, tasks, and decisions related to Jim's care. If there was tension among the siblings about who was responsible for what and how Jim's disease should be managed, family counseling could help to both alter current interactions and heal old wounds that may have been exacerbated by the present circumstances. Some of these issues pertain to blended families and were discussed in an earlier section of this chapter. These issues may also arise in caring for an aging parent whose mental functioning is declining.

Sally, as primary caretaker, may have also benefited from a caretaker support group. It is very easy for caretakers to overlook their own needs and become physically and emotionally depleted. Because of the emotional and behavioral changes that occur in dementia patients, Sally will gradually lose the Jim she loves and be left with all of the challenges of caring for a difficult patient without the benefits of their loving relationship. How much she does or does not rely on her daughters for emotional support is a decision that could be addressed in either a support group or family counseling with her daughters. A family counselor can obtain permission to exchange information with her physician and alert her or him to any biomedical symptoms she or he notices.

Liz and Barbara were in what has been termed the "sandwich" generation. They were both busy with their own families of procreation, yet were bound to their families of origin. Liz had three children at home, one quite young and with special needs. She also had two stepchildren. Although Barbara's children were both grown, she had a grandchild, a husband, and her own health problems with which to cope.

Both Liz and Barbara may have wanted or felt obligated to help their mother as Jim's disease progressed. Yet both had competing demands on their time and energy. A family counselor could help them explore ways to achieve balance in their lives, set reasonable limits on what others could expect of them, manage their own feelings about what was happening to their mother and Jim, and refer for other support services such as Meals on Wheels. Sometimes dementia treatment centers provide family support groups, but that is not always financially feasible.

Finally, Emma may have had developmental delays associated with her cerebral palsy. As with Jim, these would be organic in nature. In other words, neither individual nor family counseling could change them. However, there are a variety of services available for children with developmental delays, including speech, occupational, and physical therapies and academic tutoring. A family counselor could intervene to help the Manning-Kelly family cope with grief around Emma's limitations and also ensure that the two older children were receiving the attention they needed as adolescents. Given Christina's eating disorder, it may have been important to test the hypothesis that the family dynamics around coping with Emma's cerebral palsy had not been totally effective. Additionally, any serious diagnosis for a child may be associated with marital distress, and a family counselor could intervene to help the parents avoid such dynamics as mutual blame, reduced empathy for how the other copes, and the sense that the other is not doing enough as a product of there being simply too much to do rather than the other's unwillingness to contribute.

When a family enters family counseling, it is not unusual for one or more members to be taking psychotropic medication. Whether the prescription is written by a psychiatrist, neurologist, or primary care physician, it is useful for the family counselor to obtain permission to exchange information with the physician. The family counselor often sees the family more regularly than the physician does and is therefore able to communicate timely information, for example, about compliance or effectiveness of medication, that the physician might not otherwise learn until a routine follow-up a month or more later.

Family counselors are also in a position to refer one or more family members for a medication evaluation. It is useful to have a list of at least three psychiatrists who the family counselor trusts and with whom she or he has good working relationships to provide clients who may require medication. As with legal and other referrals, family counselors are not in a position to provide medical, legal, or other specialist advice. However, they can tell clients they recommend consultation with the appropriate professional and explain why.

Substance Abuse. Substance abuse is a mental health issue and yet also has unique physiological components associated with addiction. These were described in detail in Chapter 9.

Addiction adds a second layer to substance abuse. Clients suffering from addiction have developed a physiological or psychological dependence on the substance. Physiological addiction involves tolerance for the substance they are abusing. Tolerance means that they require more and more of the substance to achieve the same physiological reaction and suffer negative symptoms when they do not ingest the substance in that quantity. These clients cannot stop using the substance or substances they are abusing without risk of physical consequences, some of which may be life threatening. If they do decide to change their substance abuse, a physician may recommend they do so in an in-patient treatment facility where the potentially life-threatening consequences of stopping use can be treated as effectively as possible.

Clients with substance abuse disorders may require in-patient detoxification for their physical safety, residential out-patient treatment, or a 12-step group. Ideally, family counseling will be made available in any treatment program, and many 12-step programs offer groups for family members, though groups for partners and children may be separate from each other and from the abuser, rather than the conjoint family counseling you have been learning about throughout this textbook.

The Manning-Kelly family's only member with an obvious substance abuse disorder was Liz's brother, David. The information available indicates that David suffered from polysubstance abuse, meaning that he abused more than one substance. We do not know whether he was addicted and would likely have referred him to a physician to diagnose addiction and prescribe appropriate treatment.

Family counselors sometimes learn about client drug seeking, which refers to visiting several physicians for medications and then filling prescriptions at several pharmacies so that no one tracks how much medication the patient is taking. Electronic medical records somewhat alleviate this problem. However, when a family counselor is concerned about substance abuse and has consent to speak to the primary care physician about the family, it may be helpful to inform the physician about what the family counselor knows about prescriptions from other physicians.

DOMESTIC VIOLENCE

How family counselors are expected to respond when they learn of domestic violence is codified in legal statutes in all states. To review, all states require family counselors to report suspected abuse of dependents: children, the elderly, and those with disabilities. In other words, when someone is unable to get away from the abuser, the state takes over the protection of that individual.

Domestic violence between adult partners who are physically able to remove themselves is more complicated, as the abused partner is expected to remove herself or himself when physically able in terms of the law. However, in many instances, there is dependence or coercion that interferes with the victim's physical ability to leave, including the abuser manipulating or threatening the abused. Family counselors can address financial and emotional dependence, as well as the dynamics between partners that lead to manipulation and violence. It is beyond the scope of this textbook to provide a review of the various perspectives on treating domestic partner abuse. However, it is important to remember that such treatment must be within your scope of practice as a family counselor if you engage in it. If it is not, then you must ethically refer the family to someone who works with domestic violence.

Families experiencing domestic violence may need legal counsel. There are also support groups in many communities, as well as women's shelters. Partner violence directed at men is not uncommon, though it tends to be even more underreported than violence against women and so there are less resources for male victims of domestic violence. Additionally, police departments may have a domestic violence unit, which includes support for avoiding violence and not simply apprehending perpetrators of domestic violence.

Following the revelation that Mark had sexually abused Christina, the Manning-Kelly family would need legal counsel. Mark would need an attorney to guide him through the investigation that was likely to occur and to defend him if the investigation resulted in criminal charges. Liz would need counsel if she decided to terminate the marriage or in the event she was charged as a colluder in the abuse. The family and the family counselor would interact with the child protective agency in their jurisdiction. Liz and the children may also have needed legal advice or police protection if Mark refused to leave the family home.

CONCLUSION

We have reviewed eight family issues that may require services beyond a family counselor's scope of practice. These are multicultural families, LGBTQIA families, single-parent families, blended families, families with aging members, biomedical disease processes in families, mental and substance abuse disorders within families, and domestic violence. We have also surveyed some of the services with which family counselors must be familiar so that they can make appropriate referrals. We will now turn to a more specific review of resources other than family counseling that are available to families with whom family counselors also work.

Extend Your Learning:

1. Choose among the following films about families. Watch individually, as a small group, or as a class. Discuss the main issues presented. How might you work with this family? Who would you need to refer for treatment elsewhere? Why?

    Rachel Getting Married

    Ordinary People

    When a Man Loves a Woman

    The Kids Are All Right

    The Incredibles

2. Consult the phonebook or other local directory in your community. What populations appear to be served by the agencies listed? What populations are clearly missing? How would you direct a client with an issue beyond the scope of your practice in a community with limited resources?

REFERENCES

Diller, J. V. (2007). *Cultural diversity: A primer for the human services* (3rd ed.). Belmont, CA: Brooks/Cole.

Fadiman, A. (1997). *The spirit catches you and you fall down. A Hmong child, her American doctors, and the collision of two cultures.* New York, NY: Farrar, Straus and Giroux.

Lum, D. (2007). *Culturally competent practice. A framework for understanding diverse groups and justice issues* (3rd ed.). Belmont, CA: Brooks/Cole.

FOR FURTHER STUDY

Alzheimer's Disease Education & Referral (ADEAR) Center. (2012). *Alzheimer's disease fact sheet.* National Institutes of Health, National Institute on Aging. Retrieved from http://www.nia.nih.gov/alzheimers/publication/alzheimers-disease-fact-sheet

American Psychiatric Association. (2004). *Diagnostic and statistical manual of mental disorders IV.* Washington, DC: American Psychiatric Association.

Arnow, B., Kenardy, J., & Agras, W. S. (1995). The emotional eating scale: The development of a measure to assess coping with negative affect by eating. *International Journal of Eating Disorders, 18*(1), 79–90.

Atwood, J. D., & Genovese, F. (1993). *Counseling single parents.* Alexandria, VA: American Counseling Association.

Bastiani, A. M., Rao, R., Wetzin, T., & Kaye, W. H. (1995). Perfectionism in anorexia nervosa. *International Journal of Eating Disorders, 17*(2), 147–152.

Bent-Goodley, T. B. (2001). Eradicating domestic violence in the African American community. *Trauma Violence Abuse, 2*(4), 316–330.

Braithwaite, D., Olson, L., Golish, T., Soukup, C., & Turman, P. (2001). Becoming a family. Developmental process represented in blended family discourse. *Journal of Applied Communication Research, 29*(3), 221–247.

California Penal Code, Section 13700(a). Retrieved from http://www.leginfo.ca.gov/cgi-bin/displaycode?section=pen&group=13001-14000&file=13700-13702.

Cash, T. F., & Deagle, E. A. (1997). The nature and extent of body-image disturbances in anorexia nervosa and bulimia nervosa: A meta-analysis. *International Journal of Eating Disorders, 22*(2), 107–126.

Connors, M. E., & Morse, W. (1993). Sexual abuse and eating disorders: A review. *International Journal of Eating Disorders, 13*(1), 1–11.

Cooley, W. C., & Moeschler, J. B. (1993). Counseling in the health care relationship: A natural source of support for people with disabilities and their families. In G. S. Singer, L. E. Powers (Eds.), *Families, disability, and empowerment: Active coping skills and strategies for family interventions*(pp. 155–174). Baltimore, MD: Paul H. Brookes.

Doherty, W. J., & Baird, M. A. (1984). *Family therapy and family medicine.* New York, NY: Guilford Press.

Fabian, L. J., & Thompson, J. K. (1989). Body image and eating disturbance in young females. *International Journal of Eating Disorders, 8*(1), 63–74.

Family Violence Prevention Fund. (2007). *National consensus guidelines on identifying and responding to domestic violence victimization in health care settings.* San Francisco, CA: Family Violence Prevention Fund.

Gelles, R. J., & Loseke, D. R. (1993). Issues in conceptualization. In R. J. Gelles, & D. R. Loseke (Eds). *Current controversies on family violence.* Newbury Park, CA: Sage.

Gonzales, J. (2009). Prefamily counseling: Working with blended families. *Journal of Divorce & Remarriage, 50*(2), 148–157. doi:10.1080/10502550802365862

Goodkind, J. R., Sullivan, C. M., & Bybee, D. I. (2004). A contextual analysis of battered women's safety planning. *Violence Against Women, 10*(5), 514–533.

Halmi, K. A., Federica Tozzi, F., Thornton, L. M., Crow, S., Fichter, M. M., Kaplan, A. S., . . ., & Bulik, C. M. (2005). The relation among perfectionism, obsessive-compulsive personality disorder and obsessive-compulsive disorder in individuals with eating disorders. *International Journal of Eating Disorders, 38*(4), 371–371.

Harris, H. L. (2013). Counseling single-parent multiracial families. *The Family Journal, 21*(4), 386–395. doi:10.1177/1066480713488526

Holderness, C. C., Brooks-Gunn, J., & Warren, M. P. (1994). Co-morbidity of eating disorders and substance abuse review of literature. *International Journal of Eating Disorders, 16*(1), 1–34.

Howard, A. A., Arnsten, J. H., & Gourevitch, W. (2004). Effect of alcohol consumption on diabetes mellitus: A systematic review. *Annals of Internal Medicine, 140*(3), 211–219.

Howell, L. C., Weers, R., & Kleist, D. M. (1998). Counseling blended families. *The Family Journal, 6*(1), 42–45.

Johnson, C. (Ed.). (1991). *Psychodynamic treatment of anorexia nervosa and bulimia.* New York, NY: Guilford Press.

Johnson, C. (1991). Treatment of eating-disordered patients with borderline and false-self/narcissistic disorders. In C. Johnson (Ed.), *Psychodynamic treatment of anorexia nervosa and bulimia* (pp. 165–193). New York, NY: Guilford Press.

Kampfe, C. M. (2015). *Counseling older people: Opportunities and challenges.* Alexandria, VA: American Counseling Association.

Kanbak, G. A., Akalin, A. B., Dokumacioglu, A. A., Ozcelik, E. A., & Bal, C. C. (2011). Cardiovascular risk assessment in patients with type 2 diabetes mellitus and metabolic syndrome. Role of biomarkers. *Diabetes and Metabolic Syndrome: Clinical Research and Reviews, 5*(1), 7–11.

Koch, A. Y. (1983). Family adaptation to medical stressors. *Family Systems Medicine,* *1*(4), 78–87.

Koch-Hattem, A. (1987). Families and chronic illness. In D. Rosenthal (Ed.), *Family* *stress* (pp. 33–50). Rockville, MD: Aspen.

Lee, C. C. (2013). Global literacy: The foundation of culturally competent counseling. In C. C. Lee (Ed.), *Multicultural issues in counseling: New approaches to diversity* (4th ed.) (pp. 309–314). Alexandria, VA: American Counseling Association.

Lev, A. I., & Alie, L. (2012). Transgender and gender nonconforming children and youth: Developing culturally competent systems of care. In S. K. Fisher, J. M. Poirier, & G. M. Blau (Eds.), *Improving emotional and behavioral outcomes for LGBT youth:* *A guide for professionals* (pp. 43–66). Baltimore, MD: Paul H. Brookes.

Liepman, M. R., Silvia, L. Y., & Nirenberg, T. D. (1989). The use of family behavior loop mapping for substance abuse. *National Council on Family Relations, 38*(3), 282–287.

Kelly, S., Bhagwat, R., Maynigo, P., & Moses, E. (2014). Couple and marital therapy: The complement and expansion provided by multicultural approaches. In F. L. Leong, L. Comas-Díaz, G. C. Nagayama Hall, V. C. McLoyd, & J. E. Trimble (Eds.), *APA* *handbook of multicultural psychology, Vol. 2: Applications and training* (pp. 479–497). Washington, DC: American Psychological Association. doi:10.1037/14187-027

McDowell, T., Goessling, K., & Melendez, T. (2012). Transformative learning through international immersion: Building multicultural competence in family therapy and counseling. *Journal of Marital and Family Therapy, 38*(2), 365–379. doi:10.1111/j.1752-0606.2010.00209.x

Minuchin, S. (1974). *Families and family therapy.* Cambridge, MA: Harvard University Press.

Minuchin, S., Rosman, B. L., & Baker, L. (1978). *Psychosomatic families.* Cambridge, MA: Harvard University Press.

Morgan, O. J., & Lizke, C. H. (2012). *Family interventions in substance abuse. Current* *best practices.* New York, NY: Routledge.

Murray, C. E., & Graves, K. N. (2013). *Responding to family violence: A compre-* *hensive, research-based guide for therapists.* New York, NY: Routledge/Taylor & Francis Group.

Okun, B., & Kantrowitz, R. (2008). *Effective helping: Interviewing & counseling tech-* *niques* (7th ed.). Pacific Grove, CA: Brooks/Cole.

Pope, M., Pangelinan, J. S., & Coker, A. D. (2011). *Experiential activities for teaching mul-* *ticultural competence in counseling.* Alexandria, VA: American Counseling Association.

Power, P. W. (1995). Understanding intergenerational issues in aging families. In G. C. Smith, S. S. Tobin, E. A. Robertson-Tchabo, & P. W. Power (Eds.), *Strength-* *ening aging families: Diversity in practice and policy* (pp. 123–142). Thousand Oaks, CA: Sage.

Prendergast, T. J. (2001). Advance care planning: Pitfalls, progress, promise. *Critical Care Medicine, 29*(2), N34-N39.

Priest, J. B., Salts, C., & Smith, T. (2015). Special topics in family therapy: Mental illness, physical illness, substance abuse, family violence, and divorce. In J. L. Wetchler, & L. L. Hecker (Eds.), *An introduction to marriage and family therapy* (2nd ed.) (pp. 468–504). New York, NY: Routledge/Taylor & Francis Group.

Sands, S. (1991). Bulimia, dissociation, and empathy: A self-psychological view. In C. Johnson (Ed.), *Psychodynamic treatment of anorexia nervosa and bulimia* (pp. 34–50). New York, NY: Guilford Press.

Serrano, J. A. (1993). Working with chronically disabled children's families: A biopsychosocial approach. *Child & Adolescent Mental Health Care, 3*(3), 157–168.

Socholotiuk, K. (2015). Adolescent eating disorders: A contextual action theory approach to family-based counseling. In R. A. Young, J. F. Domene, & L. Valach (Eds.), *Counseling and action: Toward life-enhancing work, relationships, and identity* (pp. 223–237). New York, NY: Springer Science + Business Media. doi:10.1007/978-1-4939-0773-1_13

Steinmetz, S. K. (1977). *The cycle of violence.* New York, NY: Praeger.

Strober, M. (1991). Disorders of the self in anorexia nervosa: An organismic-developmental paradigm. In P. Johnson (Ed.), *Psychodynamic treatment of anorexia nervosa and bulimia* (pp.354–373). New York, NY: Guilford Press.

Vanderlinden, J., Vandereycken, W., van Dyck, R., & Vertommen, H. (1993). Dissociative experiences and trauma in eating disorders. *International Journal of Eating Disorders, 13*(2), 187–193.

Walker L. (2000). *The battered woman syndrome.* New York, NY: Springer.

Wooley, S. C. (1991). Uses of countertransference in the treatment of eating disorders: A gender perspective. In C. Johnson (Ed.), *Psychodynamic treatment of anorexia nervosa and bulimia* (pp. 245–294). New York, NY: Guilford Press.

Yalom, I. C. (1989). *Love's executioner and other tales of psychotherapy.* New York, NY: Basic Books.

CHAPTER 13

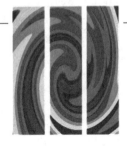

Services Available to Families

Asking for help when you need it is a sign of strength. For some, asking for help is the hardest part of receiving the help they need. For others, it is simply a matter of not knowing about the resources available. Because the family counselor is often the only link between families in crisis and the services available to them, it is important for counselors to know about such services and how families can receive them. This chapter discusses the wide array of resources and services available to families in need of support. By no means does this chapter provide an exhaustive list of what is out there for families. Family counselors should consult their local telephone directories, conduct Internet searches, consult with colleagues, and ask friends and family in order to find other sources for referring clients. They should also encourage their clients to do the same thing.

SOCIAL SERVICES

The Department of Social Services offers a wide variety of services to families, many of which are available at no cost to the families. A quick look at the Department of Health and Human Services website and at www.childwelfare.gov reveals a description of many services provided by social service agencies. There is a list from A to Z of services that help families pay bills, seek protection from abuse or neglect, find jobs, seek custody, find a day care, obtain services for their elderly parents, find housing, obtain free birth control, find physical and mental health care and much more. There are eligibility requirements for some services, but many services are free and available to the wider population. Some family clients may need assistance navigating these websites, so it is important for a family counselor to be familiar with the services available and how they work. An even better idea is to visit the local department of Health and Human Services and make contact with people who may serve as targets for referral. Building a network of referral sources will only expedite your ability to help your clients and build their confidence in being able to seek the available services.

SCHOOL COUNSELORS AND SCHOOL SOCIAL WORKERS

For many families, their children's school is the center of their community. It is where their children spend the majority of their days and where many events are held that bring the whole family together. Because children spend 8 hours a day in school, it is no surprise that the school is frequently the place where personal and family problems are noticed and attended to. In fact, many referrals to physicians, counselors and therapists, social workers, and law enforcement start at the schools. Not all schools have school counselors and school social workers working full time or even part time in the school building, but most schools have access to a counselor to which they can refer students and their families. School counselors are trained to do individual counseling, group counseling, parenting classes, consultation, and some psychological testing. Many parents do not realize the extent of their qualifications and training, but school counselors are great resources for families who are looking for emotional and psychological support.

School counselors are often available to families in the following ways:

1. Individual and group counseling for students

2. Parenting classes and other relevant topic-focused events

3. Referral resource for other services

4. Home visits if students or parents are homebound or without transportation

5. Screening and testing for learning difficulties, disorders, and referrals to other sources for testing

6. Career counseling for children

7. Conflict mediation between students, families, teachers, and staff

8. Services for homeless students and families, facilitating access to education for homeless children.

The school social worker is also an invaluable resource for families. Most school social workers are able to visit homes and agencies in order to provide services to families. For example, if a child has a medical appointment and the family has no means of transporting the child to the appointment, the school social worker can either arrange for transportation for the child or take the child to the appointment. School social workers, and many school truant officers as well, are committed to providing a free and equal education to all students, therefore, they will often move heaven and earth to get a child to school. One school truant officer I worked with would regularly take students shoe shopping, just to make sure they had shoes to wear to school. Parents don't usually have to look very far to find someone from their child's school who is willing to help.

IN-HOME SERVICES

Intensive in-home services or intensive family preservation are examples of programs designed to help families who are at risk of dividing and losing children to the justice or social services system. As the name suggests, these programs are intense, often because they focus on confronting issues and emotions in an honest and straightforward manner, and these family-centered services focus on preventing any future involvement from social services. The facilitator may operate using a family therapy model, helping family members set reasonable goals and confronting the main issues and barriers to healthy family functioning.

There may be a situation or an agency policy, such as for clients who are homebound, or for an intensive family therapy program, that involves a family counselor providing services in clients' homes. It is extremely important for family counselors to use caution when doing home visits. *If at all possible, family counselors should visit families' homes with a colleague or cofacilitator, rather than alone.* If visiting the family alone is unavoidable, the family counselor should notify others of his or her destination, the purpose of the visit, and how long the visit should take. The family counselor should also bring a cell phone along in case emergency help is needed. Families' homes can be volatile environments, especially in homes where conflict or an investigation are ongoing. Following safety precautions will help keep the family counselor safe and establish clear boundaries for the helping relationship.

JUVENILE JUSTICE AND DELINQUENCY PREVENTION

For youths who are age 15 or younger[1], the local law enforcement and, more specifically, the Office of Juvenile Justice and Delinquency Prevention offer services related to juvenile delinquency prevention. This department has a staff of court counselors who work with youth and their families to help the youth stay out of prison, develop better social skills, and learn how to engage in positive decision making. Juvenile court counselors deal with a multitude of families on a daily basis and support them through the adjudication process as well as help them find alternatives to jail time for the juveniles. Some juvenile court counselors get called upon by parents to help scare their wayward teenagers into making positive choices. The popular reality television show, *Scared Straight*, shows this approach in action, focusing on teens who have a history of risky behaviors and are often just one more deviant act away from incarceration.

RESPITE CARE AND GROUP HOMES

Sometimes parents of children with behavioral problems are looking for help with their children and need a break from the daily struggle to keep them safe. Some organizations provide respite care for families that qualify. For children who are at risk of dropping out of school and getting into trouble with the law, and whose parents are at their wits' end as to how to discipline them, some programs will provide housing for the youth for a temporary period. These programs also provide counseling, mediation, conflict resolution, and other treatment for the youth and for the parents until the family is able to function more effectively together and in keeping the teenager out of trouble and making more positive choices.

Group homes are also an alternative to juvenile detention centers and often serve as temporary housing for youth who are transitioning back into society

---

[1] The age of a juvenile served by juvenile justice programs may vary by state.

after their incarceration. Especially in cases where the family is in crisis and unable to support the youth's transition at home, the group home provides a place to learn positive life, work, and social skills, helping to ease the transition process. Because the transition back into society from incarceration can be a very difficult process, many juvenile detention programs also offer transition services specifically aimed at making this easier for the youth and their families.

WILDERNESS THERAPY PROGRAMS AND CAMPS

One of the popular alternatives to prison time for teens, wilderness camps, were on the rise in the 1990s. Also called therapeutic wilderness programs, Eckerd's E-Nini-Hassee Outdoor Therapeutic School for girls is one example of such a program still in operation. This program, located in the southeastern United States provides nonpunitive, strength-based services for girls ages 13 to 18. Wilderness programs typically emphasize personal responsibility, experiential therapy and learning, and team work. Youths are required to live in the woods for several weeks or months, often constructing their own dwellings. Most of the research on wilderness programs indicates a high success rate in decreasing young people's negative behaviors, increasing their self-confidence and independence, and helping them regulate their own emotions. Unfortunately, the challenge for these programs is that when the youth complete the wilderness training program they return to their previous environments and have a difficult time applying their newly learned skills to the old environments with the old stressors. Many of the current programs are focusing on addressing this challenge, through increasing family involvement and career development for the youth.

EMPLOYEE ASSISTANCE PROGRAMS

All federal agencies and many private companies offer emotional and psychological assistance for their employees and their families. Employee Assistance Programs (EAP's) offer counseling, usually free of charge, to their employees, their spouses, and families. Finding out if this is an option is usually as easy as a telephone call to an employer's human resources department. EAP's are often linked to wellness programs designed to keep employees happy and healthy, therefore creating a more productive workplace.

SUPPORT FOR MILITARY FAMILIES

The United States military offers a plethora of services for active duty and veteran servicepersons. The services are similar to those provided by social services, and most of them are covered at 100% through the serviceperson's insurance benefits. The Department of Veterans Affairs also continues these services for its honorably discharged veterans, and many are eligible for additional services and compensation for injuries, illnesses, or conditions sustained or developed during active duty. These services are currently being used by some members of the Manning-Kelly family. Jim, Sally's second husband and Liz's stepfather, is a Korean vet. He received a traumatic brain injury in combat and is now diagnosed with Alzheimer's disease. His family receives monthly compensation from the Department of Veterans Affairs to help cover the costs of managing his symptoms.

FAITH-BASED SUPPORT PROGRAMS

Many families turn to their spiritual communities and leaders for support. Talking to a priest, minister, or spiritual advisor may be helpful for families in need of guidance. Many clergy are trained in clinical counseling skills, so seeking their help for emotional problems within the family is appropriate. Clients should clarify the training and background of the person they're interesting in working with, in order to make sure this type of work really is something they are qualified to do. Otherwise, you might receive religious doctrine rather than objective counseling. Both have their place, but it is important for clients to be clear on what they are pursuing and what services the clergy are qualified to provide.

Several faith-based organizations offer services to families in need of support. Some of the organizations offer housing, food or food vouchers, counseling, financial support, and job training and job placement, as well as advocacy and legal counsel.

NONPROFIT AGENCIES

Depending on where you live, there is a wide variety of agencies providing services to families. These services may be focused on a particular topic, issue, or population and vary based on need and resources. You should do a local search of agencies in your community.

Here are a few of the resources within the community near our university and ones that are found in the majority of communities in the United States:

American Red Cross: International and national services to families and veterans, services include disaster relief, clothing and blood donations, and health education courses such as CPR, lifesaving, and babysitting

The Salvation Army: Offers a variety of services, domestic and abroad, including disaster relief, services for senior citizens, after school care and summer camps for children, and housing and food for homeless citizens

Meals on Wheels: Home meal delivery to senior citizens

Alcoholics Anonymous: Support group for those addicted to alcohol

Narcotics Anonymous: Support group for those addicted to narcotics

Al Anon and Alateen: Support groups for relatives and friends of alcoholics

These are services that are available nationwide, and internationally as well in some cases. In addition to the more widely known national and international services, there are also smaller nonprofit organizations that provide services to their local communities. These organizations vary by focus, sources of funding, and missions. These are also the organizations that one might find more effectively through networking with other people, rather than searching in the phonebook or on the Internet, since many of these organizations may not have the funding or staff power for advertising.

REFERRAL PROCESS

Sometimes referrals are as simple as giving a client a phone number or a name and location of an agency. Other times there is clear structure and paperwork involved. Regardless of the nature of the referral process, the family counselor must have the client's written consent before revealing client information to another professional or agency. The consent form must include the client's name and signature, whom the referral information is coming from, and what agency or individuals are allowed to receive information about the client.

STOP AND THINK:

1. Who in the Manning-Kelly family could benefit from a referral to social services or other agencies that serve families?

2. What services would be most appropriate and helpful?

3. What other family members can you think of who could use support? Where would you refer them for help?

The following are examples from the Manning-Kelly family in which other agencies may need to be involved via a referral.

First, after Christina's disclosure, the entire family is trying to support Christina as well as deal with their own feelings related to the sexual abuse. Based on the report to Child Protective Services, an assessment will begin to determine what services the family needs and what will be most helpful for Christina and her family at this time. It is possible that some members of the family will need individual counseling in addition to the family counseling they have received. While it is doubtful that Mark will come back to family counseling for a referral, he may be required to receive individual counseling based on his potential involvement with the justice system if charges are filed against him. Additionally, since Mark was the primary caregiver of his elderly parents, other resources will have to be considered for their care now that Mark will be unavailable. Most likely, another extended family member will step in and take Mark's place. However, if that isn't an option, social services or another agency that provides adult day care services will need to be consulted in order to ensure that his parents are getting the care they need.

Christina, Liz, Martin Sr., and Martin Jr. will react differently to learning about Mark's abusing Christina. Some will have more difficulties than others, and it may become apparent that a referral for individual counseling is in order.

Another example comes from Matt and Paul's family. As they are planning to expand their family through adoption, they will need support and information related to adoption, both domestic and international. Some of this information may be found at the Department of Health and Human Services website, but they may also pursue private agencies and other resources to get the support they need.

Extend Your Learning:

1. Choose a need, issue, or disorder that might prompt a family to seek support. Conduct an Internet search, Yellow Page search, or interview

someone in your community about the services available in your local community. Make a list of what you find, and bring it back to class to discuss with your classmates.

(a.) Were you surprised at what you found (or didn't find)?

(b.) How easy was it to find these resources?

(c.) How easily understood was the information?

(d.) What other services do you think need to be in place?

2. Contact a counselor in your local community. Ask him or her about his or her service referral network. What agencies does he or she refer to the most? What needed agencies or services are missing in the community?

FOR FURTHER STUDY

American School Counselor Association: https://www.schoolcounselor.org

Bandoroff, S. (2004). *Coming of age: The evolving field of adventure therapy.* Boulder, CO: Association for Experiential Education.

Corey, M. (2007). Working in the community. *In becoming a helper* (6th ed., pp. 351–373). Belmont, CA: Brooks/Cole.

U.S. Department of Health and Human Services: http://www.hhs.gov

U.S. Department of Health and Human Services, Administration for Children and Families, Child Welfare Information Gateway: http://www.childwelfare.gov

U.S. Department of Justice, Office of Juvenile Justice and Delinquency Prevention: www.ojjdp.gov

United States Department of Veterans Affairs: www.va.gov

CHAPTER 14

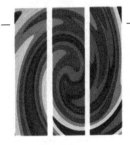

What's Next for the Manning-Kelly Family?

In this chapter, we review what we have learned about family counseling and how it applies to the Manning-Kelly family. We will also examine the challenges that remain for the Manning-Kelly family. Finally, we invite you to further explore your own theoretical orientation and your feelings about family counseling.

FAMILY COUNSELING

Now that you are reaching the end of your introduction to family counseling, it is time to review what it is and what makes it unique. Your answers to the Stop and Think questions reflect your understanding of family counseling and are crucial to any career decision you make involving family counseling. Bear in mind, however, that while an introductory class such as this one may help you decide whether you want to pursue family counseling training, it does not adequately train or prepare you to practice family counseling.

> ## STOP AND THINK:
>
> 1. What is family counseling, and how does it differ from individual counseling?
>
> 2. What makes family counseling unique?
>
> 3. Imagine yourself as a family counselor. What would you enjoy about managing and intervening in the dynamics of a family system? What might be the challenges for you?

WHAT'S NEXT FOR THE MANNING-KELLY AND JONES FAMILIES?

We left the Manning-Kelly family after the revelation that Mark had been sexually abusing Christina. Although we paused the session at that point, it was not the end of the family's story nor of their work with the family counselor.

> ## STOP AND THINK:
>
> In groups of three to five students, discuss the following questions, and then compile the answers from the entire class. This will give you some sense of the range of possibilities for the Manning-Kelly family.
>
> 1. What might have happened next for the Manning-Kelly family? Why?
>
> 2. Do you think the family would have continued to work with the same, or in fact any, family counselor? Why, or why not?
>
> 3. If you were their family counselor, and they chose to remain in counseling with you, how would you handle the fallout from Christina's revelation and Liz's and Mark's reactions?

As you may have guessed, there is not one correct answer to any of these questions but rather a number of possible trajectories the Manning-Kelly family may have taken. As it happened, Liz told Mark to move out, and the remainder of the family continued to work with the same family counselor.

Some families would have blamed the family counselor for the dissolution of Liz and Mark's marriage. Additionally, some mothers would have saved their marriages at the expense of their daughter's mental health. Mothers sometimes accept the abuser's claim that their daughter lied about being abused. Other mothers even accuse their daughters of being seductive and therefore responsible for the abuser's behavior. When families cope by blaming the victim or the family counselor or by denying the behavior occurred or was abusive if it did, they are unlikely to continue family counseling.

The family counselor found she was ambivalent about continuing to see Liz and her children. She had grown to like and respect both Liz and Christina, even though they had not always been receptive to counseling or to her as a family counselor. Alternatively, she was also unsettled and anxious following Mark's threats of legal retaliation. And finally, the family's situation was difficult, as it was extremely painful for the family members and legally fraught for both the family and the family counselor.

The family counselor noticed that she began to dread the days that included sessions with Liz and Christina. Despite these feelings, she also wanted and knew she was ethically obligated to complete her work with them. She sought peer supervision so that her ambivalence would not interfere with her work with the family and also made certain her self-care routines were in place on days when she saw them.

As a result of funding cuts, the agency to which the abuse was reported had limited resources for investigating reports of abuse. The agency was thus unable to pursue investigating the family counselor's report for 6 months. By that time, Christina had had her 18th birthday, and Mark had moved to another state. Additionally, Liz and Mark's divorce was well underway, the only relevant remaining question being whether Emma would be allowed to visit him. Because Christina was no longer legally a minor dependent, and neither she nor her siblings remained at risk of abuse with Mark in another state and her mother demonstrating her willingness to prevent him from returning to the family home, the agency concluded that none of the children was at risk of being abused by Mark. As a result, the agency decided not to use its limited resources to pursue an investigation at all.

Liz declined the family counselor's offer of referrals for legal counsel. Being an attorney herself, she said she knew she needed legal representation and also had access to a professional network that would offer her suggestions. At one point, when Liz said her fury at Mark, guilt for not seeing what was happening, and fears for the future were intruding on her sleep and sense of well-being and hopefulness, the family counselor offered her the names of three psychiatrists who could evaluate Liz's need for medication and prescribe if necessary.

Mark filed a complaint with the family counselor's licensing board, which was required to investigate all complaints against a licensee. The family counselor was investigated for the better part of a year, which caused her a great deal of anxiety and cost her a great deal of money to obtain legal consultation and representation. Ultimately, no wrongdoing was discovered.

After given a choice when Mark left the room after the revelation of abuse, Liz and Christina asked the family counselor to report the abuse with them present. Liz took Martin Jr. and Emma to her sister Barbara's house while the family counselor saw her last client of the day and then returned with Christina for the reporting.

The family counselor also asked Christina and Liz how they wanted to handle telling Martin about what had happened. She suggested several options, including Christina telling him alone, Liz telling him alone, the two of them telling him together, and any of those three things happening with the family counselor present. Liz and Christina decided they wanted to tell him together and with the family counselor present to help with his reaction. They agreed with the family counselor's recommendation that they schedule a family counseling session with Martin present as soon as possible.

Martin was concerned that Liz and Christina had requested a session alone with him and dispensed with his usual greetings.

Martin: What's going on?

Liz: There's something Christina and I need to tell you about that's probably going to upset you, but remember we're upset, too.

[Christina begins crying]

Martin: Sweetheart, what's wrong?

C: Daddy . . .

Liz: Mark has been hurting Christina.

C: Mom!

Liz: He's moved out, and I won't let him anywhere near her again.

Martin: [Loudly] What's that [Expletive] been doing to my daughter?

Liz: Our daughter, Martin.

Martin: He's not *my* husband.

FC: Martin, I cannot imagine how difficult this is for you to hear, and whatever your reaction is, it is valid. I also wonder whether it would be most helpful right now for you and Liz to discuss how you want to deal with what it means for you as parents and what you can do for Christina.

Martin: Fine, but I want to know what that [Expletive] did.

Liz: Martin, he, he . . . [To FC] Please tell him.

FC: Are you sure, Liz?

M: Tell me!

[Liz nods at FC]

FC: Mark has been sexually abusing Christina. When Christina told us yesterday, Liz asked Mark to move out, and I have reported him to [Relevant agency].

M: No! No! This cannot be. [To Liz] How could you let this happen to our baby girl? [Clenches his fists] I'm going to kill that [Expletive]. [Stands up]

FC: Martin, I'd like you to stay here for now. And I want to support your desire to protect your daughter from ever being hurt by him again.

M: I want to kill him. [To Liz] You going to let him at my son, too? Or your precious little Emma?

Liz: I told you, he's gone. And he's not going to see Emma or any of my kids again, ever, if I can help it.

FC: Martin, this is a lot to absorb.

M: [Expletive]

The family counselor made every effort to remain calm yet empathetic in the presence of the family's distress. While she was also angry at Mark, her anger was not productive for the family.

She also made a mental note to be sure before the session ended that Martin was not a danger to Mark. Family counselors are legally mandated to determine whether or not a client intends to kill someone before she or he leaves the office when a threat is made. In a situation like the one faced by the Manning-Kelly and Jones families, it is entirely possible that Martin was speaking metaphorically. In other words, his threat may have been an expression of the intensity of his anger at Mark for hurting his daughter. However, it is also possible that Martin was so enraged that he literally intended to kill Mark. If the latter were true, the family counselor would have a legal duty to report that Martin was a danger to Mark to the appropriate authorities and also to warn Mark. The duty to warn is the result of a legal precedent set by the *Tarasoff v. Regents* (1976) case in California. It was a complex case, and so a full description of the duty to warn is beyond the scope of this textbook.

Martin was very clear very quickly that while he wanted Mark to suffer he was not going to ruin his own life and his children's by physically harming Mark. He was then able to express how powerless and betrayed he felt. He also identified anger at Liz for allowing Mark into Christina's life, anger at himself for not fighting Liz for custody, in addition to the rage he felt toward Mark. He acknowledged that he would need help managing all these feelings and then forgiving both Liz and himself for not foreseeing what could not have been foreseen. Once his initial shock and anger passed, it was easier him to focus on helping Christina recover.

Martin was also upset that Christina did not tell anyone what Mark had done to her the first time the abuse happened. Christina tearfully said she did not know why she had not told anyone and that she had hoped it would stop before she had to talk about it. She said she was embarrassed and thought perhaps it was her fault. Martin and Liz were vehement that Christina was not to blame and that what had happened was hurtful rather than shameful.

Martin and Liz worked effectively together in support of Christina's healing. However, Martin decided he wanted to share custody of their children for the remainder of the time they were home, and Liz did not fight his request.

STOP AND THINK:

1. Some students have been critical of Liz and Martin for not protecting Christina sooner from an abusive stepparent. What do you think?

2. What else might the family counselor have done to help Martin?

WHAT'S NEXT FOR THE INDIVIDUAL FAMILY MEMBERS?

Most families would not remain in counseling long enough to work on individual issues following a revelation of sex abuse. Sometimes, survivors of sexual abuse seek individual counseling later in life when they discover their history is interfering with their current life. For purposes of this textbook, however, we will discuss what remains for individual family members to address, their continued work with the family counselor, and what they did following family counseling.

Christina remained in the role of identified patient throughout the family counseling. She was the one who the family had initially labeled problematic, and yet she consistently pointed out where the problems in the family system and with other family members lay. Additionally, as she began to recover from the sexual trauma, Christina was able to examine and change both her cutting and restrictive eating. She decided to take a gap year between high school and college and to use the time to work and apply for admission to college.

Christina will need to be vigilant about her life-long risk of regressing into restrictive eating and cutting during periods of high stress. She will also need to continue to recover from her sexual trauma and observe its impact on her sexuality and future relationship(s) with (an) intimate partner(s).

As attention shifted to Christina's recovery and the family adapted to Liz and Mark's separation, Emma was forced to become more independent. Her preschool teachers commented that she was growing emotionally and socially, and she began to make friends among her peers and to ask for play dates. During sessions, she began to smile at the family counselor and to play by herself while her mother talked.

Liz expressed ambivalence about the role of her career in her life. Like Christina, she seemed to be making a statement to her mother and sister about their choices. She had handled her career in a way that suggested parenting was more important than career to her, and yet she had been angry at both her husbands during their marriages for treating her work as secondary. Her residual anger at Martin also suggested that she had unresolved issues from her first marriage that need to be addressed, as well as new issues resulting from her marriage to Mark, preferably before she began another relationship. Finally, Liz appeared to be part of the multigenerational pattern of restrictive eating and obsession with thinness in the Manning family. The family counselor speculated that Liz's tendency to restrict what she ate and overexercise might be connected to her feelings about men, herself in relation to them, and thus the role of her career in her life.

Mark disappeared from Emma's life as soon as the termination of his marriage to Liz was legally settled. He moved across the country and lost contact with his parents and all three of his children. Ashley contacted Christina when Mark disappeared and eventually revealed that she had also been sexually abused by him. Mark's parents never asked what had happened between Liz and Mark. They stayed in touch with Liz, who later moved them near her so she could manage their decline.

After Mark moved out of the house, Martin Jr. reengaged with the family, spending more time at home than he had been and talking more. Because of his age, Martin's attorney advised that he would be asked by a judge where he wanted to live if his father reopened the custody agreement with Liz. So Liz reluctantly agreed to let him decide where he wanted to live. Martin Jr. elected to live with both parents, alternating weeks. Consistent with her role of identified patient, Christina expressed concern about leaving her mother and decided to continue to live with her and visit her father every weekend. Her decision confirmed the family counselor's suspicion that part of her initial refusal to go to college was reluctance to leave her mother and half sister alone with Mark.

Martin vacillated between fury and guilt. He continued to be angry and mistrustful of Liz because of her choice to bring Mark into his children's lives. He also continued to believe he had failed to protect his children and felt remorseful and angry at himself as a result. Because of this guilt, Christina's sexual trauma became a secret in his extended family. He refused to talk to Daniella about what had happened and how he was reacting to it, despite her continued emotional support. His emotional distance put a strain on their marriage, and his younger children became whiny and uncooperative. Daniella said she felt the situation had driven a wedge between her and Martin that she was helpless to change. She also expressed concern that their marriage would never again be as good as it had been, even when Martin forgave himself and Liz.

FAMILY SECRETS

Secrets are powerful, impacting those who keep them and those about whom the secrets are. Christina's revealing of the abuse that was taking place at home not only brought to light the secret suffering that Mark had subjected her to but also helped to change the negative patterns of communication between her and her mother.

Most families have secrets. Many of these secrets are harmless, such as parents keeping secret about who really puts presents under the Christmas tree (of course, Santa is real!) or brothers depending on each other to keep secret who broke mom's favorite vase. These kinds of secrets, and the people who keep them, are causing no harm to others by keeping the secret. Other secrets are potentially harmful, such as a mother asking her child to keep secret her affair with the neighbor, or parents keeping secret the adoption of their child. Secrets may be adaptive or maladaptive depending on how they impact others in the family. Most family secrets have to do with major life events such as births and deaths, personal biological facts, such as one's health, or personal thoughts, feelings, or behaviors.

Classification of Secrets by Content

One way to conceptualize family secrets is by content. Here are nine types of family secrets adapted from Grolnick (1983):

Major life events

Birth-related: out of wedlock births, abortion, adoption

Sex-related: affair, incest, rape, sexual orientation, cohabitation

Money-related: concealed income, inheritance, family business dealings, blackmail

Crime-related: past sentence, ongoing illegalities

Job-related: job firings, demotions, conflicts

Personal facts

Biological: acute and chronic illness, sexual dysfunction or infertility, inherited disorders

Functional: compulsive or ritualistic behaviors, emotions, thoughts, beliefs and attitudes, fantasies

Adaptive Secrets

It is not always easy to know if a secret is helpful or harmful to keep. The keeping and revelation of a secret will certainly affect family members differently. Certainly in many situations the keeping of secrets is necessary to protect family members, bind families together, and to lessen tension. Some secrets are important to family development, such as siblings keeping secrets from their parents. This helps the sibling relationship flourish and fosters independence. Likewise, secrets kept in the adult subsystem are also necessary and healthy and prevent children from having unnecessary anxiety about finances or relationship issues. Berg-Cross (2000) lists characteristics of these adaptive secrets:

1. The secret is known by all members of the family, or it is kept within the appropriate generational subsystems (siblings share secrets with siblings, parents share secrets with parents).

2. If generational subsystems are crossed, and a secret is shared by a parent and a child, then the secret reflects hidden strengths of family members rather than their weaknesses, such as a parent and son planning a secret birthday surprise for the other parent.

3. Finally, there is little pressure within the family and within the community to reveal the secret. Therefore, there is no undue anxiety resulting from keeping the secret.

Maladaptive Secrets

Berg-Cross (2000) also discussed secrets that are harmful to the family, promoting conflict and anxiety. These maladaptive secrets usually have the following characteristics:

1. They are secrets between parents and children that are part of long-standing dysfunctional, triangular relationships. The secret usually binds the child to one parent against the other parent.

2. The secrets reveal weaknesses or deficiencies in character, or they ridicule a family member.

3. There is a lot of pressure within the family or community to reveal the secret.

The Manning-Kelly Family Secrets

The obvious example, revealed earlier in the book, involves sexual abuse. Abuse of dependent minors, as well as the disabled and the elderly, is a complex topic beyond the scope of this book. The specific issue of Mark abusing Christina is one that has been addressed earlier in this and other chapters.

Another relevant example from the Manning-Kelly family is that of Christina's cousin, Paul, and his life partner, Matt's family. If they are successful in adopting a child, they will have to decide at what point and how to tell their child that he or she is adopted.

STOP AND THINK:

1. When do you think a child should be told that he or she is adopted?

2. What problems or issues do you think might result from keeping this information secret?

3. What cultural variables should you consider when determining how and when a child should be told about his or her adoption?

4. Who else should know about a child's adoption? Why should these people know or not know?

Adoptive Families and Secrets

Most of the research on adoption advocates telling adopted children about their birth and adoption experiences as soon as they can understand words. By making the adoption as much a part of the child's momentous experiences as birth parents would make their child's birthday, parents help their children celebrate, rather than hide their adoption. Many families celebrate something called "Gotcha Day," a day devoted to celebrating the day the adoptive parents "got" their child. This only reinforces the knowledge that the child's entry into their family was surrounded by love and celebration, rather than secrecy and shame.

TERMINATION OF FAMILY COUNSELING

There are several ways family counseling comes to an end. In some cases, families drop out of counseling, leaving the counselor wondering what happened and what she or he failed to notice or do that might have helped. In other cases, the work of family counseling draws to a close, and both the family and the family counselor feel satisfied with what they have accomplished. A third way in which family counseling ends involves the situation in which the family counselor changes jobs, moves, takes a leave of absence due to becoming a parent or her or his own or another family member's illness, retires, or dies. In these situations, the family may not be ready to finish counseling.

How the family counselor manages the final phase of family counseling, called termination, affects the outcome of family counseling for the family. No one likes to say good-bye, and encouraging the family to stay in family counseling to talk about the process is important.

When the family is finishing the work of family counseling, it is also important that they and the family counselor make time to review the process. Topics to address include the presenting problem, the family's goals for family counseling, what the family has accomplished, the tools the family members now have and can use on their own in the future, how the family might recognize when they need to use those tools or ask for a brief course of family counseling to get themselves back on track and prevent symptoms from recurring, and the meaning of the counseling relationship to the family and the family counselor.

When family counseling ends because the family counselor is unable to continue working with the family, it is important for the family counselor to be very clear that she or he is not leaving because of the family. It is also important for her or him to listen to and accept the family's reaction, including their anger. Finally, whether or not the family needs further counseling, it is important for the family counselor to provide them with names and contact information for three family counselors she or he trusts to work with them. If the family counselor's assessment is that they do require further treatment, she or he might suggest they contact potential family counselors and meet with one or more of them prior to the end of her or his work with the family, in order to establish a counseling relationship before the current family counselor departs.

Saying good-bye to a family also has an impact on the family counselor. When the family leaves precipitously, she or he may feel guilt or inadequacy about her or his family counseling ability. If the family is finished with the work they sought to do, the family counselor may feel sad. The family counselor also might feel relieved.

The family counselor we have been following experienced an array of feelings when Liz and Christina finished their work with her. Their work had been intense and sometimes unpleasant. During the process of family counseling, she had gotten to know the family well and to care about what happened to its members. She had been frightened of them when Mark threatened her and then followed through with a complaint to her licensing board and when Martin threatened to kill Mark. She had remained uneasy until she learned Mark had left the area. Most notably, though, she was sad that she would not see the family anymore or hear about the members' lives. Like many family counselors, she told them she was available for follow-up sessions, if needed, to prevent a recurrence of symptoms. Several years later, she received a call from Christina asking whether she could recommend an individual counselor in the city to which Christina had moved for college. The family counselor was delighted to hear that Christina was in college and ready to work on the impact of her trauma. After that call, however, she did not expect further contact or information.

It is important for family counselors to take time and engage in self-care to manage the feelings that arise when a family terminates family counseling. The family counselor talked about her feelings of sadness, as she had about her fear, to her peer supervision group. She also checked herself for burnout and made time for a long walk after she finished seeing clients on the day of the final session.

WHAT'S NEXT FOR YOU AS A FAMILY COUNSELOR?

Now that you have finished reading about the Manning-Kelly and Jones families, think about your overall reaction to them.

> **STOP AND THINK:**
>
> 1. What did you like and/or dislike about the Manning-Kelly and Jones families?
>
> 2. What did you like and/or dislike about each member of the Manning-Kelly and Jones families?
>
> 3. What did you like and/or dislike about the family counselor?
>
> 4. Were you comfortable with the Manning-Kelly and Jones families?
>
> 5. Were you comfortable with the family counselor and what she did?

The answers to these questions are important. They are part of the family counselor's experience working with the family. It is also part of your self-care to notice when you may be influenced by either positive or negative reactions to your clients.

Examining your reaction to the Manning-Kelly and Jones families and the family counselor is one aspect of what's next for you. The other involves your reaction to the field of family counseling after having completed an introductory family counseling class.

> **STOP AND THINK:**
>
> 1. What theory most spoke to you as a future family counselor?
>
> 2. What do you think of family counseling?
>
> 3. How do you take care of yourself when faced with ambiguity and not being able to finish work?

Some of our students find after completing this course that, while the material was interesting and may be helpful in other professions, they have no interest in becoming a family counselor. We believe that introducing people to new ideas and career possibilities and helping them acquire the information to make a decision about whether or not they are drawn to it is a successful outcome of taking the class.

Other students are drawn to family counseling and wish to pursue further training. For those students, we recommend exploring options for graduate training in the various fields that include family counseling in their training. These professions include social work, school counseling, professional counseling, marriage and family therapy, psychology, and psychiatry. Social workers, school counselors, and licensed professional counselors must complete master's degrees in their respective disciplines from accredited programs, engage in at least 2 years of supervision with a licensed professional, and pass a state licensing exam before they can practice independently. Marriage and family therapy and psychology graduate programs confer both masters and doctoral degrees, although licensure requires only the former for marriage and family therapists. Licensure also requires at least 2 years of postmaster's supervision and passing a licensing exam. In some states, master's level psychologists are not allowed to practice independently of supervision even after they are licensed, whereas a master's degree in all the other disciplines we have described allows for independent practice once the professional is licensed. Finally, psychiatry requires a medical degree, internship, residency, and licensure. Psychiatrists are trained and licensed to practice counseling and psychotherapy. They are also trained and licensed to prescribe psychotropic medication. If you are interested in family counseling as a profession, we encourage you to explore programs in multiple disciplines and the licensing laws of the state in which you would like to practice, so that you can make an informed decision about the field of study that best fits your needs.

Please note that we omitted human service studies from our list. Human service professionals generally hold an associate's or bachelor's degree when they work with families. However, they are not able to practice family counseling without graduate training and licensure.

CONCLUSION

Family counseling is unique. Unlike individual counseling, family counseling focuses on the family dynamics. In other words, family counseling focuses on the repetitive interaction patterns that occur among family members and the ways these can lead to the formation of symptoms and then impede or prevent change.

You have read about family concepts, tools for assessing families, theories that inform interventions with families, and the ethics of family counseling. You have also read about the experience of being a family counselor and issues that arise as a direct result of the work as a family counselor. And, finally, you have learned about the need for identifying resources and when family counselors need client referrals.

You have read details about a complex family as it struggled with various issues. This family's dynamics had derailed their ability to cope. Had the family counselor initially agreed to see Christina without her family, the outcome of counseling might have been very different.

STOP AND THINK:

1. What do you imagine would have happened had the family counselor agreed to see Christina alone?

2. Do you think Christina would have told an individual counselor about the abuse? If yes, do you think it would have happened sooner than it did in family counseling or later?

3. How might the diagnosis of eating disorder or depression and medication have affected Christina's life?

The purpose of an introductory course is to introduce you to the material related to a particular field of study and practice, so that you are familiar with it and can decide whether it is an area of study you would like to pursue. As you have read about the Manning-Kelly and Jones families and their family counselor, did you come to view family counseling as a field to which you are attracted or one from which you want to distance yourself? Or are you unsure? If you would like to read more about family counseling and those who formulated theories and who practice in the profession, scan the reference lists at the end of each chapter.

STOP AND THINK

Based on what you've learned about individual counseling in other classes and about family counseling in this one, which grabs you more and why?

Extend Your Learning:

1. Family Reflection Paper

When we teach family counseling students on both the undergraduate and graduate levels, we usually ask them to create a genogram (Chapters 3 and 5) and then write a family assessment paper or family reflection paper. We believe that using one's own family to exemplify the various concepts used by family counselors helps one understand them. Additionally, awareness of what is happening in her or his own family helps a family counselor avoid becoming part of the family system in a problematic way. For example, as mentioned in Chapter 10, it was easy for the family counselor to identify with Christina because she, too, had had a mother who wanted to make decisions for her beyond the time it was age appropriate. Instead of siding with Christina against Liz, which would have undermined the effectiveness of family counseling, this knowledge of her own family of origin and its impact upon her helped the family counselor avoid taking sides and instead help Liz and Christina communicate with each other more effectively.

2. Family Assessment Paper

This is an assignment we use frequently to give students more practice with the family counseling concepts. In this assignment, students choose a number of family concepts and define each one. Then students write about their own families to exemplify the concepts they have chosen.

Students often approach the family assessment assignment saying their families don't exemplify any of the concepts because they are happy and problem free. After writing the paper, they continue to find their families healthy and happy. However, they've also identified secrets or cutoffs or other issues in their extended families. We recommend that students not ask their families for information they don't already have unless they are convinced their families will be receptive to the assignment.

Additional Prompts for Class Discussion or Family Assessment Paper

What did you learn about managing ambiguity in your family?

What did you learn about self-care in your family?

What about growing up in your family prepared you to be a family counselor?

Will they make it?

What strengths have you identified that will help them in the process?

What deficits have you identified that may serve as boundaries to healing?

What information would you need to move forward with this family?

What services does this family need to help them move forward?

3. Video Examples

There are lots of videos available for students to watch full family counseling sessions online. In class or in small groups, choose an online video, or one of the videos listed below, and respond to the following questions about the family counselor's approach to working with families:

(a.) What theoretical approach or approaches does he or she appear to be using?

(b.) What are the benefits of this approach?

(c.) What are the limitations of this approach?

(d.) What did you like about the family counselor's personal style of interaction with the family?

(e.) What would you do differently if you were the counselor working with the family featured in the video?

(f.) What questions do you have after watching the video?

Selected Family Counseling Videos (from www.psychotherapy.net)

The Legacy of Unresolved Loss: A Family Systems Approach
by Monica McGoldrick

"I'd Hear Laughter": Finding Solutions for the Family
by Insoo Kim Berg

Making Divorce Work: A Clinical Approach to the Binuclear Family
by Constance Ahrons

Salvador Minuchin on Family Therapy
by Jay Lappin, Salvador Minuchin

Structural Family Therapy
by Harry Aponte

Bowenian Family Therapy
by Philip Guerin

Adolescent Family Therapy
by Janet Sasson Edgette

Tools and Techniques for Family Therapy
by John Edwards

Family Secrets: Implications for Theory and Therapy
by Evan Imber-Black

Program 3: Relationships, Families and Couples Counseling
by Ron Scott

Adlerian Family Therapy
by James Bitter

Empowerment Family Therapy
by Frank Pittman

Family Therapy With the Experts: 10-Video Series
This video includes Structural, Bowenian, Satir, Object Relations, and others.

Integrative Family Therapy
by Kenneth V. Hardy

Narrative Family Therapy
by Stephen Madigan

Object-Relations Family Therapy
by David Scharff & Jill Savege Scharff

Solution-Oriented Family Therapy
by Bill O'Hanlon

A House Divided: Structural Therapy with a Black Family
by Harry Aponte

Harnessing the Power of Genograms in Psychotherapy
by Monica McGoldrick

Of Rocks and Flowers: Dealing With the Abuse of Children
by Virginia Satir

Tres Madres: Structural Therapy With an Anglo/Hispanic Family
by Harry Aponte

REFERENCES

Berg-Cross, L. (2000). *Basic concepts in family therapy: An introductory text*. Binghamton, NY: Haworth Press.

Grolnick, L. (1983). Ibsen's truth, family secrets, and family therapy. *Family Process*, 22, 275–288. doi: 10.1111/j.1545-5300.1983.00275.x

Tarasoff v. Regents of the University of California, 17 Cal. 3d 425, 551 P.2d 334, 131 Cal. Rptr. 14 (Cal. 1976).

FOR FURTHER STUDY

Furlong, M. (1998). Finishing well. *Journal of Family Studies*, 4(1), 103-105.

Lebow, J. L. (1995). Open-ended therapy: Termination in marital and family therapy. In R. H. Mikesell, D. Lusterman, & S. H. McDaniel (Eds.), *Integrating family therapy: Handbook of family psychology and systems theory* (pp. 73–86). Washington, DC: American Psychological Association. doi:10.1037/10172-004

McGeorge, C. R., Carlson, T. S., & Wetchler, J. L. (2015). The history of marriage and family therapy. In J. L. Wetchler, & L. L. Hecker (Eds.), *An introduction to marriage and family therapy* (2nd ed.) (pp. 3–42). New York, NY: Routledge/Taylor & Francis Group.

Patterson, J., Williams, L., Edwards, T. M., Chamow, L., & Grauf-Grounds, C. (2009). *Essential skills in family therapy: From the first interview to termination* (2nd ed.). New York, NY: Guilford Press.

Rappleyea, D. L., Harris, S. M., White, M., & Simon, K. (2009). Termination: Legal and ethical considerations for marriage and family therapists. *American Journal of Family Therapy*, 37(1), 12–27. doi:10.1080/01926180801960617

Ricks, L., Hancock, E., Goodrich, T., & Evans, A. (2014). Laughing for acceptance: A counseling intervention for working with families. *The Family Journal*, 22(4), 397–401. doi:10.1177/1066480714547175

Vereen, L. G., Guay, V. L., & Burnell, B. A. (2004). Termination: "We'll tell you how it's done." In L. E. Tyson, R. Pérusse, & J. Whitledge (Eds.), *Critical incidents in group counseling* (pp. 47–51). Alexandria, VA: American Counseling Association.

Zerin, E. (1983). Finishing unfinished business: Applications of the drama triangle to marital therapy. *Transactional Analysis Journal*, 13(3), 155–157.

Index

Figures and tables are indicated by f or t following the page number.